MONKEES ARCHIVES 1

MONKEES
ARCHIVES VOL 1

White Lightning Publishing
Copyright ©2016 White Lightning Publishing

This volume reprints artifacts related to the Monkees. Through research, we believe that all pieces to be in the public domain. If you hold valid and current copyrights presented, please contact us at WhiteLightningPublishing@gmail.com with proof so that we can remove materials on future printings.

MONKEES ARCHIVES 1

BEE GEES COLLAPSE FROM 'STRAIN'

KRLA BEAT

Edition

FEBRUARY 10, 1968

Peter Tork Keeps World Guessing

KRLA Beat

Volume 3, Number 22 — February 10, 1968

TWO BEE GEES COLLAPSE IN PLANE

LONDON—Two of the Bee Gees, Barry and Robin Gibb, collapsed in a London-bound plane on their way home from a brief visit to relatives in Australia and had to be taken off the plane at Istanbul to receive medical attention.

Barry and Robin were accompanied by their manager, Robert Stigwood, who said: "They collapsed from sheer strain. We went to Australia for a holiday visiting Los Angeles en route. But for the entire time they were away from London they were being pursued by fans and they must have done a hundred and one interviews. The pressure was tremendous. On the plane soon after we left Sydney it was apparent that Barry was quite ill and Robin was little better. Their international fame has come about comparatively suddenly and I suppose they weren't geared for such pressures."

What price success?

A MONKEE UPSET

Peter Tork Surrounded By Mystery

LONDON—Two of the Monkees (but especially Peter Tork) caused quite a commotion here. After taking a brief ski holiday in Switzerland, Davy Jones returned to London and prolonged his stay on our side of the Atlantic by taking up temporary residence in a quiet but centrally positioned West End apartment.

Tork Flys Out

Meanwhile, a bearded Peter Tork flew out of London's Heathrow Airport with quite a mystery trailing behind him. Leaving with Peter were a tall, long-haired blonde and tiny baby boy. On the passenger list for their Los Angeles flight his companion was named as "Mary Harvey" which did little to clarify the situation. The baby was named as Justin.

Banner Heads

The press made much of their departure with the *Daily Mirror* headline announcing "A Monkee, A Mystery Girl, And A Baby Fly Out."

During his ten days in our capital, Peter Tork had not made any attempt to keep the girl and the baby in hiding. They accompanied him when he visited the EMI recording studios to watch Beatle George Harrison engaged upon the recording of his "Wonderwall" movie soundtrack music. When Peter gave his strictly limited number of London press interviews they waited outside in a conspicuously grand Rolls Royce. The hotel at which the trio stayed allegedly knew nothing of a "Miss Harvey" but reportedly confirmed that "Mr. Tork took a suite here with his wife and baby."

Slow Mover

The Monkees current U.K. single, "Daydream Believer," has been moving slowly but surely up our charts and is at number five as I write. After two weeks in the shops, their "Pices Aquarius, Capricorn & Jones, Ltd." album has climbed to ninth place on the LP charts.

—Tony Barrow

PETER TORK causes British to ponder the mystery

DAVY JONES has taken up temporary residence in London

MONKEES ARCHIVES 1

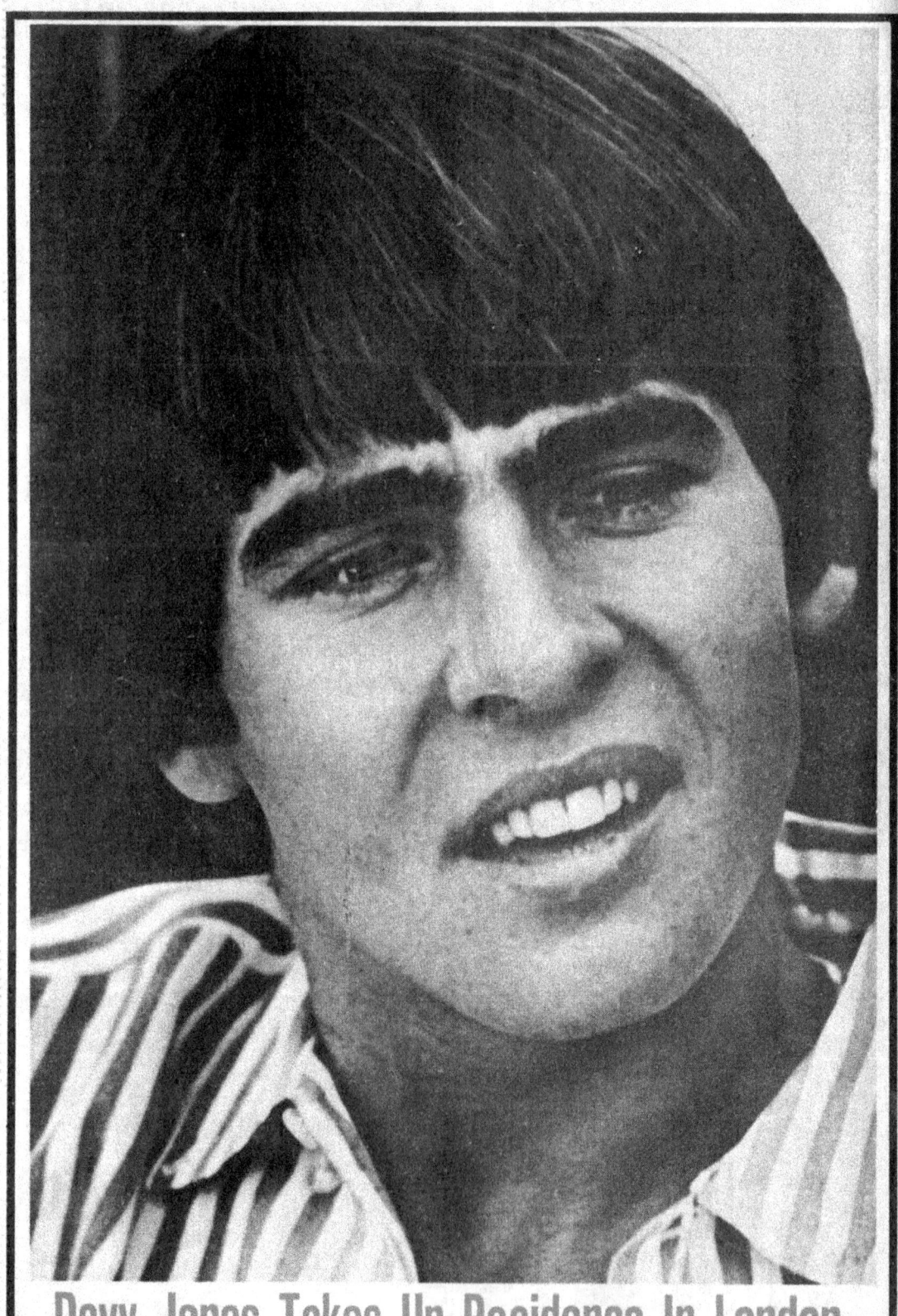

Davy Jones Takes Up Residence In London

MONKEES ARCHIVES 1

Mistaking The Four Monkees

By Louise Criscione

Just picture one very pretty princess who is about to become queen and one very jealous uncle who is determined to do her in before she reaches her eighteenth birthday. Then add four long-haired, unknown pop musicians who live together in a small but "tastefully" decorated apartment. The plot? Save the queen. The show? The Monkees. Result? A cross between Batman and Help.

In other words, a huge smash television show which no one (at least, not very many people) thought would come off. *The BEAT* ventured down to Screen Gems the other day to see this thing called The Monkees and our immediate reaction was—the show is out of sight! A complete about-face for us.

Doubtful

Approximately six months ago a gentleman appeared in the office to inform us of the show. We looked at him like he was absolutely out of his mind! A television show centered around a pop group sounded to us very much like another in a long line of hackneyed and thread-bare attempts at capturing the teen market on the screen.

Then a month or so ago teaser ads began appearing all over the country. "The Monkees is coming." "Everybody is going ape for the Monkees." "Monkee business is big business." All of which meant that somebody somewhere was prepared to spend a small fortune on four guys who had never worked together before.

Along about this time the Monkees traveled to the Stone camping grounds—the RCA studios in Hollywood—to record a single. They practically drove engineer, Dave Hassinger, (also from the Stone camp) out of his mind. They'd never recorded together before. In fact, except for Davy Jones it appeared that *none* of them had ever even cut a record! But no one was too sure about that fact so we'll just let it ride.

Anyway, when we learned that they were virtually amateurs at the art of recording we figured the record would come out sounding something like an infant group attempting to play a 12-string when they hadn't yet mastered a six-string!

Fooled Again

But we were fooled again when "Last Train To Clarksville" and "Take A Giant Step" were released. A two-sided smash and no one had even seen the television show yet!

We humbly bowed to the fact that the Monkees, despite their lack of experience as a group, had managed somehow to turn out a smash record. However, we were *not* prepared for total surrender. There was still the trite television show.

We *thought*. However, we were forced into a total surrender when we sat down in projection room 15 to view the latest attempt at teen humor. As the theme song poured out of the speakers and the four Monkees appeared on the screen in living, breathing color we admitted that there was a slim chance we had been wrong.

A half an hour later, we *knew* we had made a mistake! We know now that within a month after the show airs on NBC the Monkees will be the most talked-about "unknowns" in the country.

Probably the most familiar face among the Monkees belongs to David Jones, now known as Davy Jones but still the same English-born talent who appeared on Broadway in both "Oliver" and "Pickwick."

Most Popular

Davy tried the pop business several months ago, making the break from Broadway to Hollywood without much of a hit record but with mountains of determination. The rather short Davy will no doubt be the most popular Monkee. Because of his accent, his shiny hair, his blue eyes. Who knows?

Take a good look at Micky Dolenz and you know you've seen him before. He looks so familiar that you're bound to blow your mind trying to figure out *where* you've seen him before. Probably the next day it will hit you. He was once the blond-haired young boy who played Corky on the "Circus Boy" television series.

Micky's light blond hair has now changed to brown and he's grown quite a few inches since his "Circus Boy" days but the grin's still the same—and that's what gives him away.

Peter Tork and Michael Nesmith sort of share the honor of being totally unknown except to Greenwich Village and California folk addicts.

Ex-Folk

Peter is listed as "an ex-folk singer from the Village" and those familiar with ex-folk singers from the Village will probably recognize Peter but to the millions across the nation who will watch the Monkees, Peter will be a brand new face. Which isn't too awfully bad when you stop to consider that Peter doesn't have to face being type-cast *before* he's typecast as one of the Monkees!

Mike "Wool Hat" Nesmith has the distinction of being known as someone who used to "live at the Troubador"—a local L.A. folk club. Meaning other than the California folks no one has ever heard of "Wool Hat." But after one look at the lank, typically Southern Mike you'll never forget him. At least, you won't *easily* forget him!

Fact is, you won't forget any of the Monkees. They're big business, you know. Also talented and fresh. *The BEAT* throws up the white flag. We surrender. We're crazy about the Monkees already!

...DAVY JONES — Most popular Monkee?

'PRIVILEGE' TAKING ADVANTAGE OF JOHN?

A movie being filmed in Birmingham, England, is taking advantage of the furor stirred by John Lennon's recent remarks on Christianity.

"Privilege," a biting satire condemning conformity, centers around a plot about a young singer pushed into heading an international Christian crusade.

Although the movie has no direct affiliation with the Beatles, it is particularly timely after the massive demonstrations against the Beatles because of Lennon's religious comments.

In the film, a full-scale evangelical rally staged by the Birmingham football grounds is climaxed by the teen crusade leader singing "Return to Christ" to thousands of local extras bearing "We want God" banners.

The Birmingham rally is described by directors of the film as the "largest mass demonstration of conformity since the Nuremberg rally staged by Adolf Hitler."

Besides satirizing religious fanaticism, the film is a free-swinging attack upon British television and press managers who turn singers into pop idols.

The film marks the debut for model Jean Shrimpton and former Manfred Mann group vocalist Paul Jones. Jones plays the part of the teen idol whose affections are directed towards Miss Shrimpton.

"Privilege" has been in the works since last February. Color filming is being done entirely on location and the film is scheduled to be completed late next month in London for a February release.

...THE MONKEES (l. to r.) Davy Jones, Micky Dolenz, Peter Tork and Mike Nesmith.

DAVY JONES
Met In London By A Stampeding Mob

LONDON—Beatlemania gave way to Monkeemania as Davy Jones, smallest and only British Monkee, landed at London Airport and was greeted with a mob scene! Police said that the scene, staged by about 700 teens, revived the very worst days of Beatlemania.

The crowd, consisting mainly of girls, surged through police lines, knocked down passengers (including an expectant mother) and stampeded up and down stairs in a vain search for Davy, who was hidden in a customs room.

Frantic Officials

Airport officials were frantic and angrily rerouted other passengers because "anyone walking into that mob would risk great danger of injury." The girls wept bitterly when they were blocked from Davy and the police offered their excuse by saying that they could have done much better but many of their officers had been sent to Gatwick Airport to handle the crowds and protect Soviet Premier Alexei Kosygin upon his departure from England.

For his part, Davy could not get over the enthusiastic reception his fans staged at the airport, declaring: "I'm a very happy man. I didn't expect anything like this."

Jones' fans staged a giant sit down when police attempted to move the girls along. Davy was smuggled out of the airport in a police car and then transferred into a limousine for a ride to a London hotel. However, upon reaching the hotel Davy was greeted by another 150 girls which necessitated around-the-clock police to keep the crowds moving.

The Monkees' London publicist could not even get into his office because girls were crowding every inch of the office in hopes that Davy would appear. Davy was forced to cancel his intended visit to Manchester to see his family. "There are so many girls camped outside the house," said Davy, "I had to arrange to see my family somewhere else." Davy spent a few days in London and then headed "for the hills" where he hoped to find some "peace and quiet."

Nesmith Leaves

As Davy arrived in London, fellow Monkee Mike Nesmith boarded a plane to return Stateside and Micky Dolenz, who had originally intended to leave London for the Continent, decided instead to remain in the city. He was on hand when Davy finally arrived at the hotel.

Peter Tork is the only Monkee who did not visit England. He spent his vacation in New York.

"I'M A VERY HAPPY MAN," said Davy following airport reception.

On the BEAT
By Louise Criscione

Micky Dolenz, Davy Jones and Mike Nesmith certainly have made an impression on England during their recent vacation there. Micky was the first Monkee to land on British soil and the press lost no time in hunting him down for interviews. English or American, they're all the same and so, naturally, the first thing the British press wanted to know was whether or not the Monkees can play their own instruments. Speaking frankly, Micky said what he'd said a hundred times before—no the Monkees did not play on all their records but yes they *can* play their own instruments and yes from now on they *will* do all the instrumental tracks for their records to halt this ridiculous controversy.

As you know, Davy was mobbed at the airport and was unable to visit his family in Manchester because his fans had his house staked out. So, he arranged to meet his family elsewhere. Mike was impressed by the city of London but felt that it is too steeped in its own tradition. Peter was the only Monkee who did not go to England; he spent his time off in New York.

What a nice surprise it was to see so many pop artists in the running for Grammy Awards this year. Of course, it will be even nicer if they *win* some awards since top 40 music has been considered by many to be an illegitimate offspring of "true music."

It was Petula Clark who finally knocked the Monkees off their top spot on the British charts with her beautiful "This Is My Song." Pet, who always has something going, has now been signed for her own television series on the BBC. She's set to spend the major part of the spring and summer here in the U.S. doing personal appearances, club dates and television shows. Movie-wise, the petite international star has been offered a role in the up-coming film version of "Finian's Rainbow" but has not yet decided whether or not she will take it.

... MICKEY DOLENZ

Jealousy High

Jealousy is at its peak with groups who have not made it busily crying in their beer—not to mention, dreaming up new ways of putting-down Micky, Mike, Peter and Davy. But Monkee fans are happy—rightly so, since everything with the name "Monkees" on it is selling like nothing since the Beatles arrived on U.S. soil.

Eric Burdon best typified the feeling of most mature people when he said: "They (The Monkees) make very good records and I can't understand how people get upset about them." Eric went on to add that he digs the Monkee discs "no matter how people scream" and ended with the sound advice to "just enjoy the records" and never mind the soul-searching behind the Monkees' success. Ditto for their TV show.

Keith Relf believes that the Yardbirds are stale to the British fans. However, Keith states that the Yardbirds are not alone in their predicament. "Unless you get to the level of the Beatles or Stones," said Keith, "you all become stale to the kids after a year or two." Both Keith and Jimmy Page

MONKEE SHIRTS—Since our article about the Monkee clothiers, we've received numerous requests for "where to buy" information. Monkee shirts as shown above are available at Lenny's Boot Parlor, 1448 Gower St., Hollywood, California. Proprietor Lenny Able will send a catalog upon request. Mail orders are filled promptly. We've been seeing Monkee shirts on girls, by the way, and they're great.

MONKEES ARCHIVES 1

MONKEES ARCHIVES 1

The rumor out of the Monkee camp this week is that the group will do some straight dramatic acting on their television series next season. Of course, the zany humor and camera "tricks" will still constitute the majority of next season's episodes but a little bit of drama will also be sandwiched in there somewhere.

MONKEE DAVY JONES SUING EX-MANAGER

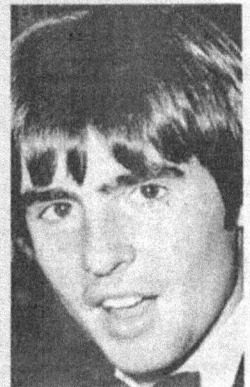

LOS ANGELES—Davy Jones, the tiniest Monkee, is having a bit of a legal problem. In a declaratory relief damage suit against his former manager, Al Cohen, Davy is asking in excess of $150,000.

In his suit, Davy alleges that the contract he signed with Cohen is not valid because Davy was a minor when the contract was signed.

He is, therefore, asking for an accounting of all the money stemming from Davy's merchandising over the past year. The action is being brought in Los Angeles Superior Court.

Davy, along with his fellow Monkees, is currently enjoying a hiatus from their popular television show "The Monkees." The season's filming was completed just before Christmas.

MICKY DOLENZ

Davy Jones Still 1-A

Monkee Davy Jones has not been declared exempt from the U.S. draft, despite the fact that English newspapers have printed that he received a 2A classification because he supports his father.

"It is absolutely untrue," stated a Screen Gems official when he learned of the claim. "We've received no word from Davy's draft board." He added that Screen Gems has no idea when Davy's classification will come up for review. He is now 1-A.

However, speculation is high that the British-born Monkee will be exempted from the draft as he does indeed support his elderly father. But the rumor that Davy may be too short for the Armed Services is unfounded. Though he stands a mere 5'3", Uncle Sam says that is tall enough.

DRAFTABLE DAVY

ART INSTITUTE OF PITTSBURGH
47th Yr. Coed. 18 & 24 mo. Diploma Course: Commercial Art, Fashion Art, Interior Design, Begin. & Adv. Vet. Appd. Dorm facilities. College referrals for degrees. Free illus. brochure.
Earl B. Wheeler, Director
635 Smithfield St.
Pittsburgh, Pa. 15222

Quiz On Monkees

Dear BEAT:
Is it really true that the Monkees don't play the instruments themselves for their records? If it is, I just can't believe it! On their TV show, they sure do a good imitation of playing.

One question which has been bothering me is, if they don't play for their records, why not? If they know how to play the instruments or are learning, why can't and don't they play them? I won't believe it! None of my friends do either.

We all think you're putting us on! Actually, I think it is all a publicity stunt! You know, The BEAT is not always right! I wish all these singing groups would stop doing such ridiculous publicity stunts. They're all silly and stupid and they never do help much anyway! Thank you for letting me have my say!

Joyce Damante

The Monkees used session musicians on their first single and album because when these records were cut they (Micky and Davy in particular) were just learning how to play. It was not a publicity stunt. The practice of using session musicians in recording is certainly not new—it has been going on and will continue as long as records are made. Some groups use them and some don't. The Monkees did; however, it's safe to say that they won't for long.

The Editor

23 x 30 MONKEE POSTER IMPRINTED WITH YOUR OWN NAME

YOUR NAME (Print) _____

1. $ 2.98
2. 5.75
4. 10.00

TED HILL & CO.
707 Paige Lane
Thousand Oaks, Calif. 91360

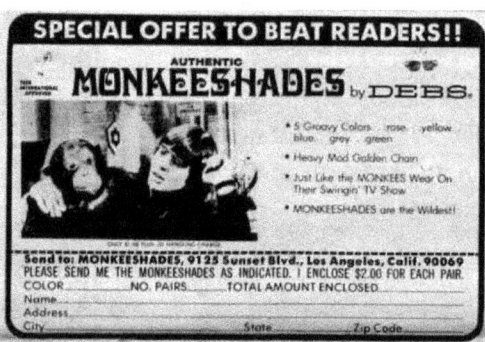

SPECIAL OFFER TO BEAT READERS!!
AUTHENTIC MONKEESHADES by DEBS
- 5 Groovy Colors — rose, yellow, blue, grey, green
- Heavy Mod Golden Chain
- Just Like the MONKEES Wear On Their Swingin' TV Show
- MONKEESHADES are the Wildest!

Send to: MONKEESHADES, 9125 Sunset Blvd., Los Angeles, Calif. 90069
PLEASE SEND ME THE MONKEESHADES AS INDICATED. I ENCLOSE $2.00 FOR EACH PAIR.
COLOR _____ NO. PAIRS _____ TOTAL AMOUNT ENCLOSED _____
Name _____
Address _____
City _____ State _____ Zip Code _____

FANS FEAR FOR MONKEE'S VOICE

HOLLYWOOD – Millions of Monkee fans have shoved Davy Jones' draft status to the back of their minds and Mike Nesmith's tonsil trouble to the front. Monkee Nesmith entered Cedars of Lebanon Hospital in Los Angeles to undergo a long-postponed tonsillectomy.

Nesmith's personal physician, Dr. Rexford Kenamer, announced that he foresaw a routine recovery period of two weeks but millions of Nesmith's anxious fans are worrying about whether the operation will change Mike's voice.

Said one young fan: "I pray that it won't change Mike's beautiful voice but, you know, sometimes a tonsillectomy will do that and I'll just die if Mike sounds even a shade different after this operation!"

During Nesmith's two-week absence, "The Monkees" television show will shoot around him. The recording sessions for their next album have had to be adjusted.

MICKY DOLENZ

Well, it looks as if the Monkees are going to receive another one — their latest album, "Headquarters," was not even released when it was ear-marked a million seller! RCA reports that initial orders for the album soared over the million mark and they have requested the RIAA to certify it as a million-seller.

The Monkees' first record was released last August and to date they have sold over 6 million albums and 6 million singles in the United States alone – which should set Monkee-haters back a notch or two.

MONKEES ARCHIVES 1

Formula For Pop Success

By Carol Deck

Ever notice how most of the successful pop groups fall into a pattern? It's almost as though there's a formula for creating a successful group.

Like, for instance, there's the genius—every group (and I'm only talking about the groups that make it—forget those that don't) has at least one genius at it's core (a John Lennon, Eric Burdon or Brian Wilson.) Some groups are lucky and have more than one genius, but it's essential that you have at least one.

Musician

Then too, you've got to have a top rated musician, someone who's mastered at least one instrument to such an extent that he's recognized by his peers as tops for that instrument (a George Harrison or a Jeff Beck.)

It's also essential that you have at least one very good looking member whom fans can point out to their parents as proof that not all rock and roll singers are ugly. You've got to have a Paul McCartney (keep calm kids, I know there's a lot more to Paul than just his looks), a Mark Lindsay or a Davy Jones. Even the Stones, who aren't exactly world reknowned for their beauty, have Keith Richard.

And every group has a quiet member—someone who says absolutely nothing during interviews and generally refuses to express his opinions on the world (Charlie Watts, Chris Dreja and Peter Tork.) These are the ones that worry reporters for we know that usually the less they say the more they think and often have great insights into the world about them but getting it out of them is like pulling teeth. These are also the ones the fans tend to want to mother.

Combinations

Well, those four are the basic essentials for a group, but there's one more that really shouldn't be left out and that is the clown. A successful group usually has one member who is a fun loving, outgoing, extroverted character who generally keeps everyone's spirits up. There's Micky Dolenz, Dennis Wilson, Zollie Yanovsky, Phil Volk. A clown may not be totally necessary, but he sure helps.

And of course you can have any combinations of the above. There's the quiet genius (John Sebastian, Jim McGuinn), the good looking genius (Herb Alpert), and the good looking clown (Herman.) And there are many top rated quiet musicians, for people who dedicate their lives to an instrument tend to be a little on the quiet side with society.

This formula, and variations of it, have proved successful with numerous groups. Look at the Beatles. They're almost a prototype of it. They've got a genius (Lennon), a musician (Harrison), a good looker (McCartney) (I know, I know there's more to Paul than just what meets the eye) and a combination clown and quiet one (Ringo — he's not the extroverted kind of clown, but he has a natural sense of comedy that may put him in the Buster Keaton category some day).

But then there's the Stones. They've got a little bit of everything, as every top group does, but they've also got the mighty mouth—Jagger—who never has played by the rules. Jagger is likely to be, at any point in the game, all or none of these all by himself.

Then There's ...

And then there's the Association, who can't be anything but tops just because they have so much of everything. All six of them are capable of genius, they've got a couple of really top musicians and when it comes to clowning, they're all out-right idiots. I suppose if you're looking for great looks, Ted will stand out and when it comes to being the quiet type, theoretically all six are capable, but Brian probably would get the credit in that department.

So you see it really isn't that hard to create a good group. You just find one member in each category, or any combinations thereof, add a lot of luck and you're on your way to your first million seller.

BEATLES have all components for success — Bob Vaughn has UNCLE.

MONKEES have a clown in the form of one Micky Dolenz.

STONES have a non-conformist.

BEACH BOYS have the "genius" of Brian Wilson.

RAIDERS have pony-tailed Mark.

ASSOCIATION number six but wish Elke Summer was lucky seven.

MONKEES ARCHIVES 1

WHERE THEY ARE

MONKEES
July 7, Atlanta, Ga., Braves Stadium; July 8, Jacksonville, Fla., Convention Hall; July 11, Charlotte, N.C., Coliseum; July 12, Greensboro, N.C., Coliseum; July 14-16, New York, Forest Hills Stadium; July 20, Buffalo, N.Y., Memorial Auditorium; July 21, Baltimore, Md., Memorial Auditorium; July 22, Boston, Mass. Boston Gardens; July 23, Philadelphia, Pa., Convention Hall; July 27, Rochester, N.Y., War Memorial Auditorium; July 28, Cincinnati, Ohio, Gardens; July 29, Detroit, Mich.

FIFTH DIMENSION
June 8-17, Bimbo's, San Francisco, Ca.; July 3, Disneyland, Anaheim, California.

SONNY AND CHER
June 14, opening of "Goodtimes," Detroit, Mich.; June 14, Steve Allen Comedy Hour, CBS-TV.

JEFFERSON AIRPLANE
June 4, Sam Houston Coliseum, Houston, Texas; June 17, Monterey Pop Festival; June 20-25, Fillmore Auditorium, San Francisco, Calif.

HERMAN'S HERMITS
July 21, Coliseum, Oklahoma City State Fair Grounds; Aug. 5, International Amphitheater, Chicago, Ill.

THE LOVIN' SPOONFUL
July 14-15, Opera House, Chicago, Ill.

SIMON & GARFUNKEL
June 16, Monterey Pop Festival; July 21-22, Opera House, Chicago, Ill.

RIGHTEOUS BROTHERS
May 29-June 14, Coconut Grove, Los Angeles, California; July 25-30, Opera House, Chicago, Ill.; September 11-17, Greek Theatre, Los Angeles, Calif.

ASSOCIATION
June 16, Monterey Pop Festival, Monterey, California; June 1-14 on vacation; July 24-30, Greek Theatre, Los Angeles, Calif.

SUPREMES
June 1-10, Shoreham Hotel, Washington, D.C.; June 11, Symphony Hall, New Jersey; June 13-26, Coconut Grove, Los Angeles, Calif.; June 29-July 19, Flamingo Hotel, Las Vegas, Nev.

TEMPTATIONS
June 2-3, Twin Coaches, Pittsburgh, Pa.; July 9-15, Steel Pier, Atlantic City.

SMOKEY ROBINSON AND THE MIRACLES
May 25-June 3, Basin St. West, San Francisco, California.

LEONARD NIMOY
June 10, Edgewater Park, Detroit, Michigan

BUCKINGHAMS
June 3, Blend, Ill.; June 16, St. Louis, Mo.; June 17, Evanston, Ill.; July 3, Leesburg, Ind.; July 4, South Bend, Ind.; July 7, Lake Schaeffer Monticello, Ind.; July 15, Lake Geneva, Wisc.; July 21, Marne, Mich.

FAMILY TREE
June 2-4, Portland, Crystal Ballroom.

BUFFALO SPRINGFIELD
June 2, Conobee Lake, N.H.; June 3-4, Boston, Mass.

TURTLES
May 31-June 9, tour of England, France, Germany, Denmark; June 24, Lagoon Ballroom, Salt Lake City, Utah.

MARVIN GAYE
May 26-June 3, Beach Club, Myrtle Beach, South Carolina.

JOHNNY RIVERS
June 2-4, Vancouver, B.C.; Edmonton, Alberta; Calgary, Alberta; June 20-30, Whisky A Go Go, Hollywood, California.

DON & THE GOODTIMES
May 31-June 15, Southwestern U.S.; June 17-25, headlining Teenage Fair, Seattle, Washington; June 26-July 3, concerts in the Seattle area; July 3, three weeks heading a Dick Clark caravan of Stars through the Midwest.

NITTY GRITTY DIRT BAND
June 6, Troubador, Los Angeles, California.

SMOTHERS BROTHERS
June 23, finish taping for first season of their TV show; July 31, begin taping for second season; July 31-August 6, Greek Theatre, Los Angeles, California.

PAUL REVERE AND THE RAIDERS
June 8, Lafayette, La., Municipal Auditorium; June 9, Shreveport, La., Hirisch Memorial Coliseum; June 10, Houston, Texas, Sam Houston Coliseum; June 11, Dallas, Texas, Memorial Auditorium; June 12, Corpus Christi, Texas, Coliseum; June 13, San Antonio, Texas, Freeman Coliseum; June 14, Lubbock, Texas, Coliseum; June 15, Amarillo, Texas, Coliseum; June 16, Tulsa, Okla., Assembly Center; June 17, Joplin, Mo., Memorial Hall; June 18, Topeka, Kan., Municipal Auditorium; June 19, Des Moines, Iowa, Veterans' Memorial Auditorium; June 20, Sioux City, Iowa, Municipal Auditorium; June 21, St. Joe, Mo., City Auditorium; June 23, Memphis, Tenn., Mid-South Coliseum; June 24, Jackson, Miss., Fairground Coliseum; June 25, New Orleans, La.; June 27, Columbus, Ga., Municipal Auditorium; June 28, Columbia, S.C., Township Auditorium; June 29, Atlanta, Ga., Municipal Auditorium; June 30, Winston-Salem, N.C., Memorial Coliseum; July 1, Chattanooga, Tenn., Memorial Auditorium

Monkee Song Men To A&M

Two songwriters credited with a large share of the Monkees' phenomenal success, Tommy Boyce and Bobby Hart, have just signed long term agreements with A&M records as artist-producers.

Boyce and Hart had a string of hits before writing Monkee songs like "Last Train to Clarksville," "I Want To Be Free" and "The Monkees Theme." The duo will make their singing debut on a forthcoming A&M single release.

Before joining the Monkee team, Boyce and Hart had over 30 of their songs recorded by Dean Martin, Little Anthony, Tommy Sands and Jay and the Americans.

BOBBY HART
TOMMY BOYCE

"WHAT DO YOU MEAN WE'RE OFF???" Yes, it's true, the Monkees appear to have had the knife comed own on their television show. At least, the official list of next season's shows has come out of NBC minus the Monkees. "Star Trek" is taking over the Monkees' time slot . . . 7:30 p.m. on Mondays.

MONKEES SET RECORD

TORONTO, CANADA — The Monkees April 2 concert here, promoted by Dick Clark Productions, Inc., sold out completely the first day tickets went on sale.

Teenagers lined up in 0-degree weather to purchase tickets at the ten box office windows of Toronto's Maple Leaf Garden. The 17,000 seat, turn-away sale resulted in gross sales of slightly more than $91,000 and constitute a new one-night record for the Monkees.

During their hiatus from "The Monkees," at least two of the members have changed their appearances slightly. Davy Jones now has a moustache growing on his upper lip and has had his hair trimmed quite a bit. It's by no means a crew cut but it is much shorter than the page-boy type style he usually wears.

Micky Dolenz has done nothing new to his hair but is in the process of acquiring a beard! However, it's safe to say that by the time "The Monkees" once again start filming all excess hair (except that on the head) will be removed!

Monkee Specials

LOS ANGELES — The Monkees, Screen Gems and NBC-TV have agreed upon a three special deal instead of the weekly series.

The reason for the new programming is due to the Monkees' popularity, explained Screen Gems studio boss, Jackie Cooper. "The Monkees grossed $2,000,000 on their last tour. They've sold 21,000,000 records. Now that's more than we're going to make in a 26-week, half-hour series that ties you up for so much time."

The Monkees plan to go on two one nighter tours next year and will produce more records. The group is presently involved in their first feature motion picture for Columbia called "Untitled."

MONKEES ARCHIVES 1

DAVY JONES FORMS OWN RECORD FIRM

BEAT Photo: Dwight Carter
DAVY'S FORMED A disc firm.

Davy Jones and his manager, Hal Cone, are going into the disc business. They formed Davy Jones Records, Ltd., and signed Vinnie Basile as the company's first recording artist.

Vinnie, 21, has been blind since the age of eight. He writes much of his own material and is a self-taught drummer and singer. His first single on the Davy Jones label will be out soon.

Old Hand

Jack Angel, an old hand in many facets of the music business including management and publishing, will be executive vice president for the East Coast. He started Herald and Ember Records. Two of Angle's biggest hits on the label were "Shake A Hand" and "Paradise Hill."

New Talent

Angel is now scouting for new talent to record on the Jones label and is searching for distributors for the company.

Davy will keep working with the Monkees who record for RCA Victor.

MONKEES AWARDED TWO GOLD RECORDS

The Monkees, those assembly line products who have created a new concept in TV programming, are now just part of a great big happy family. The family tree reads: RCA Victor, proud father; Colgems, healthy infant; and the Monkees, healthy infant's favorite toy.

The Monkees were assigned to the new Colgems label, a division of RCA, only two months ago but already everything has come up roses for RCA, Colgems and the Monkees.

Only several weeks after the release of the Monkees' first single, "Last Train To Clarksville," and their new album, "The Monkees," both discs were at the top of their respective categories on the charts.

And now both have been certified as million-sellers.

The success of the Monkees has solidified the relationship between Colgems and RCA. Commenting on the liason, RCA vice president Steve Sholes stated, "This is the first time in the history of the RIAA that a newly formed label has achieved such success with its debut releases, and we are delighted with our affiliation with Colgems."

The Monkees' single was released four weeks in advance of the group's debut on TV this fall. The record has been number one in the nation for the past two weeks.

The group's first LP was released at the same time their TV debut was aired. It was the country's top selling LP less than a month after its release.

Don Kirshner, Colgems president, is the music supervisor for all the group's recordings and music score for their TV series. Kirshner is now working on material for the Monkees' next single and LP.

The ironic part of the Monkees' disc success is the fact that the studio musicians, not the Monkees themselves, were used on both "The Last Train To Clarksville" and their album. But, apparently, Monkee fans consider it "part of the game" and continued to rush to their record stores to purchase anything with the Monkee name attached to it.

Man-Made Monkees

By Louise Criscione

Most groups happen. The Monkees were made. If they weren't intentionally created, it is conceivable that they would not exist for it is highly unlikely that the four of them would ever have met. They're about as different as any four human beings can be.

Mickey Dolenz – drummer, singer, comic and all around noise-maker left a Los Angeles technical trade school to become lead singer in a pop-rock group called the Missing Links.

Between appearances with the Missing Links, Micky took odd acting jobs which included segments of "Peyton Place" and "Mr. Novak." Being sort of a jack-of-all-trades, when singing and acting dates were scarce, Micky worked as a mechanic.

Actor's Son

Micky was born in Los Angeles on March 8, 1945, the son of an actor – the late George Dolenz. At ten, Micky began a three year run as television's "Circus Boy." When the series folded, Micky returned to school in the San Fernando Valley. Upon graduation from Grant High, he entered Valley College but transferred in his second semester to L.A. Tech-Trade. It was then that he made his first serious move toward music.

Like Davy Jones, Mike Nesmith and Peter Tork, Micky responded to an ad in *Variety* a year ago calling for "insane boys" to audition for roles in a comedy series for today's teens. And like the others, he was tested and signed because he was indeed a "Monkee," whether he knew it or not.

Although giving the appearance of being much smaller, Micky stands an even six feet and is frequently described as "athletic and restless." He shares an apartment with Davy Jones in West L.A. and drives around on a motorcycle.

David Jones, now known as Davy, left his home in Manchester, England to "become something," when he was fourteen and a half. He left with the full blessings of his father, a railroad fitter.

Davy was born December 30, 1945 with a great will to succeed. His dad knew it then and he knows it now. The tough, compact Davy headed for England's Newmarket Racetrack to become a jockey trainee. Between riding jobs, he discovered life among England's young set and explored places from which the great new musical sounds were coming. Eventually, he became part of the scene at The Cellar.

Davy's first acting job resulted from an audition at the BBC where he played a juvenile delinquent in a radio drama. This led to a steady job on a daytime series called "Morning Story."

However, he still continued at the racetrack and ironically enough it was through the racetrack that he met London theatrical executives who helped him land a leading role in the musical hit, "Oliver," in which Davy played the Artful Dodger.

From "Oliver" Davy proceeded on to "Pickwick" and won special acclaim from the American critics. Both plays were, of course, extremely successful on Broadway and were the reasons that the young Mr. Jones initially made the trip to America where he has been living for the past four years.

Not Quite

When "Pickwick" closed its Broadway run, the Colpix Record people spotted Davy's potential and signed him to a recording contract. He cut a record called "Dream Girl" which was a bomb – but not entirely because it brought him to California in time to read that ad in *Variety* and become a Monkee.

Peter Tork was playing guitar, ukelele, five-string banjo and bass before his voice changed. Later he picked up piano, French horn and other various instruments. All of which he learned to play well.

Born in Washington, D.C., February 13, 1944, Peter was raised in Connecticut. His father, H. J. Torkelson, is Associate Professor of Economics at the University of Connecticut. On two traumatic occasions, Peter himself enrolled in college with the highly respectable goal of becoming an English professor. When Peter's first try at college (Carleton College in Minnesota) failed, he returned to New England and worked for 14 months in a thread mill. When his second attempt at college turned out to be equally ill-fated, he decided to select another line of work in self-defense.

Therefore, Peter began his musical career in New York's Greenwich Village, performing as singer-musician in various pass-the-hat hideaways where the music was, at least, always new. But when money became something of a necessity, he toured with the Phoenix Singers as accompanist. He stayed with the Singers for six months, during which time he continually kept one goal in mind – to reach California.

Being rather strong-willed, Peter did come to California and was here only two months when he read the ad which made him a Monkee.

Mike Nesmith is a guitar-playing, song-writing Texan with a college degree, a solid interest in Renaissance music and the ability to shift gears to rock and roll with apparent ease. His hair rides rather long, his accent is definitely Texas-inspired and his guitar-playing is distinctively professional.

Born in Dallas, Texas on December 30, 1942, Mike traveled next to San Antonio where he attended college and expanded his knowledge of folk singing and guitar playing. When he became bored with singing the same songs, he wrote his own and upon graduation decided to seek his fortune as a folk singer in Hollywood.

Three

Arriving in Hollywood, Mike met up with a bass player named John Lundgren and the two of them set out on a road tour which had them booked for five shows a day. Upon their return, seasoned but far from wealthy, they added a third member – Bill. And the three of them traded in their folk for rock 'n roll. Mike wrote all their material and just as fame and fortune was about to descend (or so they say) the draft board arrived and Mike went back to being a single act.

His first job as a single act was at Ledbetter's, a well-known Los Angeles folk club, where he met with a tidy amount of success. It was along about this time that Mike was doing his weekly reading and ran across the famous ad.

And so, a mechanic, a jockey and two folk singers have become the hottest new group in the nation. Thanks to an ad.

MONKEES ARCHIVES 1

Millions Are Reaching Out For

THE MONKEES

PISCES, AQUARIUS, CAPRICORN & JONES LTD.

Now Available At:
**MONTGOMERY WARD
DEPARTMENT STORES**

MONKEES ARCHIVES 1

SPECIAL OFFER TO BEAT READERS!!

AUTHENTIC MONKEESHADES by DEBS

TEEN INTERNATIONAL APPROVED

* 5 Groovy Colors...rose...yellow...blue...grey...green
* Heavy Mod Golden Chain
* Just Like the MONKEES Wear On Their Swingin' TV Show
* MONKEESHADES are the Wildest!

ONLY $1.98 PLUS .02 HANDLING CHARGE

Send to: MONKEESHADES, 81 W. State St., Pasadena, California 91105
PLEASE SEND ME THE MONKEESHADES AS INDICATED. I ENCLOSE $2.00 FOR EACH PAIR
COLOR_____ NO. PAIRS_____ TOTAL AMOUNT ENCLOSED_____
Name_____
Address_____
City_____ State_____ Zip Code_____

ORDER YOURS TODAY!!

APOLOGY TO MONKEES

Dear *BEAT*:

Recently I did an extremely dumb thing. I wrote a letter to an English pop paper (the name of which shall remain nameless) and said some extraordinary things. Being the kind who has a tendency to run off at the mouth, they were extremely "witchy" things... the kind of things normally said by juveniles. Or something.

Anyway, having said them, I now regret them profoundly. My apologies to the Monkees. The funny thing is, I like the Monkees. I like their music and frankly, I like them. It isn't simply a question of "not knocking success" and their music is good; it's interesting and well done. The show, well to be honest, I can't really take it every week. But for what it is, it's acceptable.

Maybe it was because I had a typewriter and was feeling a need to try out the various little buttons. Maybe it was because being a Beatle fan (they are not my number one fave rave group... that dubious honor having to go to the "out" Lovin' Spoonful—but they are okay too. More or less), I felt a need to say something profound (I like "Penny Lane," but I can understand the dull reaction both here and in England. Some musical excitement is needed and if I had been able to condense my thoughts into smaller sentences, maybe the English paper would have printed the "digs" I included against the fab four.) Or maybe it was (and is?) a case of "feet going in where the brain fears to tread."

In any event, why am I writing to *The BEAT*? Well, you must certainly be aware of this English paper and seeing the name of one of your faithful readers "knocking" one of your favorite groups might cause a reaction—a highly negative one. And my real gripe with the English paper and I suppose with all pop papers currently is why kill a golden goose by over-exposing it?

Reading about nothing but the Monkees... seeing them every week... hearing their records until you are ready to fall to pieces is a bore. Honest. And having barely survived that kind of thing with the Beatles, do you really think I *want* to go through it again with the Monkees? Especially when Micky Dolenz insists on sounding like chubby cheeks Paulie? Sob. Not to mention scream and climb up the wall.

I said it; I'm not glad and if *The BEAT* staff sees it, please (for my sake, please) just forget it.

I'll tell you something. I read the tribute to the Monkees with glazed eyes and afterwards I did a lot of giggling. Then I think I went around for days seeing Monkee faces everywhere I looked. Ugh. It was a horrifying experience, and I don't wish to go through it again. So, please, from a faithful, loyal, highly pro-*BEAT* dedicated reader—please don't feel you have to engage in some kind of retributive (derivative of "retribution") act. Please, please, please.

Brenda

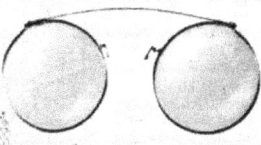

MONKEES ADDRESS

Dear *BEAT*:

I would like to write to the Monkees. Will you be kind enough to send me their address? I would appreciate it a lot.

Juana Carter

You can write to the Monkees at 1334 North Beachwood Drive, Hollywood 28, California 90028.

The Editor

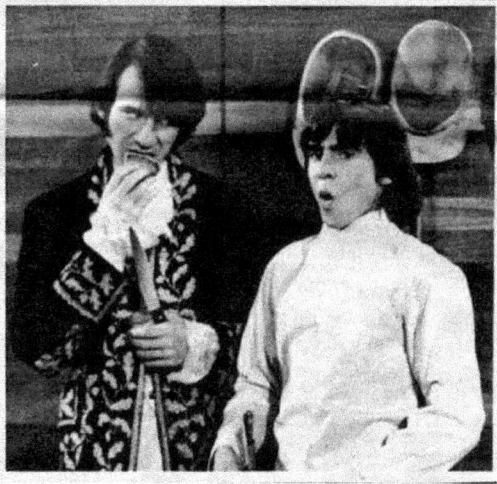

Monkees Finish First P.A. Tour

The Monkees have just finished their first public appearance tour and are now back at work on their television show.

The group, created for the TV show "The Monkees," made their first public appearances together in Chicago, Boston and New York, then returned to the West Coast.

A heavy shooting schedule for the show will curtail most performances by the group for a while.

Their first record, "Last Train to Clarksville," has been released and appears to be on its way up.

MONKEES ARCHIVES 1

BEAT EXCLUSIVE
Fan's Tale Of Meeting The Monkees

By Lori Lee

HOLLYWOOD—I could hardly believe my good luck. Within a few hours I would make acquaintance with four of the grooviest guys ever to hit the music world. It was too fabulous a thought for reality. But sure enough it came into being and here are all the exciting details of my meeting the Monkees.

Upon arriving in Hollywood at about 9:15 in the morning, I immediately sped to Columbia Screen Gems (where the television show is taped) only to find out that the Monkees were not presently filming and would not until the beginning of April.

Stick With It

Although discouraged, I refused to give up and went directly to Lenny's Boot Parlor. After hearing so much about its merchandise I wanted to browse around.

The salesman was most helpful because it was he who told me that the boys were to have a recording session at the R.C.A. Building. I rushed over there and asked the guard on duty when the session was to begin. He said that everything was set up for 10:00, which was only a few minutes away. So I waited and waited and waited patiently for a long time until someone spotted Micky's red, white, and blue Volkswagon Bus. The time was exactly 1:17 in the afternoon.

Enter Micky

Well, that just set every teeny bopper off. They all started screaming and crying as if completely out of their minds. I was terribly nervous myself but upon seeing Micky for the first time I knew that everything would turn out just great. He was comfortably attired in a pair of cut-offs, white T-shirt, brown sandals, and policeman's hat. He looked truly out-a-sight!

I hurried up and handed him some gifts picked out 'specially for his character. They consisted of several goofy Car-toon mags, a big chewy dog bone for either himself or You, and a paddle set. He then signed autographs and disappeared into the building.

Only on his second trip out to greet his fans did I notice the big difference in his appearance. Micky had grown a beard! When I later asked why, he replied that it kept his face warm. And as fuzzy as it was, it must of been doing the job just fine.

Other Monkees Arrive

Sometime later Mike arrived on the scene. He had also grown a beard which gave him a very masculine look. And, with his strong Texas accent, he was absolutely groovy. I really dug him!

It was about 3:00 when Peter showed up and brightened everyones' tired faces and spirits. It's sure hard work to have to stand from ten in the morning until three in the afternoon and still look fresh and cheerful. But, when I gave

> *It does happen—fans do occasionally get to meet their favorite entertainers. One such lucky girl is Lori Lee who spent the entire day standing outside of the studio where the Monkees were recording. Her vigil paid-off when Lori met her favorite group, the Monkees.*
>
> *This is her story, exactly as she wrote it. Lori's tale certainly proves one thing—Monkees are human!* The Editor

Peter his presents of a gyroscope top, Mad paperback, paddle-set, and poem made to order about him alone, he smiled and looked so touched that every minute of waiting seemed all worthwhile.

Great Waterfight, 1967

Everyone was now waiting impatiently for the smallest Monkee to arrive and make his grand appearance. But Davy never came. However, there was such a big commotion down at the end of the block, he was temporarily forgotten.

Suddenly, Micky came racing down the street as fast as his size 10 feet would carry him, yelling that they were after him. We all turned around just in time to see him get squirted right in the face with water by two members of the Family Tree, a groovy new singing group.

Squirting Back

Micky, being one who never lets a person get the better of him, started squirting back which was an unfortunate move for yours truly. It just so happened by some unlucky chance, the person for whom the water was intended ducked and take an intelligent guess at who got all soaking wet. You are 100% correct if you answered me. But in the end it didn't really matter because it was such a hilarious sight to see Micky get so frustrated and wet.

Still, an even funnier sight was his expression when he learned that the whole gun fight was all my fault. After Peter arrived at the building, Micky, Mike, and Rick Klein were just leaving. They returned some time later with a big package containing four or five water pistols, compliments of Mr. Nesmith. You see, besides a paddle-set and little green wool hat for his son, Christian, his gifts also included a gigantic water syringe or hypo-squirt. I wanted to see a water fight and get more than what I had bargained for. Oh well.

Three Of Four

Even with such complications, though, everything turned out just fine. I got to meet three of the four fabulous Monkees and gave them each in person several nutty gifts coming from the mind of an even more nutty person. (Davy never did show up so I left his presents at the studio. I hope he has fun tailing up with his extra large box of Corn Flakes).

And now, all I can say is, I just wish that every Monkees fan in the whole world would at some time have the same opportunity I did. And if that lucky person could have only one half the fun I had, it still could be classified as an unforgettable experience for all.

PETER AND MICKY outside Monkee soundstage in Hollywood

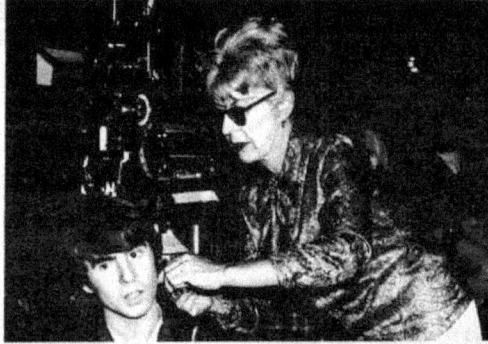
DAVY JONES receives combing hand from Sally, Monkee hairdresser

GENE ASHMAN, couterie for Monkees, straightens Mike's hat

DAVY MAD? Not really

PETER HAPPY? You can bet your life on it!

MONKEES ARCHIVES 1

U.K. POP NEWS ROUND-UP
Brian Epstein Signs Monkees

By Tony Barrow

THE MONKEES WILL STAR IN A SERIES OF THREE STAGE SHOWS AT BRITAIN'S LARGEST INDOOR CONCERT VENUE THIS SUMMER. THE DEAL TO BRING THE MONKEES TO THE U.K. HAS BEEN FIXED BY VIC LEWIS, A DIRECTOR OF BRIAN EPSTEIN'S LONDON-BASED NEMS ORGANIZATION.

It is the outcome of concentrated discussions which took place in Hollywood several weeks ago between Vic Lewis, representing NEMS, Steve Blauner, SCREEN GEMS executive, and Bert Schneider, manager of THE MONKEES.

The concerts—one show each evening—will take place at London's Wembley Empire Pool on June 30, July 1 and July 2. Top price for tickets at the massive 9,500-seater venue will be 30-shillings—which is about 4 dollars—but the cheapest seats will sell at seven shillings and sixpence (about one dollar) each.

Announcing that he had clinched the deal via a London/Los Angeles phone call, Vic Lewis said: "The Monkees will give their own hour-long show which will fill the entire second half of each concert performance. These will be the only British concerts by The Monkees and we're expecting fans to travel from all parts of the country for the occasion."

BECAUSE THE MONKEES WILL NOT BE APPEARING OUTSIDE LONDON, THE NEMS ORGANIZATION PLANS TO SET UP AN UNPRECEDENTED SYSTEM OF SPECIAL TRAINS AND BUSES WHICH WILL BRING FANS TO WEMBLEY AND RETURN THEM TO THEIR HOMETOWNS THE SAME DAY. "MONKEES SPECIALS" WILL OPERATE FROM KEY CITIES UP AND DOWN THE U.K.

According to Lewis, The Monkees will fly into London on Thursday, June 29, the day before their first Empire Pool appearance. They are expected to give just one king-size Press News Conference in London the day they arrive.

On behalf of THE BEATLES, who were tied up in the recording studio completing the final tracks for their upcoming summer LP album, I had the pleasure of collecting a bundle of Ivor Novello Awards at a ceremony held in the BBC Playhouse Theatre in London.

Awarded each year by the Songwriters Guild of Great Britain, the Novello trophies are the U.K. equivalent of your American "Grammy" presentations. As composers of "Yellow Submarine," John and Paul were awarded a Novello statuette for achieving highest 1966 record sales in the U.K.; in the "Most Performed Work Of The Year" section they had the first and second places with "Michelle" and "Yesterday."

The Novello Award for "Britain's International Song Of The Year" went to "Winchester Cathedral" written by Geoff Stevens, recorded by THE NEW VAUDEVILLE BAND.

DON BLACK and JOHN BARRY came top of the "Film Song Of The Year" section with their composition "Born Free."

Inside London pop circles the entertainment bombshell of the month must be the bid by EMI to take over the Grade Organization. EMI is the largest recording organization in the world whose roster of stars ranges from The Beatles and The Seekers to Herman's Hermits and The Hollies. Grades represent a host of top American stars plus artists as varied as Sir Laurence Olivier and Albert Finney, Dusty Springfield and The New Vaudeville Band, The Dave Clark Five and The Hollies, The Animals and Cat Stevens, Paul & Barry Ryan and Cliff Richard.

CLIFF RICHARD AND THE SHADOWS are to make a full-length feature movie with a dramatic screenplay based on the war in Vietnam... Clipped from his current album, new TOM JONES single in the U.K. is "Those Funny Familiar Forgotten Feelings"... Songstress SHIRLEY BASSEY will make her West End stage debut in the title role of "Josephine," a musical set in the times of Napoleon and his Empress... MANFRED MANN vocalist MICHAEL D'ABO joined by his wife Maggie on BBC Television's "Juke Box Jury" panel.

ROLLING STONES supported by THE MOVE at Paris Olympia concerts April 11... After May concert tour of U.K. BEACH BOYS will take vacation in Europe with their wives... JOHN ENTWISTLE of THE WHO engaged to 20-year-old secretary Alison.

BARRY RYAN (Of Paul And) has 21-year-old Caroline Walker, secretary to top deejay ALAN FREEMAN, as his current steady... "New York Mining Disaster, 1941" self-penned ballad on first U.K. single by teenage foursome THE BEE GEES. New BILLY J. KRAMER single, "Town Of Tuxley Toy Maker, Part One," another original Bee Gees composition... GEORGIE FAME to make LP album in London with COUNT BASIE'S ORCHESTRA next month... Radio Caroline selling "Your very own authentic PENNY LANE street signs" to listeners for R1.50... Probably Coconut Grove month for NEW VAUDEVILLE BAND after Las Vegas (Tropicana Hotel) appearances at the beginning of June. N.V.B. plan to spend most of summer and fall in America and may undertake October concerts with veteran LOUIS ARMSTRONG!... Watch for hefty promotion treatment from Warner-Reprise to push "Purple Haze" by JIMI HENDRIX EXPERIENCE... Former MOODY BLUE DENNY LAINE just made fantastic solo disc debut.

STEVIE WINWOOD with three-man group called The Traffic recording for Island label... "This Is My Song" back at Number One in Britain – this time version is by HARRY SECOMBE who is to play Bumble in colour movie of "Oliver!" and D'Artagnon in London stage musical of "The Three Museketeers."

BILL MOELLER(21), former road manager with Unit Four Plus Two, unmasked as WHISTLING JACK SMITH, star of Britain's fastest-selling non-vocal single of the year "I Was Kaiser Bill's Batman." Bill previously sang on record as Coby Wells but the "Kaiser Bill" single was the idea of his Liverpudlian Decca producer NOEL WALKER.

Current London Clubmanship rules that the Scotch Of St. James is only "in" if other fave clubs are too crowded. Bag O'Nails is still main rendezvous for pop stars and other night people, freshly-opened Speakeasy tipped as next month's "in" place—and not just because THE BYRDS played there!

MAMA CASS went back to America very suddenly!... New 4-man YARDBIRDS combo out with "Little Games." Group expects to undertake 7-week July/August U.S. concert tour... 3 saxes, 2 trombones and 1 French horn from SOUNDS, INC. called in for backing work on a BEATLES album track... BRIAN JONES plays sitar, organ and harmonica on soundtrack of Cannes Film Festival movie "A Degree Of Murder."

... PETER TORK AND MICKY DOLENZ prepare for flight to England.

SPECIAL OFFER TO BEAT READERS!!

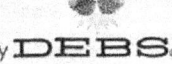

AUTHENTIC **MONKEESHADES** by DEBS

★ Created and Designed by Davy Jones in London
★ 5 Groovy Colors...rose...yellow... blue...grey...green
★ Heavy Mod Golden Cabin
★ Just Like the MONKEES Wear On Their Swingin' TV Show
★ MONKEESHADES are the Wildest!

ONLY $1.98 PLUS .02 HANDLING CHARGE

Send to: MONKEESHADES, 81 W. State St., Pasadena, Calif. 91105
PLEASE SEND ME THE MONKEESHADES AS INDICATED. I ENCLOSE $2.00 FOR EACH PAIR.

COLOR _____ NO. PAIRS _____ TOTAL AMOUNT ENCLOSED _____
Name
Address
City _____ State _____ Zip Code _____

ORDER YOURS TODAY!!

MONKEES ARCHIVES 1

If You Were A Monkee...

...YOU'D WRESTLE WITH HORSES.

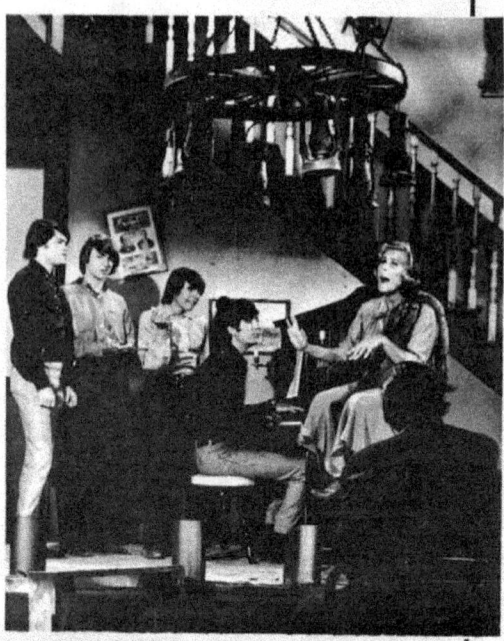
...AUDITION TALENTED (?) NEWCOMERS,

...SING TO EMPTY COUCHES

...AND INSURE GOOD RELATIONS WITH THE SERVICE.

MONKEES ARCHIVES 1

MONKEES ARCHIVES 1

The Monkees In $6 Million Suit

The Monkees had their share of trouble before they ever even hit the television screen. A temporary injunction asking for $6,850,000 and a delay in the debut of "The Monkees" was sought by two plaintiffs who charge Screen Gems with lifting the idea for the new series from them.

The plaintiffs, David Gordon (director of public relations for United Artists TV) and David Yarnell (in charge of programming and production for RKO General) claim they approached, presented and worked with Screen Gems during the past five months on a series which was allegedly very similar in nature to "The Monkees."

According to Gordon and Yarnell, the idea they presented to Screen Gems was to be named "Liverpool, U.S.A." and was to be centered around a rock 'n' roll quartet, composed of English and American members. The show was to have combined elements of comedy and contemporary music.

Gordon and Yarnell charge that in November Screen Gems informed them that the corporation was not interested in "Liverpool, U.S.A.;" however, it is the contention of Gordon and Yarnell that "The Monkees" takes its concepts and storylines from "Liverpool, U.S.A." without permission.

Court action was filed in the New York State Supreme Court and names 14 defendants in the suit, including Screen Gems, RCA Victor, Burt Schneider and Bob Rafelson (producers of "The Monkees") and co-sponsors of the show, Yardley and Kellogg.

Red Baldwin, publicist for Screen Gems, told *The BEAT* that despite court action "We're ("The Monkees") going straight ahead."

As you undoubtedly know, "The Monkees" concerns the antics of a rock group composed of four members — three of which are American and one of which, Davy Jones, is English.

Screen Gems continues to pour money and time into promoting the color series and recently held a gigantic block party at the studio to introduce the press to The Monkees. During the outdoor festivities, continuous showings of two pilot films were being held in the projection rooms.

..."THE MONKEES" (l. to r.) Mike, Mickey, Davy and Peter face a six million dollar law suit in New York.

PAT MOORE! Happy 1/100th of your centennial anniversary with KRLA! Thanks for an outasite year! Luv, Lisa and Pam, Downey.

23 x 30 MONKEE POSTER
IMPRINTED WITH YOUR OWN NAME
YOUR NAME_____
1. $ 2.98
2.   5.75
4. 10.00

NO COD's — Add 4% Sales tax in Calif.

TED HILL & CO.
707 Paige Lane
Thousand Oaks, Calif. 91360

DAVY JONES RECEIVES 1-A

HOLLYWOOD — Davy Jones, the only British member of the Monkees, has been classified 1-A by his draft board. Davy will not know until the end of July whether or not he will be called up to serve. It has been reported, however, that Davy has applied for re-classification on the grounds that he is the sole support of his father. His appeal, we understand, will take about three months to consider.

Monkee spokesmen feel that Davy will be re-classified but have stated that if he is not and is actually called up, he will certainly go.

Meanwhile, the Monkees continue filming their television series and preparing for their first concerts in England. While in Britain, the Monkees plan to tape at least one segment of their popular show.

Ho-Hum... Third Goldie For The Singing Monkees

When the Monkees go panning for gold it doesn't take them long to strike it rich.

They have a sort of ridiculous Midas touch when it comes to million-selling records. Their latest release, "I'm A Believer," has already been awarded a gold disc after only three weeks of sales.

If the Monkees ever release a single that amasses only 900,000 sales — and they haven't so far — it will be a catastrophe. Their first single and album were assured of gold awards with a record brevity.

Their first album sold so well, in fact, that RCA decided to withdraw all single copies of "Last Train To Clarksville" from the market. It didn't matter, because the disc had already sold 1,000,000 copies and the LP was selling more like a single than an album.

The album, "The Monkees," has been No. 1 in the nation since late October.

The monetary success of The Monkees' initial album prompted RCA to set back the release date on the group's second single. The response to "I'm A Believer" has been the warmest given a RCA disc since the peak of the Elvis Presley era.

And that would make a believer out of anyone.

MONKEES (l. to r.) Peter, Davy, Micky, Mike collect another one!

MONKEES ARCHIVES 1

America's Pop Music NEWSpaper

25¢

KRLA *Edition* **BEAT**

February 25, 1967

MONKEE LIFE STORIES

MICK SWITCHES GIRLS

REAL Meaning Of 'Strawberry Fields'

Switch On Fashions

BEAT Salutes The Monkees

BEAT Art: Jan Walker

MONKEES ARCHIVES 1

KRLA BEAT

Volume 2, Number 35 — February 25, 1967

SALUTES
The Monkees

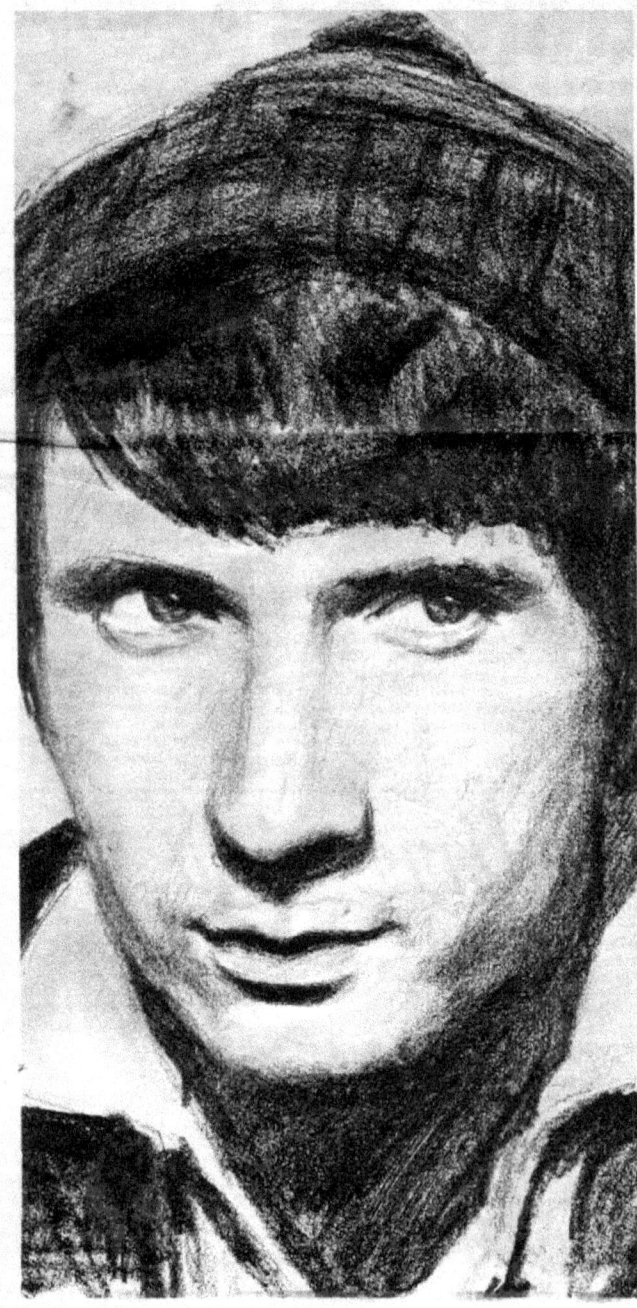

MONKEES ARCHIVES 1

Meeting 'Em Monkee By Monkee

...MICKY DOLENZ — and his dog, You.

MICKY DOLENZ was born in Los Angeles, California on March 8, 1945, the son of an actor, the late George Dolenz. Micky first entered show business at the grand old age of ten when he became television's "Circus Boy." His stint as the young Circus traveler with the pet elephant, Bimbo, lasted for three years. When the show folded, Micky returned to public school in the San Fernando Valley.

After graduating from Grant High School, Micky entered Valley College but transferred in his second semester to Los Angeles Trade Tech. His stay at Trade Tech did not last too long, however, as Micky left school to become the lead singer in a rock group called the Missing Links.

Between his jobs with the Missing Links, Micky went back to occasional acting, appearing in such television shows as "Peyton Place" and "Mr. Novak." When Micky could find neither acting nor singing jobs, he worked as a mechanic.

Like the other Monkees, Micky, of course, saw that now-famous ad in *Variety*, applied and was chosen to be one of television's Monkees. "Right now, I'm doing exactly what I want to be doing," says Micky but for his years-from-now future Micky has plenty of ambitions. He's like to go back to school, perhaps be a teacher. He'd like to produce, direct and act in his own shows. He's thought about being an architectural draftsman or an electronic engineer.

As a hobby, Micky lists photography and as for his tastes in girls — he likes girls with long hair and girls with short hair. His taste in clothes runs to double-breasted tee shirts, casual and dressy. He drives a Pontiac and digs Motown.

Micky played guitar before he ever joined the Monkees but the powers that be decided that Micky should be the group's drummer — so he took to learning the fine art of drumming.

Micky stands six-feet, is definitely on the lean side, is athletic and tends to be quite restless.

...PETER TORK — formerly of the Village.

MIKE NESMITH was born in Dallas, Texas on December 30, 1942. He was never too popular in school, due, Mike thinks, to the fact that he loved pulling pranks. Although he didn't graduate from high school, Mike entered San Antonio College which is where he met his wife, Phyllis.

Mike got a guitar for Christmas when he was 19 and immediately set about learning how to play. He couldn't read notes, so he wrote his own material. While still in college, Mike began making personal appearances, first as a country/western singer and guitarist and later as a performer of "today's sound." After college, Mike left Texas for Southern California where he teamed up with John Lundgren, a bass player, and the duo played gigs around the area. They added a drummer and became a rock group but it was very short-lived as the draft board came into the action and split up the group.

Mike joined the Air Force but as soon as his time was up he returned to the Southern California music scene at the Ledbetter's and Troubadour as a solo folk act.

Roughly a year ago, his friends urged him to answer the *Variety* ad. "I don't know why they chose me," says Mike, "but I'm glad they did because I am really enjoying everything that's happening to me."

Mike stands at six-foot one, weighs 155 pounds, has dark brown hair and eyes and is constantly seen wearing a wool hat on screen but not off. He enjoys stripping down cars, hotrodding and riding skate boards. He has a small son named Christian.

PETER TORK was born in Washington, D.C. on February 13, 1942 and raised in Connecticut. His father, H. J. Torkelson, is now an Associate Professor of Economics at the University of Connecticut. Peter's father was a First Lieutenant in the Army and was stationed in Berlin, which is where Peter spent the early part of his life.

Upon the family's return to America, they settled in Madison, Wisconsin. Since children start to school in Germany when they're five, Peter was always younger than his classmates when he returned to school in the U.S. This caused Peter to be unhappy in school and unable to make many friends because of his age.

Peter became interested in drama during high school but never played a leading role in a school play because he was too small. He worked on the campus humor magazine with his brother, Nick, but didn't become interested in popular music until he entered Carleton College with the goal of becoming an English professor. His first try at college life failed and Peter spent the next year working in a thread factory. Peter tried college again after the thread factory but flunked out at the beginning of his junior year.

Although he had played French horn in the school bands, Peter did not really go professional until he hit Greenwich Village. He performed as a singer/musician in various pass-the-hat spots in the Village and eventually landed a job accompanying the Phoenix Singers.

Peter was in Los Angeles only two months (playing local clubs) when he read the ad, applied and was made a Monkee.

...MIKE NESMITH — from Texas with love.

DAVY JONES was born on December 30, 1945 in Manchester, England. His father was a railroad fitter and while certainly not destitute the Jones family *was* on the poor side. Davy's favorite game as a child was playing doctor and because his father didn't have enough money to buy many toys, Davy made his own.

Davy remembers going to church with his family but not liking it much "because I had to sit still." He wanted to join the church choir but was rejected because everyone thought he had a terrible voice! To make up for the choir rejection, Davy would go to the hospitals and sing to the patients.

He was definitely sports-minded and when he was 13 he played on all three school football teams. Davy's mother was a pianist, his three sisters sang and Davy performed in the school plays — though he seldom captured a leading role because he was so small. One role he *did* get and loved was that of Tom Sawyer.

Davy's mother died when he was 14 and it was during that same year that he left home with his father's blessing to become a jockey. During his training at the Newmarket Racetrack, Davy acted between his riding jobs. His first acting job resulted from an audition at the BBC where he played a juvenile delinquent in a radio drama. This, in turn, lead to a steady job on a daytime series called "Morning Story."

Davy still continued at the racetrack and it was through his riding that he met London theatrical executives who helped him land a leading role in the musical hit, "Oliver." Davy played the Artful Dodger and came to the U.S. with the company when "Oliver" opened Stateside. He was then 16.

Following "Oliver," Davy stepped into "Pickwick" and it was this show which brought him to Hollywood. While here he did guest spots on several television series, his most remembered being that of a glue-sniffer on "Ben Casey."

Not many people remember, but Davy gave the singing business a try during this period, signing with Colpix and releasing a single, "What Are We Going To Do," which subsequently bombed.

...DAVY JONES — from horses to Monkees.

MONKEES ARCHIVES 1

SHOOTING THE MONKEES
Is Like Riding A Roller Coaster

..."SURE YOU LOOK like Tarzan."

..."OH, YEAH!"

..."OH, NO!"

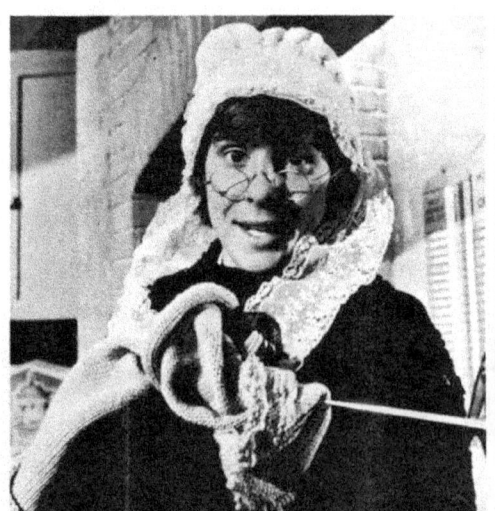
..."THE BETTER TO eat you with, my dear."

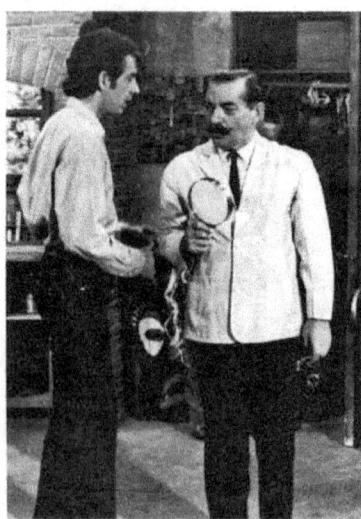
...BUT there are no Monkees here."

..."I AM TOO Super Frog!"

MONKEES ARCHIVES 1

Getting Down To MONKEE Business

Opens Exclusive Engagement
CREST THEATRE—February 15

It's all about a typical everyday American family consisting of a mother, two man-eating piranhas, several Venus fly-traps, her baby son, age 25, his luscious baby sitter and Dad, who of course just hangs around the house.

Oh Dad, Poor Dad, Mamma's Hung You In The Closet And I'm Feelin' So Sad

Rosalind Russell · Robert Morse · Barbara Harris · Hugh Griffith · Jonathan Winters

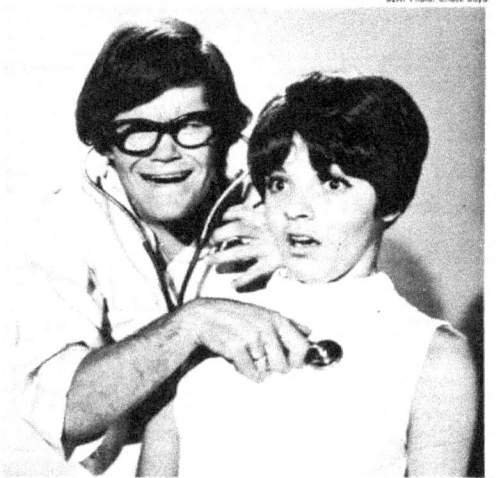

MONKEES ARCHIVES 1

Tailoring For The Monkees

By Rochelle Reed

Outfitting the Monkees is a big business! Davy, Mike, Peter and Micky own 250 pairs of pants for screen wear alone, and the sewing machines are whirring every day.

Since they began filming, the Monkees have collected some 1800 sets of clothes, and that's just a start — so says Gene Ashman, who assumes the mammoth, but fascinating task of clothing all four guys.

An expert in the field, Gene has clothed major movie stars for over 16 years, but that doesn't make him uncool — Gene knows a groovy outfit when he sees it. Or designs it, as the case may be.

Gene and a Hollywood clothier, Lenny Able, collaborated on the design of the double button shirts which have become almost a trademark for the group, and Lenny sewed them up.

Plasterin front

Lenny wound up making numerous sets of the shirts, which have a "Plasterin front" and not double breasted front, Gene explained. The guys own them in four different colors — burgundy, Navy blue, gold and cream.

With the shirts, the Monkees generally wear Herringbone or Gambler's Stripe (larger than pin stripe) pants and, of course, boots. Their trousers, tapered and fitted especially for each Monkee, are cut about two inches higher than the usual hip-hugger design but give the appearance of being the real thing.

The Monkees are seldom forced to go through tiring fittings. Early in their careers, they were measured by the studio tailor shop and the shop presents each haberdasher with exact figures from which he cuts the clothes. The Monkees themselves drop by only if special tailoring is needed.

Gene describes Monkee clothes as the "Mod-Western look." An appropriate tag, it sums up the slightly English clothes Davy wears, the Western garb favored by Mike and the in-between styles worn by Micky and Peter.

Different Styles

Though the Monkees' clothes usually look identical on television, closer examination reveals they are cut differently for each member of the group. While Davy wears his modified English style suits, Mike's may be three button, Peter's one button and Micky's double-breasted.

"We wanted something not strictly Carnaby Street," Gene explained, adding that many Carnaby costumes are "absolute plagiarism of old period costumes,"

The main idea, he went on, is to "complement the Monkees rather than make them unique." In other words, Screen Gems wants the Monkees easily identifiable to everyone, and not freaks or clothes horses. They also want each Monkee to be an individual, and wear clothes fitting his personality.

Future Monkee shows will hold changes and additions to the Monkee wardrobe. New shirts have just been completed, and are a distinct departure from the double button style. The basic front design this time is a V-shape, designed to make the shoulders appear wide and then narrow down at the waist.

..."MOD-WESTERN"

...GAMBLER'S STRIPE PANTS

...MODIFIED ENGLISH

...TIE-SCARF COMING UP

The shirts, made in a cotton Chambray material, have been sewn up in three colors.

Gene has also designed a "tie-scarf" for the Monkees. Somewhere between an ascot and a tie, it is worn close to the neck like an ascot or can be draped underneath the collar, like a scarf or tie.

Both Lenny and Gene agreed that "the guys have great taste." Davy and Mike especially are noted for knowing when they try on a suit whether it looks right or not. "They are 99 per cent right," Lenny added.

But can you ever imagine the Monkees getting their clothes dirty? Happens all the time, says Gene. And each night after filming stops, all the Monkees clothes are dry cleaned and returned to the set by the next morning.

In their private lives, the Monkees dress very much as they do on screen. Davy just recently, purchased some modified bell-bottom trousers for his vacation, along with several shirts.

Though Monkee styles are less extreme than many worn by pop groups, they are definitely trend setters. In fact, Gene predicts that within several months, people all over the world will be switching on with the "Mod-Western Look."

THE ASSOCIATION
NO FAIR AT ALL
V 758
From
Their Album
RENAISSANCE
Valiant RECORDS

MONKEES ARCHIVES 1

BOYCE AND HART:
What It's Like Cutting The Monkees

By Eden

"We've had many, many funny experiences with the Monkees in the studio, beginning with the first session we ever had with them. We *met* them at the studio for the first time after we'd written the first three songs for the pilot, which hadn't been made yet. The guys had just been picked – in fact, we sat through about 97 interviews when they were picking the guys."

The young man speaking was Bobby Hart – one half of the successful Boyce-Hart songwriting team that has become internationally famous for their work with the Monkees as writers and producers.

Seated in a conference room down the hall from their Hollywood offices, the boys were reminiscing about some of their early experiences with the phenomenal young quartet. Bobby continued:

Bad Quartet

"We finally met the four of them in the studio and they decided they were going to try to sing our song, the Monkee theme – except, they had *never rehearsed it* – I don't think they ever saw the song until that time! They weren't really that enthused! It sounded like a *bad barber shop quartet* at that time!"

"They hadn't been together too much and they were just getting to know each other, so they were nervous too," Tommy injected. "Right," agreed Bobby, "it was a new thing for all of us." "We were kind of nervous that night too; and *we* sounded like *bad barbers!*" concluded Tommy.

"And then we all got into a wrestling match on the floor," Bobby remembered. "It was kind of a *disaster* – it lasted about an hour and then we all gave in!"

Tommy took over the story here and explained that: "Recording with the boys is very interesting; we look forward to it. They're sort of relaxed now, so when we go to a recording session, it's not like a regular recording session where everybody's up-tight and real nervous; we just get very, very relaxed and we always have fun.

"Micky's a comedian and he cracks a lot of jokes and does a lot of imitations – like Jonathan Winters and stuff like that. They're *all* funny – Peter and Mike and Davy."

Both Tommy and Bobby agreed that one of their funniest experiences was cutting the "Gonna Buy Me A Dog" track on the first album. Tommy remembered: "Most of that song was like an ad-lib, all this talking – it was Davy and Micky just sort of ad-libbing because they really dig each other, and they just started ad-libbing throughout that song. Davy started saying things back to Micky, and Micky kept saying things back to Davy during the song and it was so funny that we decided that we should leave that in. That's the way they were on television and that's the way they *are*; they're very funny."

Bobby added that: "If you've heard that cut on the album – well, *every* song that we recorded with them started out that way. They have fun with everything they do."

At this point, Tommy and Bobby decided to sing *their* version of the tune for me, and in an attempt to find the right note (K minor, I think!); Bobby suddenly got up from the table and very quietly walked over to the corner of the room and stood on his head, humming the note of C, and looking much like an inverted human pitch fork! The Monkees are not the only comedians in this group!

"They're On"

Once he managed to return himself to an upright position, Bobby continued to speak about his four zany friends: "They're funny constantly; they're *on* all the time, just as long as there is anyone around to watch, they're *on!* From the first time we met them until now, they've always been *on*. It's like continual unbelievably funny things, one after another. They're always doing something funny!"

Tommy and Bobby have spent some time on tour with The Monkees, and Tommy recalled one funny incident which occurred on the road recently. "We went with them to Phoenix and after the show, there were about 15,000 people there running and screaming: Bobby and I were in a limousine trying to get out of the crowd, and about 40 of them jumped on top of the limousine. They were sitting on top of the car, and the guy was driving down the street and there were girls' feet and arms hanging off the top and we were going about 30 miles an hour; there were people hanging all over the top and they were crushing the top in – they pulled out the aerial and broke the air conditioning and the radio – and we rolled down the window and said, 'Hey girls – we're going on the *freeway* in a minute and you'd better jump off!' And we were riding right down the *middle of town* and there were *30* girls all over the car! They were just hanging on and it was a very wild thing; but, they finally jumped off and nobody was hurt."

Hysterical Girls

Bobby picked up from there: "There were always girls backstage who fainted, and they were carried out on stretchers and ambulances – some of them were hysterical and some of them just wanted to meet the Monkees. But many times I saw, mostly Micky – sometimes Davy, and sometimes one of the others – go over and put his arm around a girl who was particularly overcome and comfort her. Micky's very good with the kids – if there were a choice, he'd go out into the crowd and associate with the kids rather than running."

Tommy and Bobby both feel that the images which the public has of the four Monkees are actually quite close to what they are as human beings; they really are warm, generous, funny, fun-loving guys "when they are at home." Most importantly, both boys agree that the Monkees are four of the best friends they have – and four of the grooviest guys *anywhere.*

... "WE MET THEM after we'd written the first three songs."

... "THEY'RE FUNNY constantly."

... "THERE WERE always girls backstage."

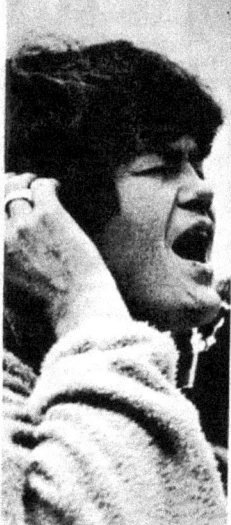

... "MICKY'S A comedian."

"WRESTLING on the floor."

Mobs, Chaos, Knockers — For Monkees What Price Fame?

By Louise Criscione

Davy Jones is not physically big anyway—not that it matters much how huge you are when you find yourself the object of so powerful a fan force that they'd tear you apart like a piece of paper if given half a chance.

"I don't mind admitting I'm frightened by this whole thing," said Davy. "Frightened" has to be the understatement of the century. "Terrified" would be much more appropriate.

When "The Monkees" recently took a three week break from filming, Davy, Micky and Mike headed for England. Mike didn't stay long, Micky extended his visit several days but it was Davy who caused an uproar England won't soon forget—and all because he wanted to visit his family.

Mob Scene

Met at the London Airport by a mob 700 strong, Davy was hidden in a customs room while police attempted (unsuccessfully) to move the crowd along. Driven out in a police car and then transferred into a limousine, Davy arrived at the hotel only to find over a hundred fans encircling the entire premises.

But the worst was yet to come. Davy's father lives in Manchester and his fans know it. Consequently, when Davy arrived at his family's home looking for a little peace after the chaos in London he found anything but. "We found that there were hundreds of them (fans) outside the house," said Davy. "We made several attempts to stop so that I could go in the house but it was too dangerous. The girls had already smashed the front gate."

Impersonation

In desperation, Davy dressed up as a woman, got some neighborhood kids to walk along with him as if he were their mother and succeeded in getting around to the back of the house, climbing a fence and making it inside. Davy didn't think the fans knew he was there but it made little difference as they merrily went about their business of smashing all the windows and breaking down a door. A phone call brought every available police car to the Jones' residence and the risky job of getting the girls out of the area and Davy safely out of the house got underway.

Davy left uninjured but disgustedly reported: "In a whole week, I've been able to see my father for just two hours." Lovely price for fame. "If they can cause so much damage to the car, what would they do to me?" asked Davy. Not much. Break an arm, a leg, smash a head. Not much at all.

Those of you who think the Monkees are already rich are wrong. They reportedly make a flat $400 a week on the show and another 30 per cent of the gross from their personal appearances—after all expenses are taken out. Of course, they make record royalties—but, generally, royalties are notoriously late in arriving.

The future for the Monkees is assured for at least another year. Their television show has been picked up for another season, they're set to make a movie, they've been booked to play the World's Fair in April and, of course, they will continue recording and making personal appearances.

In the far away future, Davy thinks he'll stick with acting, Mike and Peter will go solo and Micky will become a comedian. As for the knockers who have been constantly chipping away at the Monkees, Micky, Peter, Mike and Davy sort of shrug their shoulders at the inevitability of success bringing jealousy and whistle on their way to the bank.

Ad Lib

The scripts for their show are more of a guide line than a Bible. Roughly 85 per cent of the series is strictly ad lib. Whole scenes are discarded if the Monkees don't feel they're right and each Monkee changes his lines if they don't suit his personality.

The Monkees each have their own dressing room which assures them of at least a small domain of privacy, though the set itself is always overrun with visitors who pay no heed to the "closed set" sign which is obviously more of an ornament than a law.

Home-based in Hollywood, the Monkees have little or no trouble with wild mob scenes, although their fans stage all-out searches to find their homes and phone numbers. The grapevine system is amazing and fans knock on Davy's door at all hours of the day and night. But compared to the mess in England, Davy's apartment is a real bed of tranquility.

Safe At Home

The Monkees are rarely bothered in clubs and are relatively free to come and go as they please. In fact, Davy and Micky once visited a Sunset Strip club and were not even asked for so much as an autograph the entire evening! Another time, Micky went to an after-hours club and no one seemed the slightest bit ruffled because a Monkee was in their midst.

Once out of Hollywood or once on a stage, however, everything changes. Mob scenes break out with regularity, extra squadrons of police are needed, objects hurled through the air manage to hit at least one Monkee (not to mention unfortunate fans seated in the line of fire) and pandemonium reigns supreme. "When something like that happens," says Davy, "you feel you want to walk off."

But you can't. You're a star and it's all part of the game.

MICKY THE TOUGH GUY? Not on your life — he's a comedian.

DAVY AND HIS dad — long ago when there was privacy.

PETER TORK AND LEAH (Cass Elliott's sister) on the Monkee set.

MIKE NESMITH PUTS on a serious face for some guitar playing.

Lenny's Salutes The No. 1 Group In The United States

LENNY'S BOOT PARLOR

1448 GOWER STREET

HOLLYWOOD, CALIFORNIA 90028

WRITE FOR FREE CATALOG

MONKEES ARCHIVES 1

America's Pop Music NEWSpaper 25¢

KRLA Edition BEAT
JANUARY 28, 1967

MONKEES SURPASS BEATLE SALES!
See Page 1

MONKEES ARCHIVES 1

Monkees Top Beatle Record!

The Monkees are one up on the Beatles. The four Monkees have broken the existing Beatle record by selling over three million copies of their first album, "The Monkees," — more than *any* previous Beatle album has sold!

"Last Train To Clarksville" has sold well over the one million mark and "I'm A Believer" has already passed the two and half million point. Meanwhile, advance orders on the Monkees' second album, "More Of The Monkees," indicate that it will, in all probability, outsell their first LP.

Controversy

Ever since the Monkees first graced the nation's airwaves, they've been the object of heated controversy with one side claiming the Monkees are nothing but Beatle imitators while the other side stoutly proclaims the Monkees are *not* imitators but an original, talented group.

Perhaps the only objective way to decipher who is the world's top group is through the number of discs sold and the number of attendance records set. Judging popularity on that basis, the Beatles are still the number one group. However, in the span of only four months, the Monkees have already topped the Beatles in the number of albums sold — leaving only single records and personal appearances to go before they officially take-over the Beatle crown.

With two and half million copies of "I'm A Believer" sold in the U.S. alone, the Monkees are not even near the all-time Beatle record of five million copies of "I Want To Hold Your Hand."

Monkee personal appearances have been necessarily limited due to the filming of their television show. However, they have managed to break away for short tours — their last grossing $159,753 in only four concerts. They still have quite a way to go before they top the Beatle records of selling-out such places as Shea Stadium in New York and the Hollywood Bowl.

The Monkees have managed, though, to cause the same sort of wild hysteria which goes hand-in-hand with a Beatle concert. Their first personal appearance, in Hawaii, saw the Monkees playing before a packed audience while wave upon wave of anxious Monkee fans hurled themselves bodily at the stage.

Mob Scene

"Fifty cops were fighting them off with clubs," said Davy Jones, recalling the mob scene in Hawaii. "I don't want any part of that. But I suppose they have to do it. If the girls got to us they would tear us apart."

Up until December 31, the Monkees belonged exclusively to the U.S. but now their television show is being aired over the BBC and "I'm A Believer" sold over 400,000 in the first week of British release.

(Turn To Page 5)

...MONKEES READ fairy tales and sell over three million albums!

RUMOR HAS IT DAVY JONES was originally intended for part.

Movie Script Big Decision For Monkees

The Monkees were already discussing plans for their first movie last week as they arrived back in California from their smash personal appearance tour of Hawaii.

Still in search of a suitable script, the boys agreed that after their unique TV series they would have to be highly selective.

"We want it to be as different a movie," said Micky Dolenz, "as the series was to TV. And we want to bring back a lot of the old Hollywood glamour and excitement with it."

The foursome first realized their national popularity when they were greeted by a mob scene on their first outing in Hawaii.

Back in California, however, Mike Nesmith admits the Monkees still have a way to go. He was refused admittance at Martoni's in Hollywood.

"I agree I looked kinda scruffy in a blue jean jacket and with this long hair," he said. "That's why I asked if we could come in. When they said no, we went to the Villa Capri!"

Whether you like it or not, the Monkees are very big business. On their just-completed U.S. tour, the boys grossed a neat $159,753 in just four cities. Davy Jones took time off before the tour to visit England, where "The Monkees" is now being aired on the BBC, and left his native country in the wake of all sorts of predictions that England would soon follow America in proclaiming the Monkees one of the biggest groups on the scene.

However, being a Monkee is not *entirely* peaches and cream — though about 90% of it is! While certainly a popular show, "The Monkees" ran into early rating problems but recently picked up enough ratings to virtually assure it of another season on television.

But the four Monkees find themselves in the position of being the objects of some rather heated jealousy from other pop groups. Davy admits that the Monkees take quite a bit of chopping from groups who have had to work long and hard in all sorts of dives in order to make it big and, therefore, resent the fact that the Monkees had it all made for them. What the other groups *don't* realize, according to Davy, is that: "We're not a group, we're an *act*." A popular act, Mr. Jones, a *popular* act. And that, in essence, is the difference.

...PETER TORK

MONKEES ARCHIVES 1

FIRST PRESS CONFERENCE
Monkees In London

By Tony Barrow

In four days of happy but hectic activity The Monkees met between three and four hundred press, radio and TV people and presented their stage show before a total of 50,000 British fans.

They flew into London from Paris minutes before midnight to be greeted by a roof-top crowd of 300 fans perched high on the balconies of Queen's Building at London's Heathrow Airport. To make sure that those fans had a good chance of seeing the group, Micky, Davy, Mike and Peter broke away from their own ring of security personnel, vaulted over a set of steel barriers and raced across towards Queen's Building with a score of news photographers and TV cameramen in hot pursuit.

During the four days and nights which followed, thousands of fans besieged both the Royal Garden Hotel (where the Monkees' entourage took over most of the heavily guarded fifth floor) and the Empire Pool, Wembley, North London (where the group made its series of five appearances).

The Press Conference, held in the huge Buckingham Suite Ballroom of the Royal Garden Hotel in Kensington, was attended by representatives of almost every European newspaper, magazine and news medium including more than a hundred photographers. As is the convention at these curiously frightening affairs, the standard of questioning was far from high. Yet, the Monkees, facing an ordeal of this type for the first time in their brief group career, coped well with the battery of banality, coming back with brisk ad libs or lengthy explanations according to the mood of each question.

These are assorted extracts from the 20-minute exchange between Monkees and writers:

You come here surrounded by a sort of mythology about being a pre-packaged group and under considerable attack from the critics. Does this matter to you?
PETER: *No, it doesn't bother us that we come under attack. As far as we're concerned you can't help that. These stories about us being a pre-packaged group, I mean in the sense that you mean the words, it is quite true.*
MICKY: (Applauding) *Jolly good!*
MIKE: *It's pretty much the same way everybody else forms a group whether it's John Lennon walking down the street asking Paul, Ringo and George to join him or whether it's someone putting an ad in a paper. You've got to start somewhere.*

What thoughts have you all given to what you're going to do when the series goes off?
DAVY: *We know it's sold for another year in America and we have a pretty good chance of making it another year after that. Then we'll be tired of being Monkees, I should think, in about six years from now but we'll still be playing together I suppose.*
MICKY: *We'll probably go off and do different things — like one of us or two of us, and then three and then four. Whichever way the wind blows.*

DAVY AND PETER ARRIVING IN LONDON.

Is the feature film you're going to make an extension of your TV series or made on an entirely new concept?
MICKY: *We'd like it to be an entirely new concept. If you've any ideas please let us know. Anybody ... mail 'em in!*

Micky, after you've finished your TV series are you going to continue with your pop career?
MICKY: *I intend to stay in some field of entertainment. I'd like to get in production and movies and records and shows and films and making candle holders on my lathe and I'm getting into electronic music and I've just bought a mock synthesiser and I'm trying to discover anti-gravity and all kinds of things like that.*
PETER: *It took him six months to learn to say "synthesise."*

When you prepare for a press conference like this do you antici- pate the line of questioning and do you agree on a certain line the answers ought to take?
MICKY: *We've never had a press conference like this. It's the first one ever. It's really neat too.*

Did you do any preparation for it?
DAVY: *We had breakfast this morning!*
MICKY: *We've been asked the same questions before but not in this kind of a circumstance.*

I'd like to ask Davy just how far his plans as an independent record producer have gone and if he is recording groups who are they.
MICKY: *The Beatles.*
DAVY: *Yeah, I have a group called The Children. They're a Texas group, six boys and one girl. We cut three tracks at a recording studio in Hollywood. It turned out well.*

Have you any plans to grow any
(Turn to Page 19)

MONKEES
(Continued From Page 1)

The Monkees intend to insure their already snow-balling English popularity by flying over around the first of February for a ten day visit aimed, primarily, at radio and television promotion.

If all goes as planned, the Monkees will make a three week return visit to England on a tour with the Troggs during August. However, this tour is still in the negotiation stage.

Whether the Monkees manage to overthrow the Beatles or not, at least they have the satisfaction of knowing they've come the closest yet.

Monkees Hold First Press Conference—But In England

LONDON — The Monkees held their first-ever press conference, and in England yet, before more than 400 journalists who showed up for what was to kick off the group's United Kingdom tour.

Bert Rafelson, one of the creators of the Monkees, said he expects the group to gross over $85,000 on the tour. A world tour is predicted for next year, and a for-sure set of concerts has been scheduled for the Orient in February.

Rafelson may film the concerts, although the release date for such a production is not known. There's a good chance that Screen Gems may do the flick for movie-house distribution.

European Press Meets Monkees

(Continued from Page 3)

facial hair in the near future?
PETER: *I can't stop myself! No, I'd like to grow a beard one of these years.*
MICKY: *We can't. The Beatles did it already.*
PETER: *We'd be accused of imitating. Ha! Ha!*

Mike, do you think it's a good thing for you to take your wife on tours?
MIKE: *I think it would be kinda dangerous.*
Why?
MIKE: *I'll let you figure that out!*

Davy, there have been reports that you're unhappy about being a Monkee, that you're restless and that you feel you could now afford to go solo. Have you any plans to do that this year?
DAVY: *No, I don't. I might as well clear it up now by saying I am NOT leaving the Monkees and I'll be with them as long as they're Monkees. That's all just rumours.*

The Beatles have admitted to taking L.S.D....
MICKY: *Ah! There it is! That was the one we were waiting for!* (Laughter) (continuing) ... *also two of The Rolling Stones who are on drug charges claim that drugs help them in their work. Judging by one of two of the tracks on the Beatles' LP it gives some people inspiration. Do you think it necessary for pop groups to take drugs?*
MICKY: *Do you like The Beatles album?*
Yes.
MICKY: *Well?*
But do you think it is necessary?
MICKY: *No.*
Do you take them yourselves?
MICKY: *Coffee. I drink coffee. That's about the worst drug I take.*
PETER: *I took aspirin once. It destroyed my head and provided me with a lot of inspiration. I'm gonna write a song.*
MIKE: *I have a real problem. I get high on one-a-day vitamins.*
MICKY: *I drink chlorine with ...*
DAVY: *Ex-Lax does it to me. It keeps me going all the time. No? O.K.!*
MICKY: *No, I don't think anybody needs anything. It's just whatever is right for whoever is involved.*

MONKEES ARCHIVES 1

A Day in the Life of.....

MONKEES, Peter, Micky, Mike and Davy rehearse as Shieks for upcoming television segment.

The MONKEES

Only a couple of years ago, a day in the lives of Davy Jones, Mike Nesmith, Micky Dolenz and Peter Tork would have been a colorless thing indeed. For Peter and Mike, little-known folk singers, Micky, a former child actor, and Davy, an ex-apprentice jockey, one day was pretty much like any other — until, that is, they were brought together as the Monkees.

Today, two years and unaccountable record hits later, they are the most popular vocal group in the country and on the move constantly. A day in the life of the Monkees is divided between recording sessions, screen shootings for their television series, live performances on stages across the nation, and, if they are lucky, an occasional break for rest.

A day in the life of Davy, Mike, Micky and Peter is anything but dull today, as the pictures on this page show.

MIKE — Thoughtful interlude.

DAVY — At poolside break.

ABOARD PLANE, Monkees rest for concert

PETER — Swinging from a tree.

CROWD meets boys outside hotel.

MONKEES ARCHIVES 1

BUSY MONKEE SUMMER

Monkee fans all over the country mark your calendars for what will be the top rock event of the summer. Dick Clark Productions is sending the fab foursome around the country during July and August for a string of one-nighters, according to an announcement by Rosalind Ross, DCP's executive director.

The Monkees will play some of their many recent hits at 31 single appearances and are set for a three-day stand at Forest Hills Tennis Stadium in New York during mid-July. Here is the Monkee's tour schedule:

July 7, Atlanta, Ga., Braves Stadium; July 8, Jacksonville, Fla., Convention Hall; July 11, Charlotte, N.C., Coliseum; July 12, Greensboro, N.C., Coliseum; July 14-16, New York, Forest Hills Stadium; July 20, Buffalo, N.Y., Memorial Auditorium; July 21, Baltimore, Md., Memorial Auditorium; July 22, Boston, Mass., Boston Gardens; July 23, Philadelphia, Pa., Convention Hall; July 27, Rochester, N.Y., War Memorial Auditorium; July 28, Cinn., Ohio, Gardens; July 29, Detroit, Mich., Olympia Stadium; July 30, Chicago, Ill., Stadium; Aug. 2, Milwaukee, Wisc., Arena; Aug. 4, St. Paul, Minn., Municipal Auditorium; Aug. 5, St. Louis, Mo., Kiel Auditorium; Aug. 9, Dallas, Texas, Memorial Auditorium; Aug. 10, Houston, Texas, Sam Houston Coliseum; Aug. 11, Shreveport, La., Hirsch Memorial Coliseum; Aug. 12, Mobile, Ala., Municipal Auditorium; Aug. 17, Memphis, Tenn., Mid-South Coliseum; Aug. 18, Tulsa, Okla., Assembly Center; Okla. City, Okla., State Fair Arena; Aug. 20, Denver, Colo., Coliseum; Aug. 25, Seattle, Wash., Seattle Center Coliseum; Aug. 26, Portland, Ore., Memorial Coliseum; Aug. 27, Spokane, Wash., Coliseum.

DAVY JONES NIXS RUMORS

Rumors that Davy Jones is going to play the title role in the screen version of Lionel Bart's "Oliver" have been vigorously denied by the firm making the picture, Romulus Films. British newspapers have carried stories suggesting that Davy wants a vacation from the Monkees to accept the part.

A spokesman for Romulus said there is no truth whatsoever in these reports and that Davy's name has not even been mentioned. He called such speculation nonsense since Oliver is the role of a child.

Another rumor that the Monkees and the Beatles will split the bill in a "Battle of the Giants" concert has been strenuously denied by both Nems and Screen Gems.

Davy Jones released a single recently using Bob Dylan's "It Ain't Me Babe" backed with "Baby It's Me." Both tracks are from a previous Davy Jones LP.

Davy Draft Upsets U.K.

LONDON: "Dear President Johnson: We are very much against writing you this letter but it seems necessary because you plan to draft Davy Jones of the Monkees." It goes on. "We know maybe Davy won't protest but if you don't draft him, he won't have to."

It is a letter, signed by 2,000 fans and handed to the U.S. Embassy in London by a crowd of 150 angry teens. One placard read, "Singer not soldier, Monkee not guerilla."

Said an 11-year-old girl, "It's all very well to say get out there and fight, but he's too small. He only weighs about eight stones, eight pounds (120 lbs.) and what would the Monkees do without him?"

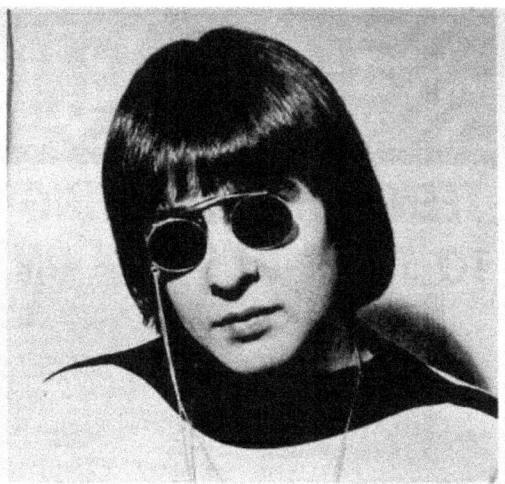

DICK CLARK SIGNS MONKEES FOR EAST

LOS ANGELES — Dick Clark Productions has announced that they will promote a series of three concerts by the Monkees at the Forest Hills Tennis Station in New York.

Dick Clark will host the shows which are set for July 14, 15 and 16. The Monkees will do one show per night in the open-air 14,000-plus seat arena, which will be scaled to gross over $300,000 for the three days.

Just in case of rain, Clark has also rented the Stadium on the nights of July 17, 18 and 19.

Monkee Lets Secret Slip

That harmonic accompaniment behind the Monkees on their TV show and deluge of records is coming from a source other than Mickey Dolenz, Davy Jones, Mike Nesmith and Peter Tork.

One of the Monkees admitted the well-kept secret last week in an interview with New York Times reporter Judy Stone. He said, however, the group does its own singing.

An unnamed Monkee is quoted as saying, "Studio musicians were used for the recordings, although all the boys do play guitars and Micky is learning to play drums."

The BEAT has learned three of the Monkees' back-up musicians are members of the New Order, a Warner Bros.' instrumental group. They are guitarist Jerry McGee, bassist Larry Taylor and drummer Bill Lewis.

Had a nice chat with the Monkees the other day and managed to come up with a real scoop for you Monkee fans, especially you Mickey Dolenz fans. "I'm gonna buy a helicopter! They're groovy, they're so out of sight!" exclaimed Mickey. "They fly right over the roofs and you can stick out your foot and hit people in the head!" And where is Mickey going to keep this helicopter of his? "On the roof." Naturally.

All kidding aside, though, the Monkees are really a great bunch of funny guys. They're one of the dying few who still get a kick out of signing autographs and talking to fans, etc. A groovy change from a lot of the swell-headed, in love with themselves groups which are making the scene today.

Two A Week

The ones who really amaze me, however, are Tommy Boyce and Bobby Hart. They write the material for the Monkees and are supposed to come up with two new songs for each segment! Which is a heck of a lot of writing, you must admit. And besides all the writing for the Monkees, Tommy records as a solo artist for A&M Records and Bobby has his own group. Gluttons for punishment? Maybe, but just think of all the money they must be making!

Brian Jones was supposed to have broken his hand so badly that he would be out of action for the next two months. It must have

... MICKEY DOLENZ

Good news for you Monkee fans this week. It looks as if Screen Gems and Columbia have finally worked out an agreement whereby the Monkees will make a movie. The deal supposedly is that Columbia will be allowed to make a Monkee movie if Screen Gems receives exclusive rights to turn "The Professionals" into a television series! The theory of "give a little, get a little" put to good use.

Hearts Club Band" album ... Big U.K. press stories manufactured from unfounded rumour that DAVY JONES might play "Oliver!" in movie version of the Lionel Bart musical.

DORS presented with a demand for 160,000 dollars by British tax authorities ... From recently issued album of pre-Monkees solo recordings by DAVY JONES, Pye Records have now put out his

... MIKE NESMITH

MONKEES ARCHIVES 1

Monkees To Be TV's Beatles?

Will the Monkees be to television what the Beatles are to the recording industry – the biggest thing to hit the screen since commercials? Screen Gems thinks so and accordingly has signed Davy Jones, Mike Nesmith, Mickey Dolenz and Peter Tork (collectively known as the Monkees) to an exclusive seven year contract.

Says Steve Blaunder of Screen Gems: "We plan to give them the same publicity treatment as the Beatles in every respect. With 30,000,000 people watching them regularly Monday night they should be bigger than the Beatles."

Movies

The studio also announced that under the terms of the contract, they will produce one or more feature films starring the Monkees. The group's first film is scheduled for shooting during the summer of '67 when the television show takes it's "vacation" from filming. Other movies will be made depending on the success of the series.

However, that success seems assured. Screen Gems has spent a small fortune on the Monkees and, from all indications, it is paying off with big dividends.

Following the show's debut on NBC, The BEAT questioned roughly a hundred young people who had seen the show. The overwhelming majority of the teens were enthusiastically in favor of the Monkees, both as actors and as singers.

At random, then, here are some of the comments we received. "They're really groovy, I especially love Davy Jones. He's so darling."

"I thought the show was great. It's kinda like 'A Hard Day's Night' but it's even better 'cause it's in color and we can see it every week."

"I liked it but it was a little corny in parts. The guys are groovy, though, and I hope they have one of those interviews at the end of the show every week. That was the best part – except for the commercials. They were funny, too."

Fresh Ideal

"I dug it because it's a fresh, new idea for a television series. I think it's good for at least two years, maybe even longer. Of course, next year we'll probably have a show like that on every single station but like the Beatles, the Monkees will always be the most popular because they were first."

"I luv 'em. Mickey and Mike are so funny and Davy's so cute and Peter's just so . . . Anyway, even my parents liked the show and

(Turn to Page 5)

THE MONKEES (l. to r.) Mike, Mickey, Davy and Peter have been signed to an exclusive seven year contract by Screen Gems with movies also in the offing. Their first feature film is scheduled for the summer of '67.

The Monkees On Top?

(Continued from Page 1)
they promised not to laugh at me when I sit in front of the television and drool at them!"

"They're great. I dig the show. That's all."

"I wish it was on for an hour. It seems like it just comes on and then it's over. I also wish I had a color television."

And so the comments went – on and on and on. No one could think of anything particularly bad to say about the show, other than the fact that the plot was not all it could be. However, it was felt that the excellent camera work and the show's funny bits more than made up for the lack of script.

Therefore, the Monkees, according to your opinion, are "in" solidly as far as their television show is concerned and, from all reports, they're not bombing out as recording artists either. "Last Train To Clarksville" is making it's way up the charts all over the country and their first album, "The Monkees," is giving record stores a gigantic headache – you seem to be buying it faster than they can stock it!

Monkees Finish In 'Clarksville'

Would you believe it? RCA is spending money on someone other than Elvis Presley! The recepients of the latest bit of RCA promotion were the Monkees. The label, distributors of the Monkees' Colgems material, took the group on a ten day promotional tour which wound itself up in Del Mar, California where the city's name was officially changed to Clarksville for the day.

During the whirlwind tour, the four Monkees visited Chicago, Boston and New York. "We got mobbed in New York," Mickey Dolenz told *The BEAT* but when pressed for details admitted, "Well, we weren't exactly *mobbed*. But the girls tried to get us and we had to have guards and the whole bit. It was really groovy!"

Obviously excited about the group's newly-found popularity, Mickey continued: "We really don't know where it's at yet. I mean, like we just got back from the tour and then we got up this morning, flew down to San Diego, took a helicopter to Del Mar and now we're on a train to L.A.!"

The Monkees' tour was more to meet the press than anyone else, revealed Peter Tork. "Mostly we just talked to reporters. In one city we did about twenty minutes on stage but in each city we had special showings of one of the series' segments," said Peter.

Concerning the tour, about the only thing Davy Jones had to say was: "I'm tired." And it's no wonder! Besides the tour, the four Monkees have been keeping themselves busy filming their NBC television series and recording the new songs (skillfully penned for them by Tommy Boyce and Bobby Hart) which are included in each segment of "The Monkees."

Their first album, also titled "The Monkees," has just been released and neither Mickey, Davy, Mike nor Peter could seem to get over how fast the radio stations across the country were jumping on it. "You know, this morning," started Mickey but was forced to stop for a photographer. Photos taken, he tried it again: "Picture this. It's six in the morning, right? I'm in bed and the alarm goes off and the radio comes on and they're playing "The Monkees Theme." I think, 'what? I'm dreaming again!' But they're really playing it!"

Meanwhile, their debut single, "Last Train To Clarksville," is steadily climbing up the nation's charts and that, too, came as something of a surprise to the group. In fact, they couldn't decide whether to call it the "Last Train To Clarksville," or the "Last Train To Home, Girl."

"It's good we decided on Clarksville," laughs Peter. "Can't you just see the major saying: 'I now proclaim this the city of Home Girl?'"

Not quite – but we can see the Monkees taking over the world!

MONKEES ARCHIVES 1

Draft Looms In Monkee Future

HOLLYWOOD — If anything splits the phenominally popular Monkees, it will be the United States Army! And the Monkee closest to being called up is Britain's Davy Jones.

Davy, although still a British citizen, is eligible for the U.S. draft because he lives and works in this country. He's due to take his Army physical shortly but everyone connected with the Monkees is confident that Davy will not be called up.

"Eligible"

The Monkees' American publicist refused to comment on the subject, except to say that Davy is "registered and eligible." However, the group's English publicity office was a bit more talkative. "Obviously Davy doesn't want to go," said publicist David Cardwell, "but he certainly won't kick if he is called up. He has no plans to appeal against it, as far as we know."

Another spokesman for the Monkees said: "It is true that Davy is eligible for service, but the fact that he has dependent relatives and is not of the required height will almost certainly exclude him."

Needless to say, the millions of Monkee fans all over the world are keeping their fingers crossed but in the end it will be entirely up to Davy's draft board whether or not he is called up.

On the record front, the Monkees' fantastic sales pace has not lessened at all. As usual they were awarded a Gold Record simultaneously with the release of their latest single, "A Little Bit Me, A Little Bit You" b/w "A Girl I Knew Somewhere." The single had orders in excess of 1.5 million copies at the time of its release and was immediately audited and certified by the RIAA.

Since August 16, 1966 the Monkees have sold over six million albums and nearly six million singles in the United States alone.

Meanwhile, the Monkees have landed right in the middle. of a $35,000,000 lawsuit filed by Don Kirshner. The Monkees themselves were not named in the suit filed by the former executive of Screen Gems/Columbia music. However, the suit revolves directly around them as Kirshner charges that he was "fired without cause" from a five year contract signed last August and that Columbia Pictures and Bert Schneider, Monkees' manager, were involved in a "conspiracy" against him.

Allegedly, the story is that Schneider asked Kirshner to leave "The Monkees" television show because of a disagreement over how the group's music was being handled on the show and also over who was getting the credit for the music.

A further allegation is that the Monkees would like to write more of their own material instead of using the compositions of other writers. Of course, no one is kicking (indeed, can kick) about the Monkees' sales figures.

Denials

For their part, both Columbia and Schneider emphatically deny that there is any foundation to Kirshner's allegations. A statement issued by Columbia said, in part: "in the opinion of our counsel the suit is totally without merit and the personal charges which Mr. Kirshner has made against the individuals are wholly groundless. We are confident that the court will agree that the actions were well justified and that the corporations acted within their legal rights and in the best interests of their stockholders."

Schneider said only that "there is no basis whatsoever for the accusations."

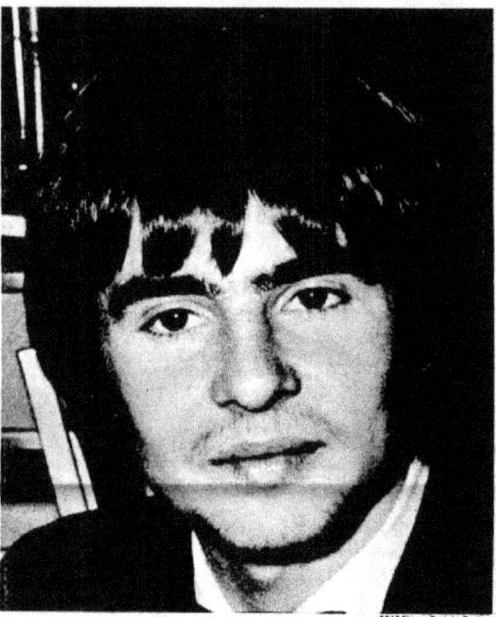

...DAVY JONES will go without a fight if drafted

THE MONKEES—LAST TRAIN TO CLARKSVILLE (Prod. Boyce & Hart) (Writers: Boyce & Hart) (Screen Gems, Columbia, BMI)—All the excitement generated by the promotion campaign for the new group, which debuts on a fall TV show, is justified by this debut disk loaded with exciting teen dance beat sounds. Flip: "Take a Giant Step" (Screen Gems, Columbia, BMI). Colgems 1001

TELLY TIME

DON'T MISS the MONKEES' 60-minute special on NBC-TV when it swings your way at the end of March. JULIE DRISCOLL, BRIAN AUGER, FATS DOMINO, LITTLE RICHARD, JERRY LEE LEWIS and the CLARA WARD SINGERS will be among the many guest stars. (As of this writing, the **exact** date hasn't been set — so be sure to scan your **TV Guide!**) Attention PETER TORK fans: Be super-sure that **you** see the MONKEE spec, cos this may be PETER'S **last** appearance as a member of the MONKEES. (PETER will be seen without his beard again — he shaved it off after rehearsals)! . . .

MONKEES ARCHIVES 1

MONKEES ARCHIVES 1

Monkee Session Revisited

Because people are more apt to believe what they *see* than what they hear, we've decided to disprove the "story" that the Monkees do not sing on their own records by printing these pictures of the Monkees taken at the RCA Victor recording studios in Hollywood.

As you can see, Monkees will be Monkees no matter where they are! So, sandwiched in between all the hard work which goes into recording, Davy, Mike, Peter and Micky manage to get a bit of Monkeeshines going. Helps relieve the pressure, you know!

These pictures were taken during the session which created "A Little Bit Me, A Little Bit You." The song was penned by Neil Diamond who also wrote "I'm A Believer" for the Monkees. Jeff Berry, who incidentally happens to be Neil's producer, again took on the producing chores for the Monkees.

BEAT Photos Courtesy of RCA Victor

MIKE, PETER, MICKY AND DAVY wait to hear playback on a take of "A Little Bit You, A Little Bit Me."

...DAVY AND MICKY indulge in a little game of "catch the imaginary ball."

"I ONLY THOUGHT if we changed it here..." Producer Jeff Berry doesn't seem to see the light, but Davy's making sure Jeff sees him!

DAVY AND PETER rehearse their background music.   **INTENT LOOK** crosses Mike's face during playback.   **...THAT'S IT**, guys, I'm through for this session."

MONKEES ARCHIVES 1

HERB ALPERT clutches Grammy
BEAT Photos: Dwight Carter

MICHELLE AND JOHN toast the occasion

BEHIND THE
GRAMMY AWARDS

DAVY JONES sits alone at his table but not for long!

NOMINEE LOU RAWLS

TWO PAPAS, ONE MAMA happy over their Grammy.

HOLLYWOOD – The 1966 Grammy Awards went off in the International Ballroom of the Beverly Hilton Hotel with very few surprises, a bit of glamor and a lot of talk.

The big winner was, of course, Frank Sinatra who managed to cop awards for the Album of the Year, the Record of the Year and the Best Vocal Performance – Male.

The Beatles, Mamas and Papas and the New Vaudeville Band represented the pop field in the list of Grammy winners and, in fact, John and Michelle Phillips and Davy Jones presented awards this time around.

Davy Jones showed up with the beginnings of a beard and mustache and Michelle appeared in a floor-length gown accompanied by her husband, John neatly attired in a tux. Quite a change from the usual Mamas and Papas outfits.

Ray Charles received the biggest ovation from the crowd when he was named winner of the Best Rhythm & Blues Solo Vocal Performance and the Best Rhythm & Blues Recording.

Bill Dana took off his Jose Jiminez voice for part of the night and took on the master of ceremonies chores for this year's awards.

Performing the nominated songs were Jack Jones ("The Impossible Dream"), Roger Williams ("Born Free"), the Anita Kerr Singers ("Michelle"), Julius La Rosa ("Somewhere My Love") and Keely Smith ("Strangers In The Night"). As you know, Paul McCartney and John Lennon won the Song of the Year award for their "Michelle."

Herb Alpert, last year's big winner, walked away with two awards and when Bob Newhart failed to show, Davy Jones took over his spot to present the two biggest awards (Song of the Year and Record of the Year) with June Hutton.

LOUISE, DAVY, CAROL

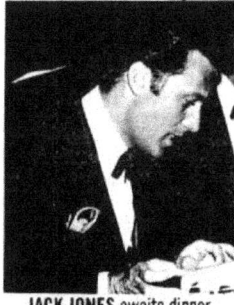
JACK JONES awaits dinner

...AWARD WINNERS POSE WITH HERB ALPERT.

DAVY JONES SMILES with Keely Smith

JACKIE DESHANNON

A VERY HAPPY PAPA JOHN

...JODY MILLER AND SHEB WOOLEY.

RAY CHARLES

MONKEES ARCHIVES 1

CHIP DOUGLAS INTERVIEW

CHIP DOUGLAS TALKS ABOUT THE MAKING OF PISCES, AQUARIUS, CAPRICORN AND JONES, LTD.

CHIP

Chip Douglas, at just 25, is one of today's brightest producers and has produced both the Monkees' albums, Headquarters and Pisces, Aquarius Capricorn and Jones, Ltd.

Chip was born in San Francisco, California and moved to Hawaii with his family when he was three years old. His father was a doctor on a sugar plantation on the north shore of Oahu.

When Chip was older he came to Los Angeles and joined the MFQ. He later played bass for the Turtles and last year was asked by the Monkees to do their record producing. Many hours went into their latest and greatest album on Colgems; and Chip recounts the interesting details below.

How long did you and the Monkees work on the new album?
Well, really it's been on and off since we finished the last one.

Were there any big plans made before you started actual work on it?
No, there's never any chance to plan *exactly* what you want to do, you just do what has to be done. Recording comes third on the list as far as the Monkees go. First it's shooting the TV show, then touring, and finally we squeeze in a little recording time.

Was it hard recording the album in different cities?
It took a while to get used to each studio, maybe a couple of hours more than usual. For the most part they were on tour and doing a lot of singing, so the vocals came off pretty good. We only recorded vocals on the road and they came out a lot better because the boys were doing a lot of singing and their voices were used to it, so they could hit a lot higher notes.

Why did you decide to leave in the talking before the songs start?
We probably shouldn't have left it on "Daydream Believer." The disc jockeys don't like the talking at the beginning, because it's hard to cue up. I just mixed everything down for an album. I wasn't thinking about singles. Then, they decided to put "Daydream Believer" out as a single. I completely forgot about the talking intro on that, but it's just as well anyway.

We try to leave as much of the talking bits on as possible, because it's a little something extra for the listener. I think the Monkees should do a lot more of that sort of thing. I think it would be groovy if they had about six numbers where they weren't even singing—just talking and doing bits. Hank, our engineer and I went over some of the left over tapes the other day and there's a lot of funny stuff left. They'll probably go on the next album for sure.

How did you come to use a Moog synthesizer on the album?
Micky found it. He heard of it somehow and he went over to some guy's house who had one. Micky has been interested in electronic music for some time. The guy who had the Moog did the score for "Forbidden Planet" some years ago and he was showing

MONKEES ARCHIVES 1

it to Micky. The Moog synthesizer is an electronic thing which duplicates any kind of sound. So Micky bought one. He played it on one tune, and we all dug it. Then we thought it would be kinda neat to have a jazz solo on this other tune, so we got Paul Beaver, the guy who built it, to come down and play it. He does some work around Los Angeles with his Moog, like he did the news breaks for KHJ radio and the sounds at the end of Screen Gems' films are done with the Moog synthesizer. It's just breaking into pop music.

Did the Monkees have fun experimenting with it?

Micky was having a ball on this tune "Dayly, Nightly", so we let him go four times on it, and just kept overdubbing stuff all over the place. Then later we sorted it out on the tape and I just brought up the best parts on the final track.

Who chose the name for the album?

I don't remember who it was exactly. It seems that one of the Monkees was on the phone and Lester Sill, who publishes their music, and I were discussing what we were going to call the album. Someone had thought of the idea "Monkees 4 U." But then one of the Monkees came up with "Pisces, Aquarius, Capricorn and Capricorn, Ltd." For some reason, I don't know how it started, the name just popped up from nowhere in the office and someone said, "How about Pisces, Aquarius, Capricorn and Jones, Ltd."? I laughed, and I thought, "That's great!" All the Monkees thought it sounded groovy, so that's what they called it.

Can you recall any funny incidents while recording this album?

There was the time that Ann Moses and her friend came in and clapped on "Daydream Believer" and that was pretty funny, because we had to do it several times because you have to clap a special way.

We had many, many hilarious hours riding to and from the studio in New York. The scene with the girls following the limousines was incredible. They'd follow us all the way into downtown New York.

Once a little girl got in the limousine with Davy and she didn't even know what to do. She just sort of jumped in and there she was face to face with David Jones for the first time! And Davy had one of those shocked looks on his face. She didn't know what to do, so finally she grabbed him and locked her arms around him and wouldn't let go. Finally we let her out a little ways away from the crowds. I'll never forget that!

Also, there's a whole bit that's not on this album that Micky did ad lib. Micky does this whole comedy thing where he starts talking about the Walls of Jericho and he does a whole thing on that. I've got it on tape and we edited it and put it together and it's really funny. Then Davy's trying to play a French horn in the background and it's very funny.

How did you come to include pieces like Peter's tongue-twister, which aren't really songs at all?

Peter has a bunch of those things he does every once in a while. One is called "Alvin," that his brother wrote. "Alvin" didn't get on this album, but it's very funny. Peter did that "Peter's Percival..." thing for me one day and I cracked up and I thought, "How great, we'll stick it on the album!" I wish we could have more of them, but we didn't have the time.

How did you get Mike's voice to sound so different on "Don't Call On Me"?

That's just another side of Mike Nesmith. He just sings that way. He had been saying for some time, "You ought to let me sing a ballad." And everybody would say, "Okay, great." So finally he came up with this ballad and everyone said, "Hey, great song, let's do it!" So we cut the track on it.

Did you use a special effect to make his voice sound different?

No! It's just him, one take, no doubling, no nothing. He's just singing really soft and close to the microphone.

(Continued on Page 51)

MONKEES ARCHIVES 1

CHIP DOUGLAS INTERVIEW
CONT. FROM PG. 49

Whose voice is the most difficult to record?

Mike's is the hardest to record when he sings out. It's a lot better since he's had his tonsils out. His voice is very hard to get crisp. It sounds kind of fuzzy all the time, but that's the way it is. Only when he gets into a certain register does it start popping through and he has to really sing hard and intense in order to get the words across. So his, sound-wise, is the hardest.

Some people still question the Monkees' ability to play their own instruments. Did they play on this album?

Sure. Sometimes we may use strings and things like that, and they can't do those things. But the basic tracks they do themselves. There's at least a couple of them there on the tracks all the time. Maybe not all four of them exactly, only on every little thing, but they do their own backing tracks.

Why do you record mostly at night?

Well, first of all, they work during the day. Also, their voices get warmed up at night. They don't really like to record during the day. Micky doesn't. He doesn't like to come in before six in the evening and then he likes to work until about two a.m. Everyone is different. I like to record during the day. I believe you can get the most done because you're freshest in the early part of the day, as far as tracks go, and then get into vocals in the evening time.

How much time would you say goes into one album track from start to finish?

I'd say maybe 18 or 20 hours for each tune. It can be as much as 24 or 25 hours. Sometimes it's four hours, but usually because we can't record every day when we come in we have to start from scratch. We have to go through all the sounds on the instruments, get the arrangement down and things like that. The Monkees don't like to practice outside the studio. They like to rehearse right in the studio.

Do you see the boys much outside the recording studio?

Sure, as much as possible. I go over to their houses and talk about the songs first and then it's always a good idea to plan out what we want to do. We're doing that more and more now—getting together and talking about the songs. It works out a lot better.

Have your impressions of the Monkees changed after working with them for over a year now?

No. I hold the same high opinion of each of them that I always have.

Who are some of the other artists you are working with?

I'm producing a group called the Dillards, whose single should be out around the first of the year. Their sounds are like an updated bluegrass-rock; and I think the record we're working on now is going to be a gigantic success.

I'm also working with a group whose name isn't quite set yet because they may be adding another member. John Stewart and Buffey Ford is what they call themselves at the moment. John wrote "Daydream Believer."

You have redone several of the Monkees early tunes, do you think you'll re-record "Valerie"?

It's quite possible.

There was talk of putting out a Monkee album recorded live at one of their concerts. Do you see this in the near future?

We recorded them live at three of their concerts with the act they did for the summer tour. Some things came out good and some things didn't come out so good. Mainly the big appeal in a live album is in-between the numbers all the clowning around. The excitement with all the kids screaming is groovy, but it's not that great sound-wise. Live rock and roll things are very difficult to record, but it's really groovy. There're no immediate plans and no release dates, but we will quite possibly put some of it on the next album.

MONKEES ARCHIVES 1

What's New With The Monkees?

Davy Jones and Micky Dolenz

In a nutshell, it's this—**Mike Nesmith**'s got a swell new LP, on the Pacific Arts label, called *From a Radio Engine To The Photon Wing* (how's that for a title?) that's going gangbusters on the charts! It's spacey and mellow, and typically **Mike**! **Peter Tork** is working on a book, along with writer Ellen Mandel, and **Davy Jones** and **Micky Dolenz** have been touring the country with a **Monkees** revue! 16 caught up with *these* two zanies for a chat!

Davy and **Micky**, very pleased with the success of the **Dolenz, Jones, Boyce and Hart** revival of the old **Monkees** hits, *and* with the success of *The Greatest Hits Of The Monkees* LP, decided that some of the **Monkees** had to go out on the road to meet their fans—so they did just that! What resulted was a fantastic, lively show which thrilled the oldest and youngest of the **Monkees** fans! **Davy** and **Micky**, the most consistently visible **Monkees** on the music scene, are very pleased that the reruns of the old **Monkees** TV programs have brought about such a demand for their talents. **Davy** had been busy working for the Disney studios, and playing tennis and horseback riding, while **Micky** got involved with his own production company—it makes lots of commercials! **Micky**'s also done a lot of commercials out on the west coast for a chain of clothing boutiques. But now, both fellas have got **Monkees** on their minds! As a matter of fact, if 'ya promise not to breathe a word of this to anyone, there's even talk of a new **Monkees** TV special which would reunite the four original members **Davy, Micky, Peter,** and **Mike**! How's that for a scoop?! **Micky** says, he wouldn't mind doing a new series, if that's what *you* want him to do. So what do ya think? Wanna see the guys do a show together on TV? If ya do, why not let them know! Write to **Micky** care of the **Micky Dolenz Fan Club**, 115 University Ave., Los Gados, Ca., 95030. You can also write to **Davy**—and let him know how you feel—at P.O. Box 85429, Hollywood, Ca., 90072. If they get enuf of your letters, they'll take 'em over to **Mike** and **Peter**—and who knows? We just might have started another **Monkees** craze!

INSIDER

Comeback Kids

The recent resurgence of The Monkees—both on the concert circuit and in MTV reruns of their zany '60s comedy series—has even surprised the "Prefab Four" themselves. "We weren't prepared for this," ad-

mits the group's Micky Dolenz (above). "Suddenly we found ourselves one of the hottest acts of the summer." Ironically, the group's new-found success comes just as Columbia Pictures Television has decided to manufacture a new group of Monkees. The real ones are less than thrilled. Says Dolenz: "We don't understand why they're doing it. It's unnecessary, untimely and diluting everyone's energy."

MONKEES ARCHIVES 1

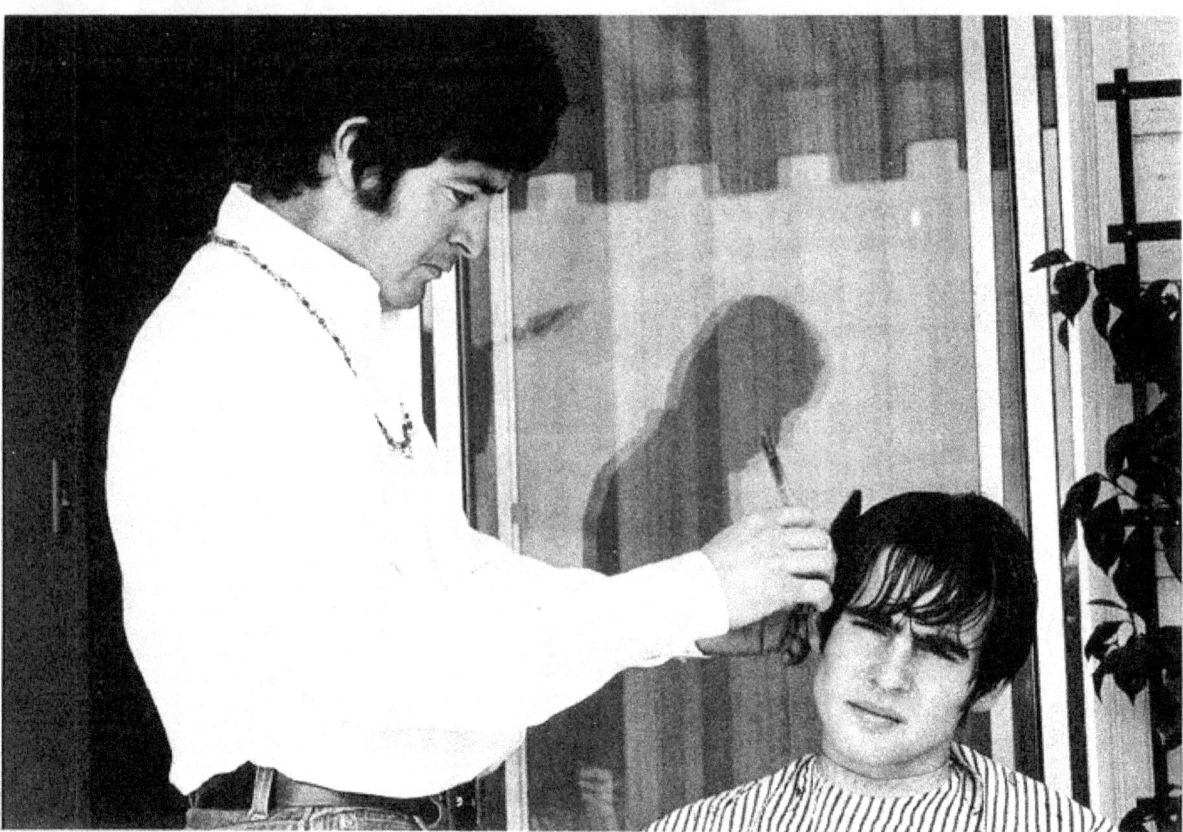

Manny Garcia, his personal barber, trims Davy's hair once a week and cuts it once a month. Usually, Manny will take his talented scissors over to Davy's house. While Davy relaxes in complete privacy, Manny carefully snips at one of the most famous heads in the world.

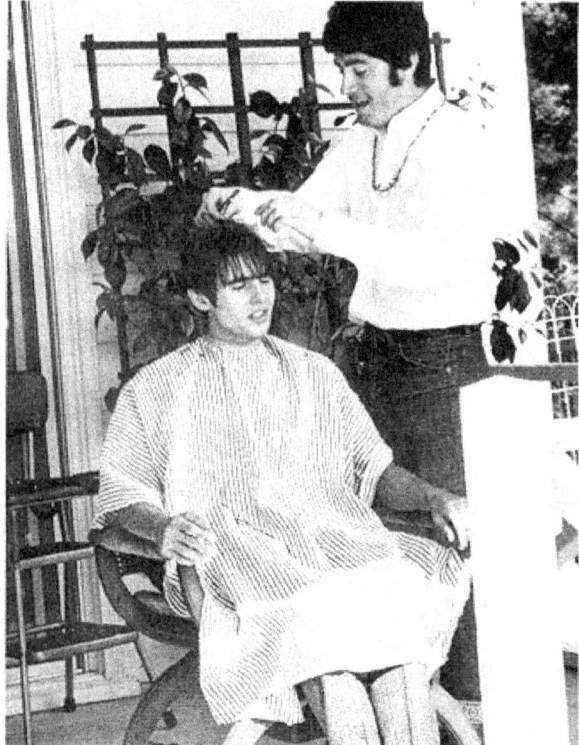

Sitting on his own porch, Davy takes a fast twenty winks, knowing that Manny will trim his hair perfectly.

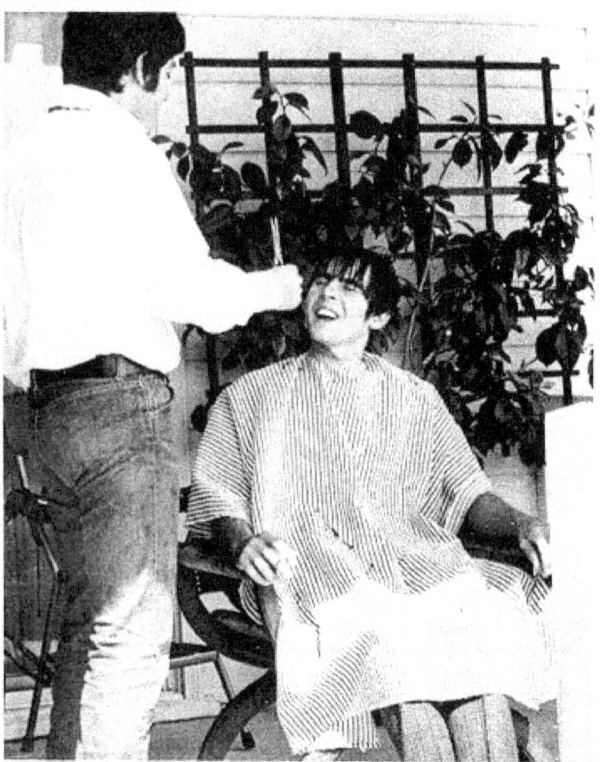

Davy and Manny have become good friends, and Manny knows how to keep his best-friend customer smiling.

MONKEES ARCHIVES 1

Davy's hair is wet because for the kind of haircut he gets (a scissors cut) his hair is much easier to cut when it's moist.

Davy's sideburns are trimmed every week. Here, Manny makes sure that they're exactly the way the Jones boy likes them.

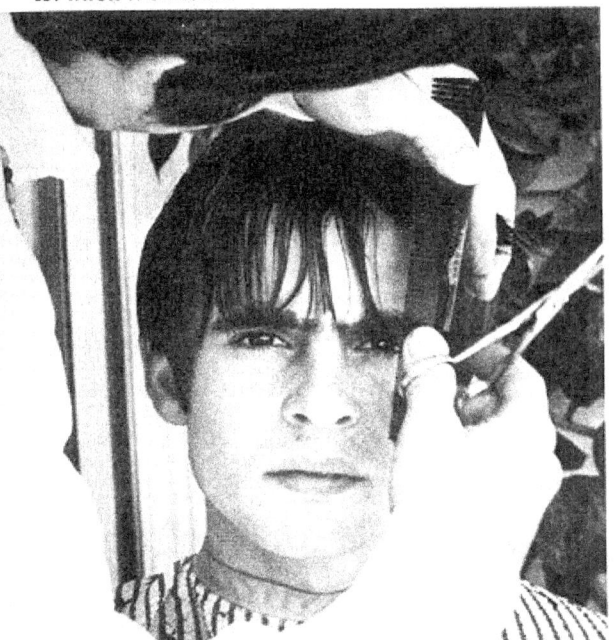

"Look, FLIP, no hair!" In the final shot of this exclusive FLIP series, Davy smiles right into our candid camera, having shared a very personal part of his busy life with you.

Now you can order

DAVY'S FIRST LP
Stores can't get it!

**DAVY SINGS EVERY SONG
A RARE COLLECTOR'S ALBUM
HURRY! SUPPLY LIMITED**
(Please order only as many as you need!)

☐ Send me_____ NEW DAVY LP(s)
Enclose $5.75 for each.

Send this ad with your name
& address with Zip Code & money to:
DAVY'S FIRST LP
P. O. BOX 3031 F
HOLLYWOOD, CALIF. 90028

SEND 50c FOR RUSH HANDLING

MONKEES ARCHIVES 1

How The

Because the Monkees' homes are the only places where they are *not* Monkees, Davy Jones, Peter Tork, Micky Dolenz and Mike Nesmith have probably put more of their real selves into their homes than any other facet of their lives. For this reason, by taking a look at how they live you can actually see a little more of the person behind the image.

More than any of the other Monkees, Mike's home is a total extension of his philosophy and the realization of the dreams he had of "home" as a boy.

POOR CHILDHOOD

Mike grew up in the very poor section of Dallas, Texas. His mother worked to raise her son like other children, but still Mike felt the sting of having raggedy clothes, the feeling of hunger and the hope of something better for him and his mother.

Along with Mike's longing for something better came his present philosophy which is greatly influenced by his religion, Christian Science. Both he and his wife, Phyllis, believe that if you desire material things and you have them, then they become less important. So, they spared no expense in building their beautiful home.

MIKE'S GORGEOUS HOME is what he's always wanted. The peace and quiet that Phyllis needs to raise the children is right here. There's a lovely yard to run in and the privacy Mike needs to do his composing. The Nesmiths have also become very gracious entertainers at home. It's a groovy experience to be invited here for a party.

Monkees Live

PETER'S PAD
Peter Tork lives in the smallest and simplest house of all the four Monkees. He has mentioned, "When I went to look for my first house I thought of hills and cool green." And so he found it.

Material objects to Peter are the least important things in his life, so his house and its furnishings are simple, yet very, very comfortable. Peter is currently looking for a bigger place since his current house can't accommodate all his friends.

MONKEES ARCHIVES 1

MICKY'S WONDERLAND

Micky Dolenz has a "thing" about children—he loves them, he loves their fairy tales and he would love to be one again. The house in which he lives is probably the closest he'll come to returning to childhood himself.

Mick's house sits half-way up a steep hill in Laurel Canyon and looks like a cross between a Swiss Chalet and the gingerbread house from Hanzel and Gretel. He's currently building treehouses for the trees behind his house; and when he entertains he's a very warm host who makes sure that everyone is having fun at all times. He serves his guests popsicles of all flavors and entertains them by showing movies like "Alice in Wonderland" in color. But as you can see, Micky's house is a wonderland all on its own.

MONKEES ARCHIVES 1

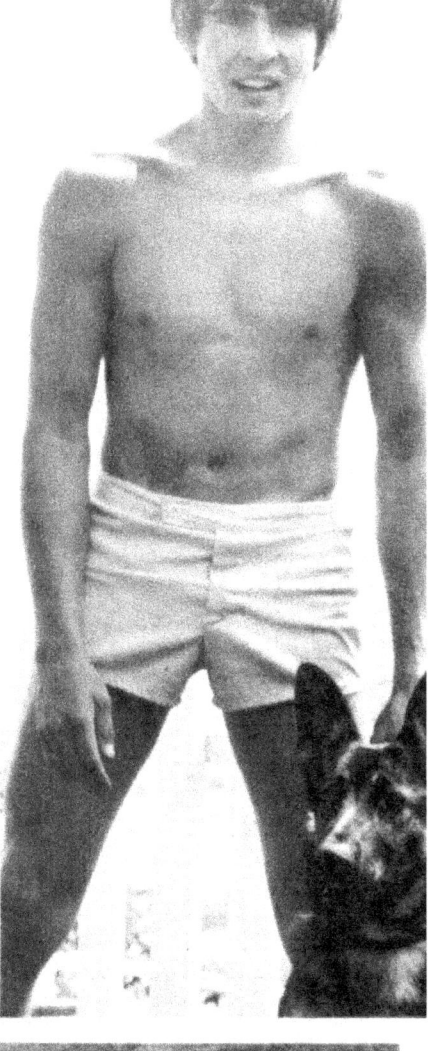

ENGLISH COTTAGE

If Davy Jones' house is an extension of him, as he says it is, then you'll know right away his heart is still in England. He chose the house he now owns because to him it looked like an English country house.

At first Davy had a full-time housekeeper and cook, but when he missed doing those things himsef, he let them go. Now he does almost everything himself. This is one of the ways Davy relaxes. Like the other Monkees, the times they seem to enjoy most are those spent at home with friends and family, because the houses themselves are sort of friends, too!

MONKEES ARCHIVES 1

The Difficult Art Of Being A Monkee

Read on and see why it isn't always groovy being famous!

Groovy things happen to the Monkees—everyone knows that. They get fame, fortune and travel. Except for the ground rules laid down by Screen Gems when they are filming something, they can do almost anything they want.

Like, if Peter suddenly decided he wanted to visit the North Pole on a vacation, he could—providing he got back in time for shooting or a tour.

But sometimes, the Monkees can't even eat dinner in peace. And when that thought sinks into your brain, you begin to realize that being a Monkee can be a difficult art!

PHOTOGRAPHERS' RACE

Take for instance the Grammy Award Presentations in Hollywood back in March. All the Monkees showed up except Peter. Davy was with a girl named Linda, Mike and Phyllis were there and Micky attended with Samantha.

They all sat at a round table—but then all the tables were round—at the far end of the huge California Room of a plush hotel-convention center called Century Plaza. Though the Monkees had obviously been seated at that table to keep them somewhat out of the way of traffic, it looked like a Los Angeles Freeway at 5 p.m. once the guys sat down.

The minute they arrived, photographers and reporters all but ran over to their table to peek and stare and take pictures. In fact, light bulbs were flashing so rapidly it actually seemed like high noon in their corner.

MONKEES ARCHIVES 1

GUYS ARE TIRED

Now look at it from the guys' point of view. It's nice to get attention, but not after you've spent an entire day—about 12 hours—on a movie set. They were really tired, and they all looked it.

They had to go to the presentations whether they wanted to or not because some of their songs were up for awards and in Hollywood it's considered extremely bad manners not to show up—unless you're a Beatle, perhaps. Anyhow, the Monkees had to rush home from the set, scrub off their make-up and get dressed up once more so they could sit at an awards presentation until midnight or so.

It might not have been so bad if they hadn't been on camera, so to speak, all night long, too. The minute they pulled up in their cars, the photographers were all lenses, shutters, flash bulbs and light meters.

SMILE PLEASE

And just imagine trying to keep your cool all the time! Not only can a Monkee not frown or even look bored or puzzled at the proceedings, he has to smile 24 hours a day. To top it off, some bright young starlet probably just stepped on his toe and he can't even flinch. After all, just think what it would look like to have a big photo of a Monkee frowning while some lovely young thing was standing on his right foot. Every paper in the country would probably run it—and that would be only a little embarrassing!

But back to the story. After the Monkees had fought their way through the crowds and finally collapsed at their table, they discovered their problems had just begun.

Have you ever tried to eat a salad before 1,000 eyes—or cameras? It's not easy. Everyone at the Monkee table had to keep his mind on the fact that each bite was liable to wind up being photographed —and nothing looks worse than seeing a picture of yourself in a paper while you were trying to maneuver a tomato slice into your mouth, or try not to leave cracker crumbs all over your portion of the table. Doesn't do much for the appetite.

FREEDOM OF SPEECH?

But perhaps the hardest part of the whole difficult art of being a Monkee is that you can't always say what you think. Well, you *can*, but because you're a Monkee people don't let your remarks slip by lightly.

When Davy Jones was reading off the nominations for Best Documentary Recording Of The Year, he came to "Open Letter To My Teenage Son" by Victor Lundberg, and most teens know what they think about that!

Well, so did Davy and when he had to read the title off as one of the nominees, he just couldn't take it anymore. Right before hundreds of people, he thought about it for half a second and finally blurted out, "And I hope it doesn't win!"

EAT YOUR WORDS

Well, if anyone else had said the same thing, probably no one in the audience would have said a word. But a Monkee! People just couldn't believe it and they started whispering and talking and Davy probably wished he could take back his words.

So the difficult art of being a Monkee demands that you watch your tongue at all times.

After the presentations, all the Monkees probably wanted to do was go home and go to bed—it was midnight and they had to be up at least by six if not earlier.

But they had to smile and wave to photographers and not look too disappointed when they lost out to other singers in the categories for which their songs were nominated.

It was a pretty tiring evening for all concerned. And it wasn't particularly unusual either. The Monkees have to go through that sort of thing more often than they'd like. The difficult art of being a Monkee is sometimes enough to want to make all four of them take a vacation to the North Pole, and stay forever!

MONKEES ARCHIVES 1

BARBARA HAMAKER TALKS ABOUT HER GROOVY JOB WITH THE MONKEES!

Last month Barbara told you how she got her wonderful job with the Monkees. This month you're going to hear all about her exciting adventures on tour!

That's lucky Barbara above with her four favorite friends.

EXACTLY WHAT DOES YOUR JOB WITH THE MONKEES ENTAIL?

Mainly it involves the press and what people say about the boys. We send out releases, let people know what's happening, who's buying what car, who's going to what country and we take care of who goes on the set. We make sure there are pictures on file so when some desperate columnist calls us we can rush out a picture.

Also, a large part of my job is keeping the files on everything that's written about the boys all over the world. I have a complete file of clippings from around the world. It entails volumes of work. I must say London has overwhelmed me with their clippings. The press there must be fantastic.

WHAT WAS YOUR JOB ON TOUR?

I was sort of an assistant to Marilyn Schlossberg and Ward Sylvester; that was my main job. A lot of times I would set up interviews with the coming radio stations. I would call ahead and say, "Are you ready for Mike? He's on his way down." And I would call ahead to the hotels and make sure all the reservations were straight.

WHAT PREPARATIONS HAVE TO BE MADE AT EACH HOTEL?

We had to have four deluxe singles for the boys and they could not be near an elevator or an exit. They had to be together, preferably at the end of a hallway. Either Ward, Marilyn or Jim, our head security man, had to have a room next to them.

The first time I had to do this ended up disasterously.

One hotel didn't have a floor plan and trying to get a floor plan over the telephone is almost impossible. So I thought that we needed four deluxe singles and in my mind the four deluxe singles were more important than their being together. Well, I found out it's the other way around.

So I called ahead and I thought I had it all set up and we got there and there was absolute pandemonium. This floor had about 50 rooms and we were scattered everywhere and there were hotel guests everywhere. I was so upset because I had no idea of why it didn't work out.

After that wild experience, I had to get a floor plan and get the room numbers and I called ahead and said, "I want Nesmith in this room, Jones in this room, Tork in this room . . ." and they would confirm it and then I'd give everyone their room number before they got off the plane and they would make a bee line for their room.

MONKEES ARCHIVES 1

DO YOU REMEMBER ANY CRAZY THINGS THAT HAPPENED ON TOUR?

Well, the Monkees gave me a birthday party and it was a total surprise! It was our last night in New York. Marilyn and I had dinner with the manager of the hotel, who was the most wonderful man. I had bought some paints that day and so after dinner I went back to my room and I was painting for about three hours.

It was about 10 o'clock and Marilyn called me and said, "Will you come down to the hospitality suite, I want to talk to you." And I thought, "Oh, no, what have I done wrong now?" So I went in and there was this big cake and everyone was in there and they all had signed this big card and it was really beautiful.

Then Micky showed us some slides he'd taken of the tour and they were very funny. He has very bad vision and usually wears glasses, but he didn't then. So he kept adjusting the projector to his vision and Peter kept hitting him on the head saying, "Micky, I can't see it!" and so Micky would put his glasses on and adjust it again. He had some fantastic shots from the tour.

DO YOU REMEMBER ANY FUNNY INCIDENTS ON THE PLANE?

Micky helped us serve dinner one time. Lynne Randell and I would help serve the meals because we didn't like to just sit, so one night Micky walked around and served the trays of food with us.

One night Davy Jones asked me to go to the movies with him and a few other people. Would you believe this, I was making beads and I said no. I didn't go because I'd already seen the movie.

WHAT ARE SOME OF THE THINGS YOU DID FOR THE BOYS ON TOUR?

I made all the plane arrangements for their trek up to the Indian reservation in Wisconsin. I'd always check with our pilot to find out what field we were at and where we should meet the plane after the concerts, because we always rushed out of the city we were in right after the shows.

DO THE MONKEES TAKE AN INTEREST IN THEIR PUBLICITY?

Yes. Peter is very conscious of the press. The man at the Columbia bookstand just outside the lot tells me that Peter comes down there regularly and reads almost every news, not fan, magazine on the rack. Then he comes up to the office and he likes to go through my files on the different tour cities. Right now he's very interested in Japanese magazines.

David likes to send things to his father. Micky doesn't pay much attention. Except for a while, he was very concerned about his hair. He wanted to make sure that only the most current pictures were printed.

(Continued on next page)

MONKEES ARCHIVES 1

DO ANY OF THEM HAVE ANY QUIRKS ABOUT WHAT IS WRITTEN ABOUT THE MONKEES?

Mike doesn't like the name, "Wool Hat." I think the main thing is that the boys take offense if a magazine doesn't give them justice and credit for playing their own music.

Peter does get very upset if his viewpoints are stated incorrectly, because he has very strong views about things. I guess Peter and Mike are the most conscious about the publicity, they really come up to my office and ask to see certain magazines.

HOW DO YOU FEEL ABOUT THEM NOW AS PEOPLE?

I feel like they know me and I know them. I think whenever a star meets a civilian, or whatever you want to call them, it's always hard for them to see anything but a fan. I think each one of them is a nice individual. They're all so different.

They're very good friends and they understand each other, but they're like anybody you meet. They work together. They're individual people. If I met someone at school, I wouldn't want to spend 24 hours a day with them, even if I really liked them. I think some people expect the Monkees to really live together. It just so happens that each of them, in their own ways, have their own ideas. They're so individual and each one is a strong person.

They are great friends and the associate producer raves day after day about how beautifully the boys work together. He comes up to my office and says, "I don't know what I'd do without 'em! They did that scene so perfectly, they knew exactly what they were doing and they moved so great, they're so agile." And he just goes on and on, and they are great.

HOW IS IT THAT YOU SEE THEM DAILY?

As an example, the other day a disc jockey from Japan came and I took him and his two companions down to the set. Peter turned out to be out of the scene for the moment, so he came over and talked to them. He was really excited. I usually see them on the set when I take a reporter over. Almost always they break for an hour at lunch and almost always one of them will come up to my office to have a look at some press clippings. David is the one I see the least of because he has so many projects he's working on. Micky is always driving around or doing something, so I usually just run into him. Peter comes up most often because he's always looking for magazines.

MONKEES ARCHIVES 1

DO YOU LIKE YOUR JOB NOW?

Oh, yes! Because it's not just a secretarial job, it's everything combined. It's so interesting, I couldn't even think of asking for a better job in the line I'm in. In this line, it's about the most creative and free and most interesting job I could have. I'm not a good secretary, by any means. My skills are not good and I was not trained for this. I don't like typing, it's a drag, but my job is interesting because of the people I work with.

DO YOU WATCH THE MONKEES ON TV NOW?

I usually try and read the scripts and I usually visit the set. I love to watch the show in the screening room, because that way I can see it in color. Just before we left on tour I saw a lot of the rough cuts, which I liked. It was really very interesting. By all means, my image of the boys has certainly changed from a year ago!

WHAT THINGS DO YOU DO IN YOUR SPARE TIME?

I love to sew and I make a lot of my own clothes. I like to make baskets, it's very interesting. My mom was a kindergarten teacher, so all my life I've done that stuff. Then I love to make mobiles. I make mobiles out of little plastic crystals. I usually make a lot of my own Christmas presents. My favorite medium right now is tissue paper. I love to make collages and paper flowers. I've made a lot of pictures out of tissue paper. I like to make my own candles as presents. Lately, too, I've been making so many beads, they're coming out my ears!

CAN YOU REMEMBER ANYTHING ELSE FROM TOUR?

I had been going to these hobby shops along the tour and one day we were in one city, I think it was Memphis. I mentioned to Tad, one of Micky's friends, "I'm going to the hobby shop this morning, do you want to come," because I knew he wanted to get some things. "Maybe Sammy and Micky will want to come," he said. So it turns out that we went in a limousine and the whole works. Ward Sylvester came and Micky and Samantha. We ended up spending about 95 dollars or something outrageous like that. Micky bought all this leather; and we had Sam's kitten with us. So we brought all this stuff back and put everything in the middle of Micky's bed at the hotel. Micky and Sammy were pounding away on this leather they bought and I was making beads. Tad's beading away and the kitten is running around. Then we ordered lunch from room service and the cat was eating the lunch because we were so involved we didn't stop to eat. It was really freaky!

MONKEES ARCHIVES 1

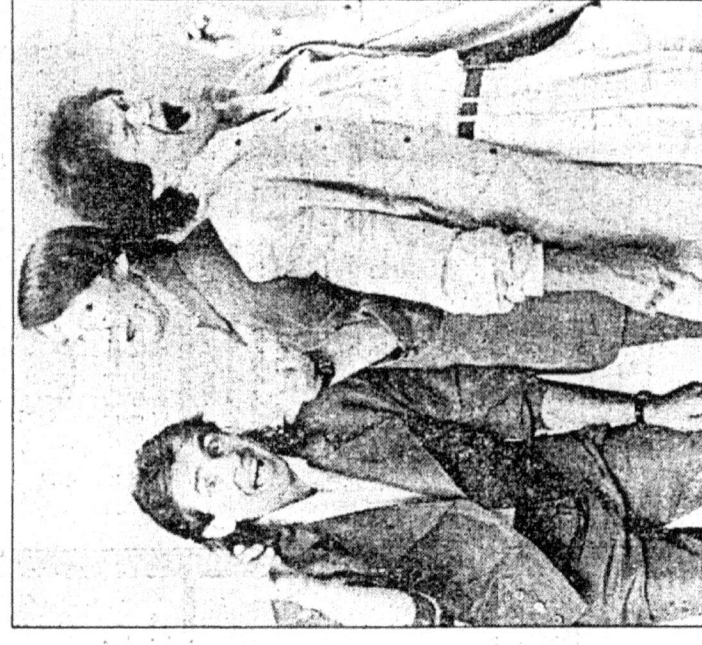

Monkees Davy Jones, Peter Tork, Micky Dolenz

They're Too Busy Singing....

When Davy Jones tries to put all the pieces together in his mind, he finds plenty of quirky wrinkles in the pop-star fabric.

Here he is turning 41 next month, the pint-size Monkee who fell in love in our living rooms every week on TV's first sitcom about a rock group.

He's on his second marriage. He's on the road again with two of the guys who helped make "I'm a Believer" a slumber-party anthem for millions of preteens two decades ago.

He's also the father of three girls, one of whom is about the right age to squeal over the January issue of 16 Magazine — in which Jones is the featured pinup.

"I don't know what I'd feel like if my 15-year-old came home with a 41-year-old man," Jones said last week, musing about the age range of '80s Monkees fans.

When the TV series debuted in 1966, many Monkee maniacs — including myself and my two sisters — were struggling through grade-school spelling tests. (My sister Jeanne was 8 and wouldn't leave for school without kissing Peter Tork's goofy grin on a life-size poster on her bedroom wall.)

Kathy Haight

NIGHTLIFE

In a climate of gushing '60s nostalgia, today's fans include grown-up versions of the original faithful, plus new generations born after the band broke up. All are making the group's 20th anniversary tour a phenomenal success.

Extended from four months to six, from 75 cities to 200, the tour is selling out nationwide. There are still some tickets left for Sunday's 7:30 p.m. show at the Charlotte Coliseum, which is two stops away from the Dec. 3 finale in Bethlehem, Pa.

On the road with the Monkees in 1986, vitamins and elastic knee braces have replaced marijuana. Wives and kids have replaced groupies, and fans are throwing bras on stage, unlike '60s shows, where lots of fans were too young to wear them.

Last week, in a snowbound recording studio outside Worcester, Mass., Jones picked up the phone for a 30-minute chat — his tart British accent full of bemused delight and keen business calculations about the Monkees then and now.

After facing years of abuse for being a plastic TV band that didn't play its own instruments, the Monkees are ridiing a wave of critical and commercial vindication that includes seven albums on Billboard's Top 200, a sellout tour and plans for new albums, books, tours, TV or feature films and an offer for a revival of the Broadway show "Helizapoppin."

Even industry cynics admit the Monkees are "hip by association": The group's songs were written by pop stalwarts like Neil Diamond, Carol King, Tommy Boyce and Bobby Hart. The TV show's producers went on to do "Easy Rider" and "Five Easy Pieces." The writer for the group's '68 feature film "Head" was a young actor named Jack Nicholson.

See MONKEES Page 4D

MONKEES ARCHIVES 1

Monkees Still Singing, But To New Generation

Continued From Page 1D

"I feel it's some kind of reward I've just gotten," Jones said of all the recent attention. "I have just won first prize after all these years, after early on in the Monkees days when the studio made all the money and the record company made all the money and everybody ripped us off.

"All of a sudden, it's being 20 years older, and Micky Dolenz and Peter Tork and I now having more in common and being closer than we ever were. We've all been married, been divorced. We all have children (a total of nine, between the ages of 3 and 18). We've all had individual careers, individual highs and lows to contend with. And now we're all back there together. We're approaching it in a very professional and honest and friendly way toward each other."

They're also smart enough to take advantage of the existing bull market on Monkees paraphernalia.

Jones, who's spent his years since the Monkees raising horses and doing musical comedy and club gigs, is recording a solo album and has an autobiography due out next year. He has even added streaks of orange to his carefully moussed hair.

Along with Dolenz, 41, a TV producer-director in England, and Tork, 44, a musician and music teacher who fought alcohol and drug dependencies after leaving the Monkees and served a brief prison term for hashish possession, Jones will begin work on a new Monkees album after the trio wraps up its U.S. tour.

Ex-Monkee Mike Nesmith, 43, a film and video producer who inherited $25 million from his mother (she invented Liquid Paper) isn't touring with the group. Jones thinks the band's popularity has endured partly because the TV show used innovative video techniques that have been embraced and embellished in today's rock videos.

Beyond that, Monkees songs still hold up well as solid pop tunes and the Marx Brothers-style humor of the TV show has proved itself in syndication — attracting new generations of fans.

Though band members aren't thrilled with plans for a "New Monkees" TV show, using young actors to recreate the premise of the original program, Jones, Dolenz and Tork are determined to ride their wave of success as far as it will take them — and to bring their kids along for inspiration.

"My 5-year-old is ridiculous," Jones said, excusing himself from the phone for a few words with his youngest daughter, Jessica. "She runs security for me sometimes. She's always saying,'Daddy, you must sign these autographs.' They've been waiting all the time.' She's very aware that people are interested in me and makes sure I don't forget that it's a first-time experience for that particular person. She helps me stay fresh. Kids do that, you know."

■ IF YOU'RE GOING

The Monkees play at 7:30 p.m. Sunday at the Charlotte Coliseum, 2700 E. Independence Blvd. Gary Puckett and the Union Gap, Herman's Hermits and the Grass Roots will open. Tickets are $15.50, $17.50. ($17.50 sold out.) Box office: 372-3600, 10 a.m.-9 p.m. today and Saturday, 1-6 p.m. Sunday. To charge by phone: 332-4806 same hours.

tell somebody you
LOVE
about the
BIRDS
the
BEES
and the
MONKEES

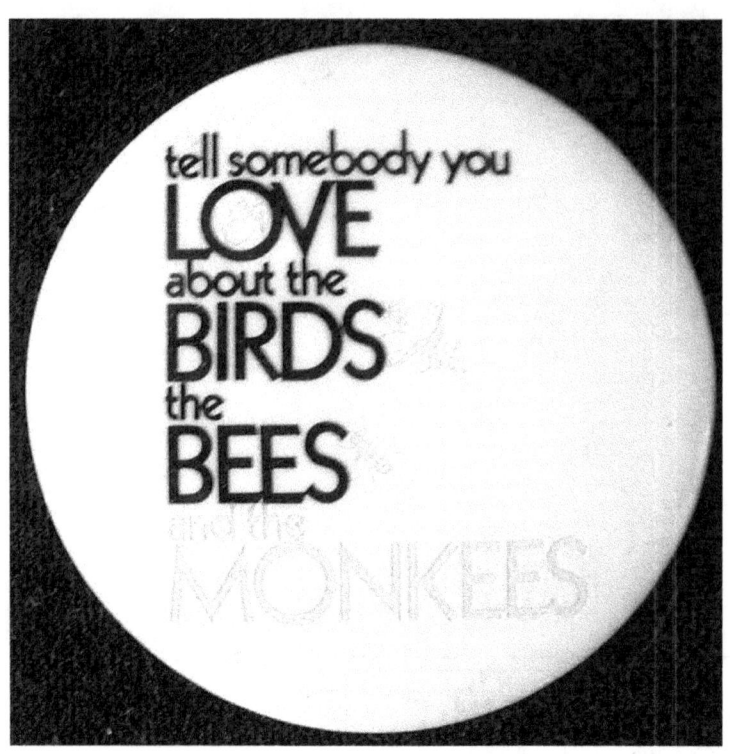

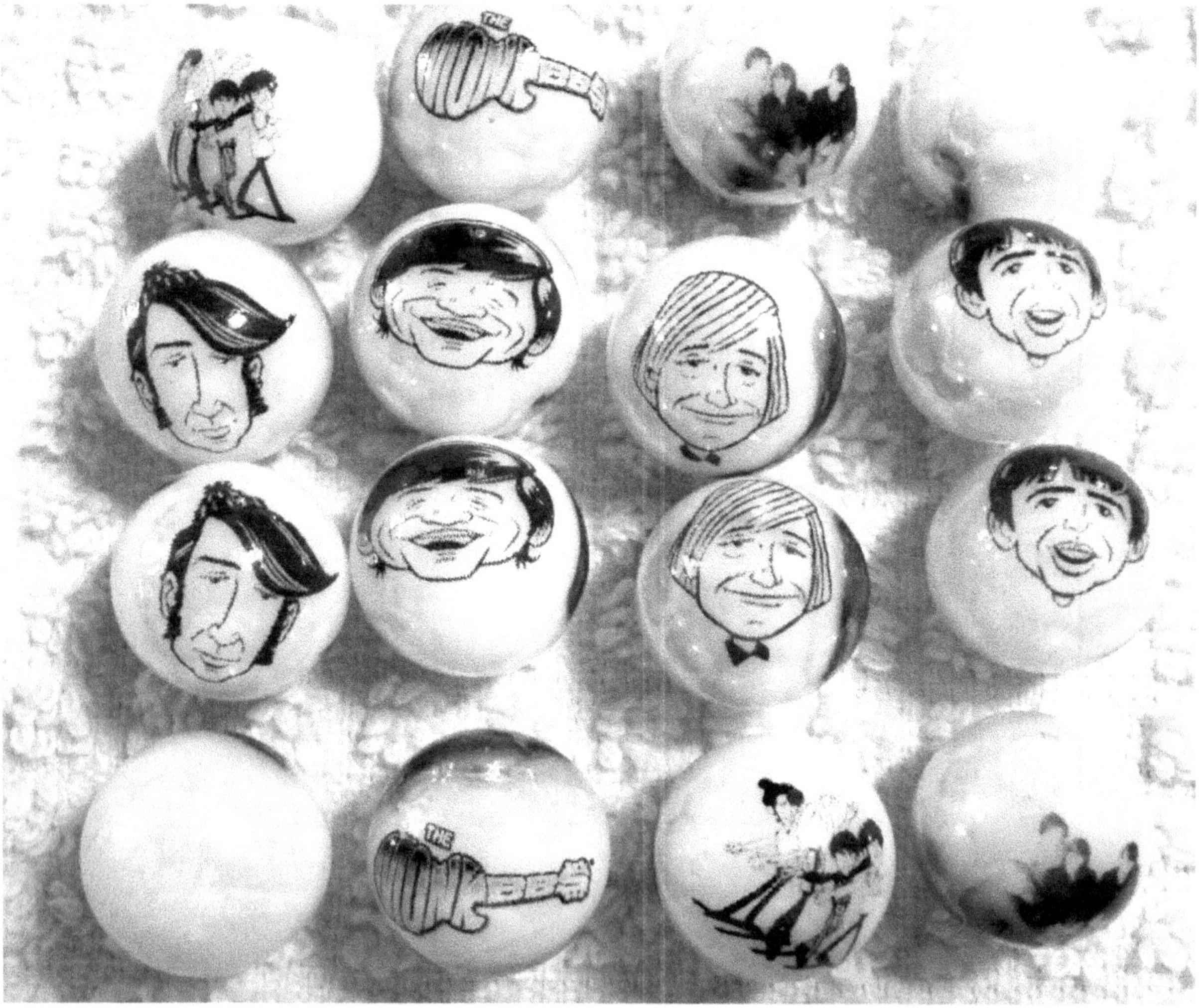

MONKEES ARCHIVES 1

A SPECIAL NOTE TO MONKEE FAN CLUB MEMBERS:

Micky and David asked that I drop you a note and tell you about the new MONKEES record . . . OH MY, OH MY. It was just released and we hope you will be hearing it on your favorite radio station.

You can help make their new record a big hit. Telephone, or write your favorite disc jockey and ask them to play the record. **If they don't, keep calling.**

In case your local record store hasn't stocked OH MY, OH MY yet they can order it by referring to COLGEMS Record No. 66-5011 distributed by RCA.

Let's all pitch in and help the new MONKEES record become a big hit.

Joan Davis
MONKEES NATIONAL FAN CLUB

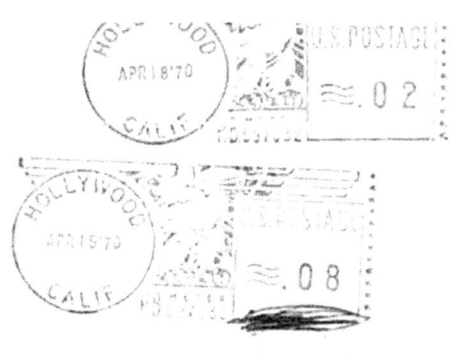

MONKEES ARCHIVES 1

New management

The Monkees have had several changes of personal management during the past hectic three years.

They have also been involved in many different business enterprises, including publishing, recording and film companies.

They have now decided to concentrate their efforts to promote the Monkees as a group and they have appointed David Pearl and Brendan Cahill as their personal managers.

David Pearl, as our regular readers will already know, has been Davy's personal friend for many years. Brendan Cahill met the boys when he acted as their chauffeur in 1967

CASH GUEST

Mike recently appeared as a star guest on the Johnny Cash Show, which is the top Country and Western television programme in the United States.

As you probably know, Mike is a great country music enthusiast and it gave him a marvellous opportunity to play some of his "rural blues"

What's he doing now?

Apart from making several short films for television, Peter Tork has gone into the restaurant business. He recently bought a Soup Kitchen in Greenwich Village, which is the hippie centre of New York. Tork's eating place is rapidly becoming a big meeting centre for artists and musicians in the area.

MAY TOUR POSTPONED

Just when everything seemed set for the Monkees first major tour of the leading European countries, the news broke that it had been put off until later on in the year

Main reason for the postponement was that the boys had decided to form a seven-piece backing group now that Peter Tork has left.

The group is going to be called The Goodtimers Band Ltd. Several of the members are reported to have played on previous Monkee sessions, particularly the private ones in their own home recording studios.

VALENTINE FOR MONKEES

Many of Britain's top popsters make a point of looking up the Monkees whenever they visit California. Donovan dropped in during his recent State-side visit and ended up staying for four whole days. Most of the time was spent in Micky's recording studio working on new song ideas.

Before he left, Donovan gave the boys a song which he had written specially for them called "Valentine Angel" It has never been recorded before and the Monkees reckon that it is one of the most beautiful numbers that they have ever heard. It is one of their main choices for a future single.

GAVE ZILCH AWAY

You will remember that many months ago we reported that Davy had opened a boutique in New York with the unusual name of Zilch.

The Monkees Monthly asked him how Zilch was going recently and he came up with the surprising news that he had given it away.

Apparently, he found that he couldn't spend enough time at the shop due to all his Monkee commitments, so he decided to give the whole lot, lock, stock and barrel, clothes and all, to the Neills.

In a way, this was a "thank you" from Davy for all they did for him when he stayed with them in America.

MONKEES ARCHIVES 1

MONKEES ARCHIVES 1

IN HAWAII

Aloha! It's Davy's adorable head peeking out from a "mountain" of leis – the traditional gift for every visitor to the magical Hawaiian Islands!

Here are zany Micky and Honolulu's super groovy deejay, Mike Hamlin of Radio KKUA, listening to the Monkees' great Colgems' single **Listen To The Band**.

After 45 fantastic minutes on KKUA Radio, the tempestuous trio decided to "get away from it all" by taking a leisurely stroll through one of the beautiful forests of Honolulu.

No—it isn't Steve McQueen doing a daredevil stunt! It's Mike getting some exercise and fresh air as he zooms along one of Hawaii's white white beaches!

MONKEES ARCHIVES 1

The Monkees

遂に来

マイク・ネスミス

デーヴィー・ジョーンズ

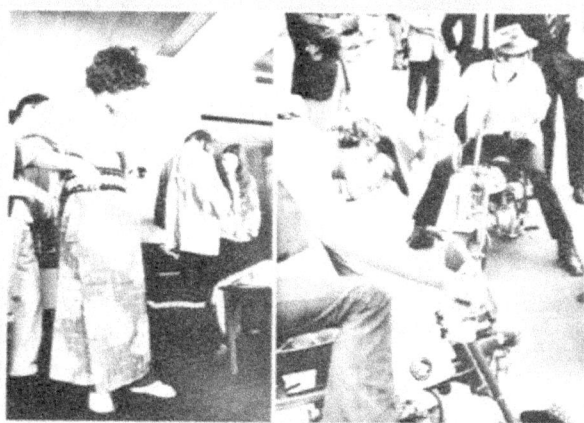

右上は羽田空港で飛行機のタラップに立った四人
右二番は歓迎会場にくつろぐ四人

何度か来日を伝えられながら、ファンの期待を裏切ってきたザ・モンキーズが、遂に日本公演のため、9月30日午後1時7分羽田着のカンタス航空機で来日した。ミッキー・ドレンツ、ピーター・トーク、デーヴィー・ジョーンズ、マイク・ネスミスの順でタラップに現われたモンキーズは、約1000人の警官による万全の警備のうちに宿舎の東京・赤坂のホテル・ニュー・ジャパンに直行した。

記者会見は10月2日午後1時から、ホテルの大宴会場で行なわれた。ザ・ビートルスやS・コネリーに匹敵する大規模なものだった。

待ちに待った舞台演奏は10月3日東京・武道館での公演からスタ

MONKEES ARCHIVES 1

た！ ザ・モンキーズ

ミッキー・ドレンツ

ピーター・ノーク

来日してのデーヴィー

ト、ワーワーキャーキャーさわ
ぐ少女ファンの前に、上品なグレ
ーのスーツでいきなり高い舞台に
現われたモンキースの4人、ト
ムが割れんばかりのエレキのサウ
ンドをひびかせて合声練本にこた
え、会場はたちまちものすごい熱
気にあふれた。あざやかなプロロ
ークの演奏が終わるや、今度は一
人ずつ次から次へと独特の服装に
替えて登場、迫力あるソロにパン
チをきかせ、ファンもモンキース
も一体となって約一時間にわたる
興奮状態がつづく、あまりのうれ
しさに体をふるわせ、泣き出すフ
ァンも少なくなかった。　　かく
てダイナミックな演奏でファンを
たんのうさせた一行は、関西公演
を終えて帰国の途についた。

撮影・本誌写真部

●特別会見記は118自

モンキーズ記者会見

MONKEES ARCHIVES 1

WHY PETER LEFT

Of course, there were rumours. There always ARE rumours surrounding any internationally popular group. One of the earliest rumours was that Davy Jones was "definitely" planning to leave the Monkees. That one was put down very fast ... but then the stories about Peter Tork and HIS future plans started.

Just rumours. But every so often a rumour hardens into actual fact. And the fact, as we all know, is that Peter HAS left the group and now plans to carve out a career either on his own or with a new bunch of buddies.

It's been a shock. In a tight-knit group like the Monkees, every member has a special part to play. From the start, from those very first television half-hours of zaniness, Peter developed his own personality and his own following. Remember what the others used to say about him?

Said Micky, on his very first visit to London: "Three of us more or less play ourselves in the series. The odd one out is Peter Tork. Off-stage, he's a real serious guy who thinks a lot about things like religion and the problems in the world and that kind of thing. But in the series he throws off all that and becomes a dumb-but-likeable sort of character who is always doing the wrong thing at the wrong time. He kinda moons around with a lovesick expression on his face—not like the REAL Peter Tork at all."

SERIOUS LOOK

But from the middle of 1966, that moon-like face of Peter's was much photographed. Sometimes with a serious off-stage sort of look on it; sometimes with that boy-next-door grin that somehow split the face into two ... a grin that showed through in his eyes as well.

Don't worry—that face will continue to be much photographed in the future. But not, alas, as part of that quartet of merriment and music that was the original Monkee set-up. And it's my job this month to try to explain just how it was that Peter decided to quit and go in search of pastures new.

First, we must understand exactly what goes on in a group like the Monkees. Though there has to be a certain amount of freedom for the performers themselves, it inevitably becomes a bit restricting. A bloke with imagination, and Peter sure has a lot of imagination, can kick in his ideas and, if they're for the good of the group as a whole, then those ideas are accepted.

But any decision has to be made for the good of the group as a whole. And Peter didn't always see it that way.

So ... it's no secret that Peter, of all the boys, DID start to feel a little bit hemmed in. He played it pretty cool as the boys were put into orbit as the most shattering pop success of the last couple of years. But towards the end of last year he decided to go his own way.

There were lots of early signs. There were little quibbles about exactly WHAT kind of music the boys should produce for their records. All the way through they hinted that they would like more freedom to develop in the way they knew best. There was all that early criticism about what they actually did on their records and this was hurtful to Peter because he was an accomplished musician in his own right and had earned a living by playing round the folk-type clubs, armed with his banjo and a collection of songs.

SURPRISED

Elsewhere in this issue members of the Brian Auger Trinity reveal how surprised they were to find that Peter was so well up in musicianship ... they, too, had been taken in by the critics who found it hard to say anything

MONKEES ARCHIVES 1

MONKEES ARCHIVES 1

A VERY PERSONAL INTERVIEW WITH

SAMANTHA sat, toying with a king - size filter, smiling a lot—obviously very happy, if a bit tired. Enviable sun-tan, built up in the smilingly sunny climes of Hollywood. Here, with baby Ami Bluebell, to meet up with her folks again, have the odd business chat—then back to her main duties these days as Mrs. Micky Dolenz.

Remember Sammy's television image? Always there, on "Top Of The Pops', at the shoulder of the disc - jockey of the week, but never saying a word. Some people even put it around that she couldn't talk. Well, she can. She's full of views and theories—and full of deep-rooted convictions about the big future ahead of the Monkees.

She talked first about her own business interest—a boutique called One Of A Kind. "It's still going well," she said. "We make the patterns, design the clothes and have salesmen out selling them. Sometimes I serve there myself. But we switched in mid - stream in terms of the market we were catering for....

"We originally did the usual older teenager and early 'twenties clothing. Then we got lots of letters from kids aged between 10 and 16 and they rightly pointed out that we were leaving them out of the main fashion ranges. They had to go to the main department stores, where their sizes were available—they had to go for the mass-produced lines. So we got right in on that younger market and it is working out fine."

Sammy switched to more personal news and views about the Monkees in general ... and Micky Monkee in particular. She talks with an engaging mixture of American drawl and sharp North-country attack. "One day Micky and I might go to live in Mexico," she said. "Micky keeps saying he is fed up with California, but you know Micky—he changes his ideas round every other day or so. But Mexico is becoming more European all the time. It's cheap to live there, and there are great labour forces. People say it is a police state, but I don't know about that. Maybe it is the only way they can do it to start off, but you can't keep people down like that all the time.

"To anyone who hasn't seen 'Head' yet I'll just say that I think you'll like it. Now this is gonna sound like the proud wife talking but, really, Micky's scene where he meets up with the Italian Army in the desert is really one of the biggest highlights. You know how you can feel kinda embarrassed when you're watching someone you know up there on the screen — well, I didn't feel one little bit embarrassed watching Micky. I think he's a natural in the acting business. I've felt bad, deep inside, seeing him in some things — like some of the television shows — because I felt it really wasn't him, if you see what I mean. But now I'm convinced ... he should be an actor. He

MONKEES ARCHIVES 1

has all the talent he needs. One day, I'm sure, he'll concentrate on being an actor.

"But the boys, as a group, have really got into the recording scene these days. They're really involved — in a way, for the first time since they hit it big. And they have their band, the Good-timers, which creates a really good show now. I'll tell you this — there are people who are always ready to write off the Monkees, but you should hear the reaction they've got on some of their shows on the recent tour.

"Why, they had one big appearance at Forest Hills ... and they were asked to make a return trip there even before they'd done the first engagement. That's how big they were at the box-office. Surely that sort of thing is what really counts ... not a few nasty comments in some of the newspapers.

GREAT SHOW

"On stage now they don't play instruments so much — though Mike still does a fair bit. But they do a great show. What really hurt them all, specially Micky, was when they were called Plastic People in the *Daily Mirror* here. That really hurt. I mean, it's just not true ... people who know them, who see them work, know how unkind that is. You take Davy, he's a real professional. I'll tell you this: he's never been late for a show in the whole of his life.

MONKEES ARCHIVES 1

"People forget so easily. Like I say that Micky should become an actor. Right — well, I've seen some of the things he did, in film clips, as a five-year-old. He was tremendous — really. Doing a Mexican accent at the age of five. You know?

"For rehearsals, Davy rented an old theatre, somewhere where he could get away from things. He just loves being up there on a stage. And they've rehearsed in the Red Velvet Club... Micky was singing there every night before he even became a Monkee. And, of course, Mike was doing the same thing at the Troubadour. Plastic people? It's just ridiculous...."

FRIENDLY

"I've settled in well in America. I'm very friendly with Phyllis Nesmith and we do quite a lot of entertaining. But the Monkees, generally, don't do much clubbing. It's never really been the scene in Hollywood. More like the 'out' crowd get in the clubs. But sometimes some tourists we know want to go, so we tag along. The Factory is okay, but people are always asking for autographs. The Daisy is the most exclusive...."

Samantha fingered her cross-over, entwined wedding ring and threw in a quick: "I really miss Micky right now." And she went on: "The Monkees ended the television series simply because they felt stale at the way it was going. But it should be remembered that the Monkees is rather like a trade name. That is the product—but each individual must feel free to do what he wants outside the group. That's what they do, and it works out well.

"Mike really is doing a lot of writing and he's a very clever producer. 'Listen To The Band' is all his thing. And, of course, he has signed a production contract with Dot. He really is involved with new ideas in recording — techniques, that kind of thing."

And what about Micky then? Said Sammy: "Oh well, the acting thing first of all. But tell you what— he loves filming. Acting on film, yes ... but I've an idea his real ultimate ambition is to become a director. He did one of the television shows, you know, and considering it was his first time he did it very well indeed. People were there, trying to give him advice, but he said nope, it's my job right now, and if it's a flop then I want me to have all the blame.

"He's not really a stage actor. He is much more at home in the movie world— but then, of course, that's where much of his experience has come from.

"Now Davy is different in that he's just a natural for stage work. I never knew anybody who really works at his career the way he does. He's rehearsing all the time. His dance sequence in 'Head' is another of the stand-out sections, a really big hit with the fans.

"That's how I see their future ... but with all the action on the group side as well, of course. As for Micky and I ... well, I'd like at least two more children. But an alternative is to adopt two—you know, give a good home to two kids who really needed it.

"I know Micky's talking to you on the transatlantic 'phone for this issue, so I won't cut too much across his ground. But we're listening a lot to classical music these days at home. I don't like Brahms or opera, for instance, but mostly the both of us have a pretty wide taste. That psychedelic stuff rather aggravates me ... a lot of it is rubbish.

GOOD GUITARIST

"You know Micky was, and is, a good guitarist. But then he had to start drumming for the television series. At first he didn't know much about it....

"Now people come up to him and say that he's really becoming a drummer. That knocks him out. And it also goes to show that the Monkees, as a group and individually, are always going forwards, learning new things, trying to put on the best of all possible shows."

Time for Sammy to go. A quick trip to Manchester where Ami Bluebell was waiting for her. And then back to America. Said Sammy, by way of stressing the point: "Sure do miss Micky. Yes, I do."

MONKEES ARCHIVES 1

MONKEES ARCHIVES 1

Davy Visits his Horses

A big smoke screen was erected by Screen Gems to hide his real movements during Davy's recent visit to England.

The main reason for this was that they wanted to protect Davy's father from any extra strain. As you know, he is pretty ill and if a huge crowd descended upon his home every time his famous son pays a quick visit, it could have a very bad effect. So, while he was supposed to be firmly ensconced in a country house in Berkshire, Davy went home.

While he was in the North he decided that it would be a good opportunity to go and see how his two horses, Chicomono and Pearl Locker, were getting on.

He had intended to make the trip on Tuesday, June 11th but he received an urgent request from Belle Vue, Manchester to have his handprints recorded in concrete for posterity. So, he didn't set off until the Wednesday. He and David Pearl drove up in a Mini-Traveller and arrived at the stables in mid-afternoon.

His horses are trained by Basil Foster in a stables in

Davy makes the same face as Pearl Locker.

the centre of a small village called Middleham which is situated right on the edge of the Yorkshire moors, about 15 miles west of Catterick. One of the outstanding features of the village is an old castle where Richard III lived. The young princes (you remember the ones who were murdered in the Tower of London) also spent their early years there. The stables where Davy's horses are trained is called Glasgow House and is situated bang opposite the castle.

The first thing Davy did after saying 'hello' to Basil and the other people around the stable when he arrived, was to strap his saddle on Chicomono and ride him up to the moors.

When he came back, he said how marvellous it was to be on the back of a thoroughbred once again and what was even more exciting —his very own horse. He unsaddled, groomed and fed Chicomono and then fed his other horse, Pearl Locker.

Although Davy had not ridden a horse for several months, he still sat Chicomono like a professional jockey. But, afterwards when

Davy mounted on the back of Chicomono before his gallop on the Yorkshire moors.

he was talking about the ride he said that a lot of his muscles ached. This is because a jockey puts a tremendous strain on muscles which you normally don't use much. He spent a long time talking to the stable boys. As usual, his memory was fantastic, he had forgotten nothing and knew everyone's name.

Then, everyone went into the house, sat down for a cup of tea and talked about the future.

Davy was full of plans for Chicomono who had already shown that he had tremendous promise by finishing second in a race at Thirsk. He certainly thought it wouldn't be long before he would be leading him into the winner's enclosure. By the time tea was over, the news that Davy was at the stables had spread and a big crowd had gathered to say 'hello' and get his autograph.

When he had finished signing Davy went indoors to wash and then walked up to the White Swan pub in Middleham and played darts until 10 o'clock. Then, it was time for him to set off back to Manchester as he had to catch a plane to America the following morning.

Davy's a great jockey   and owner !!!

BELOW: Davy after he returned from his gallop on the Yorkshire moors.

MONKEES ARCHIVES 1

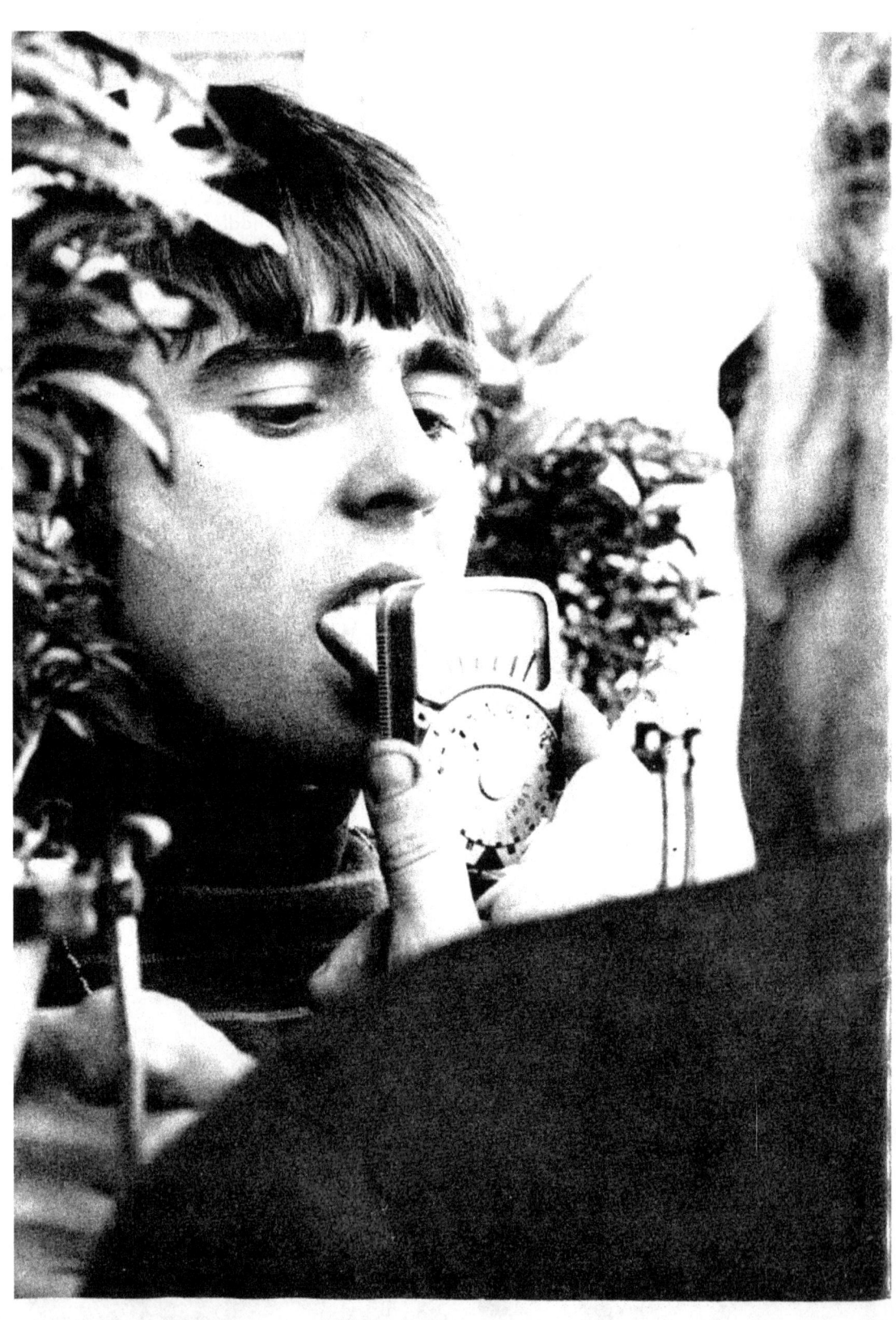

MONKEES ARCHIVES 1

WHAT NEXT?

Well, it's a question worth posing isn't it? We've all heard so many rumours and counter-rumours . . . headlines POSITIVELY stating what is going to happen to the four greats who've rocked the show business scene so much during 67 and 68.

But there's such a lot of guess-work going on around the boys. To get a clear picture of the situation, I must briefly hark back in time to those weeks when the whole pop world went Monkee mad.

At the start of it all Davy, Micky, Mike and Peter were going to play the parts of four zany young musicians in a series on television. Whether they played and sang as WELL as acting was purely a matter of luck. Yet there had to be music, obviously, in a series about a modern pop group . . . so a record was made. And it was a staggering big hit.

SIX GOLDS

Consider what has happened since then. Total record sales of more than twenty million. Six gold discs for singles and six for albums in the States. Plus that weekly half-hour show on television which was eventually sold all over the world. Plus tours that have busted box-office records—and nobody who saw the boys at Wembley Pool last year can forget the incredible impact, the energy, the personality of the boys "In-person" act.

So back to our question: what next for the Monkees? One could argue that they've done just about everything they possibly could. And if they felt they'd reached that point . . . well, maybe they'd also feel they might just as well split up and go their separate ways.

In fact, though, we know they DON'T feel that way. BUT . . . their future plans must be rather flexible right now for purely business reasons. When that television series started, the boys were getting around four hundred dollars a week each. Since then they've become a multi-million dollar industry in their own right . . . and, more important for them, have developed an amazing sense of confidence in what they are capable of doing.

So now we have them in the throes of a dispute with Screen Gems, who originally sorted out the television series. How this will work out is anybody's guess. And certainly it is not for us to go into the why's and wherefore's of the dispute.

But it HAD to be mentioned here because any business dispute simply is bound to interfere with the future. The boys, for all we know, are dead sure what they want to do next . . . but there may be things that are holding them back on the contract side.

Now let's dig a little deeper into what COULD happen. First, they are determined to buy themselves a lot more time. When one considers the pressures, the sheer pace of their career thus far, one can only marvel at the fact that none of them has collapsed with some kind of breakdown. Fortunately they each have the constitution of an ox—and have managed to keep going even if they've felt like collapsing and not working for a month or two.

NEW THINGS

Time IS all-important. They want time to work out new ideas and get new things going on records. They want to explore the wider aspects of show-business. Remember what Davy Jones said on this: "One day we would like to do a whole show at, say the London Palladium. For we are essentially a performing group. We're a film-making group who got into a musical groove. . . ."

In fact, Davy went on to say: "First of all we were four actors together. Now we're four actors and four

When this photographer stuck his light meter in Davy's face he promptly got it licked!

MONKEES ARCHIVES 1

musicians. We've been changing as people, but some of the things we've been doing have not shown just how much we've changed."

It's no secret now that the Monkees weren't completely happy with every episode of their TV series. Sure, they knew it was a massive job to come up with a new half-hour segment each and every week—but they still didn't like the way that certain parts, like at the beginning of the programme in a series, were the same week in and week out. They wanted TIME to work out something different but right from the start they simply had to work to a tight schedule and more or less do what they were told.

OLD HITS

Hear Davy again: "We know we're doing a world tour. Some of these countries haven't seen us before, so we'll be singing 'I'm a Believer' and all the old hits, but I'm pretty sure it'll be the last time we include such material. Otherwise the world will get the impression that we're strictly limited, whereas in fact we've been building our ability all the way."

What they want then is TIME . . . and Freedom! More freedom, anyway, to do what they want. Through circumstances completely beyond their control, they've come up against terrible criticism . . . over the series, over their records. It comes from inside pop music and television—because we know that their efforts have, in any case, delighted millions of fans. But the boys WANT that artistic appreciation. They want the so-called experts to see that they have the power to appeal to all age-groups and types of people.

There's been talk of the three big TV spectaculars to be made in America. Fair enough, because the boys themselves would like to see the Monkees projected in this way. But until contracts are settled, how can anything be really certain? They want to work on TV with artists drawn from other parts of the business—but again how can they be sure it will all come off?

Says Davy again: "We only want what is due to us. Our last tour, grossed two million but we only made a tiny percentage of that . . . well, something has got to be changed. For us the next twelve months will be hard, I'm not denying that. We want to do the world tour and hope we'll be allowed to do it.

"We're the Monkees, right now. There's a lot to do in that direction, if only we get the time and the freedom to do it all. In twenty years time, we might not be the Monkees. But for now there's no point in everybody asking if I'm going solo or anything, because there are three other guys, my three buddies, back there who are in it with me."

They've made their first full feature film and as you'll have read elsewhere in Monkees Monthly, it's very much THEIR own effort, Many of the stunts and ideas came swelling from the boys' own brains to a large extent.

PRIDE

But talk to any of the Monkees and you get an instant sense of pride in what they have managed to achieve, artistically, despite having to work schedules that would frighten off most performers. They're specially proud of their stage act—and of the plans they are creating right now to make it even more spectacular.

I believe we can look for quite a few changes of image. They'll stay the Monkees, but will not be projected in the same way via records or television.

But the TV shows, live appearances and records will all come flowing our way just as soon as the ink is dry on those new contracts. So lets hope everybody signs them real quick!

Mike looking over the Sho-bud guitar factory when he was in Nashville, Tennessee.

MONKEES ARCHIVES 1

MONKEES ARCHIVES 1

MONKEES ARCHIVES 1

MIKE TALKING!
ON THE TRANSATLANTIC PHONE

Once upon a time—or possibly twice upon a time—Mike Nesmith was the most highly organised person one could imagine. He used to keep notes about his appointments, a diary about his activities... and every day came and went without a hitch. But then he became a Monkee and, short of inventing his own thirty-six hour day, he found himself forgetting things.

And then he became a highly musical Monkee, too, which meant he spent every spare moment listening to new sounds, some created by himself, in studios, And, as is to be expected, life became even more disorganised.

Which is a rather roundabout way of explaining that Mike's Trans-Atlantic phone call came in a trifle late. Would you believe a great deal late? Ever so late? But in any case all was forgiven as soon as that dark-brown Texan voice purred into my ear and said:

"Jackie, I sure am sorry. I guess I should have tied a knot in my throat to remind me to call, but what's happening is this. I've been playing over some tapes we made down in Nashville, Tennessee, and the truth is I've gotten so interested in trying to create new sounds that when I get into my record-listening clothes I clean forget the time.

"You do understand, don't you? Well, fine. Say, how are the folks over in London. How's the gang on Monkees Monthly? I miss the scene there, but I guess I ended up the only one in the group who actually spent the vacation working. I heard about some things from Davy and Micky, who had a groovy time in London.

"I'd have liked to have gone over with them, but I'm really so hung up on the recording scene that I just hadda spend a lot of time in the studio. It was all work down there in Nashville. But I've had a bit of a vacation recently—went fishing... I just sat there and switched my mind off. When I kinda came to a few hours later I felt refreshed like after a whole day's sleep. Maybe I was asleep!"

Me: Were you completely happy with the album "The Birds, Bees and Monkees"? We all thought it was fantastic.

"Well, that's nice of you to say so. Yes, we felt it was easily the best album yet. Maybe the most thrilling part of it was summed up in the sleeve reference 'produced by The Monkees'. It meant a break. It meant taking charge of the recording side of things and that's what we've always wanted. Next one will have it split neatly between the four of us... three tracks from each. That way you'll get a greater variety, we hope, with several different styles and approaches.

"I really do feel kinda immersed in the recording business. The tracks on the 'Birds' album I was most closely involved in were 'Auntie's Municipal Court', and 'Tapioca Tundra' and 'Righting Wrongs' ... and what was the other one? Mmm... Oh I remember, 'Magnolia'. Well, you'll hear all kinds of strange noises like surface noises, even a needle swishing across the L.P. It's kinda horrible I guess. And if you think they're there by mistake. well, you're wrong. It's all part of this deliberate experimenting I feel myself getting into right now.

"I guess on the whole I was happy with 'Wichita Train Whistle', too, which is out here. Most of the reviews have been pretty good, which is gratifying. Dot SLPD 516 is the album number—I may have a bad memory for some things, but I've got that engraved on my mind. A free plug is a good plug."

Me: Saw some weirdo pictures of you from the film, Mike. Strung up in the air on the end of wires, like some Monkee-type flying ballet.

Mike: "Oh, yeah. That was kinda scarey. Looking at that sort of thing, you'd think it was easy. Like flying without a propeller, but in fact it's only too easy to tip right over and lose control. You have this harness thing round the hips and legs and what you have to do is hold your breath and hope that the guy working the strings doesn't nip off for a quiet smoke or somthin'. Really there's quite an art in learning how to balance your body."

Short pause hereabouts while there was a lot of crackling and sounds that somehow sounded like frogs being strangled, or something. A few seconds of nothing at all, then Mike came back on:

Me: Do you still like chocolate brown?

"Sure. That Radford Mini I had shipped over from England I had painted chocolate brown. And I also have a Jaguar XKE... same colour. Now you're not going to ask me what is the significance of this chocolate brown thing, are you!"

Me: Yes, I am.

"Uh, huh. Well... I can't really give you an answer. I just LIKE chocolate brown, that's all. I went off the bright colours—for cars, specially. I started feeling a bit sombre and I figured that chocolate brown matched my mood. Maybe it's just that you don't see too many chocolate brown cars!

"But now I just wanna go back to my recording scene. Down there in Nashville, I produced some pop-country tracks which I thoroughly enjoyed. That's THE centre for C and W music, as you'll know. Come to that it is one of the most important recording centres in the world.

"Most of my tracks are basically instrumental, using things like violins and guitars—all kinds of guitars. There's a new special pedal steel guitar they've got in the studios there and it gives a great raw-edged sound to music. The musicians there in Tennessee are quite magnificent. I don't know too much about British recording techniques, but I'd be interested to compare them one day."

Me: Does that mean we can REALLY expect a visit from you in the near future?

"Hey, hold on there! Don't rush me. Seriously, though, I'd like to re-visit old places in London and have a look at the scene. But I'm sure you'll understand right now that nothing is absolutely certain at our end of the line. We have a few backstage problems to cope with—I guess you'll have heard a bit about that. But the way we four guys think is this. We hate raising hopes among fans. We know, and appreciate, that you want to meet us again. We're gonna do what we can to oblige. But to keep making promises... then breaking them. Well! we don't like to do business that way, Jackie, and we hope you understand.

"But London is high on our list of priorities, believe me. And just as soon as we know when the visit is likely to be, you'll have me on the phone to you. And I won't be forgetful like this time, I promise. Because, in any case, news of a return to London would be so exciting that I wouldn't be able to keep it to myself."

Me: Just so long as you DON'T forget, Mike.

"Listen, Jackie, don't think me rude but I must get going now. Some buddies are coming round to hear some tapes and I hate to keep them waiting. I've got some great stereo equipment here, you know... sometimes we listen to music halfway through the night. Like it is now! Love and peace to all of you there in Britain. It's been real nice talking to you again. 'Bye."

And mad-keen producer Mike went back to his beloved music. So he was a bit late with the call! So who cares?

'He says he's come to cut off the phone!'

MONKEES ARCHIVES 1

JULY 69   Monkees   No. 30

Monkees

2/6

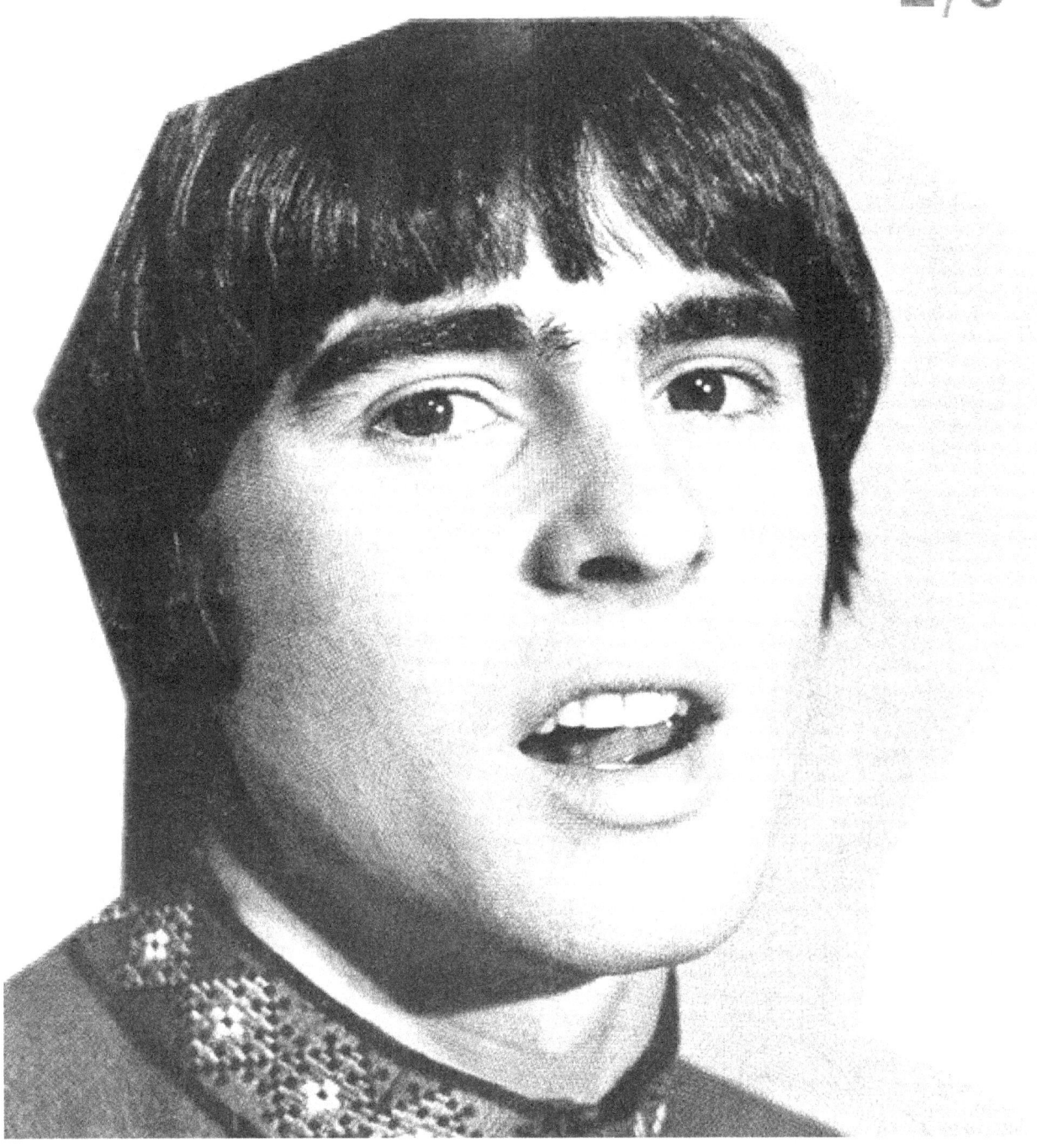

MONKEES ARCHIVES 1

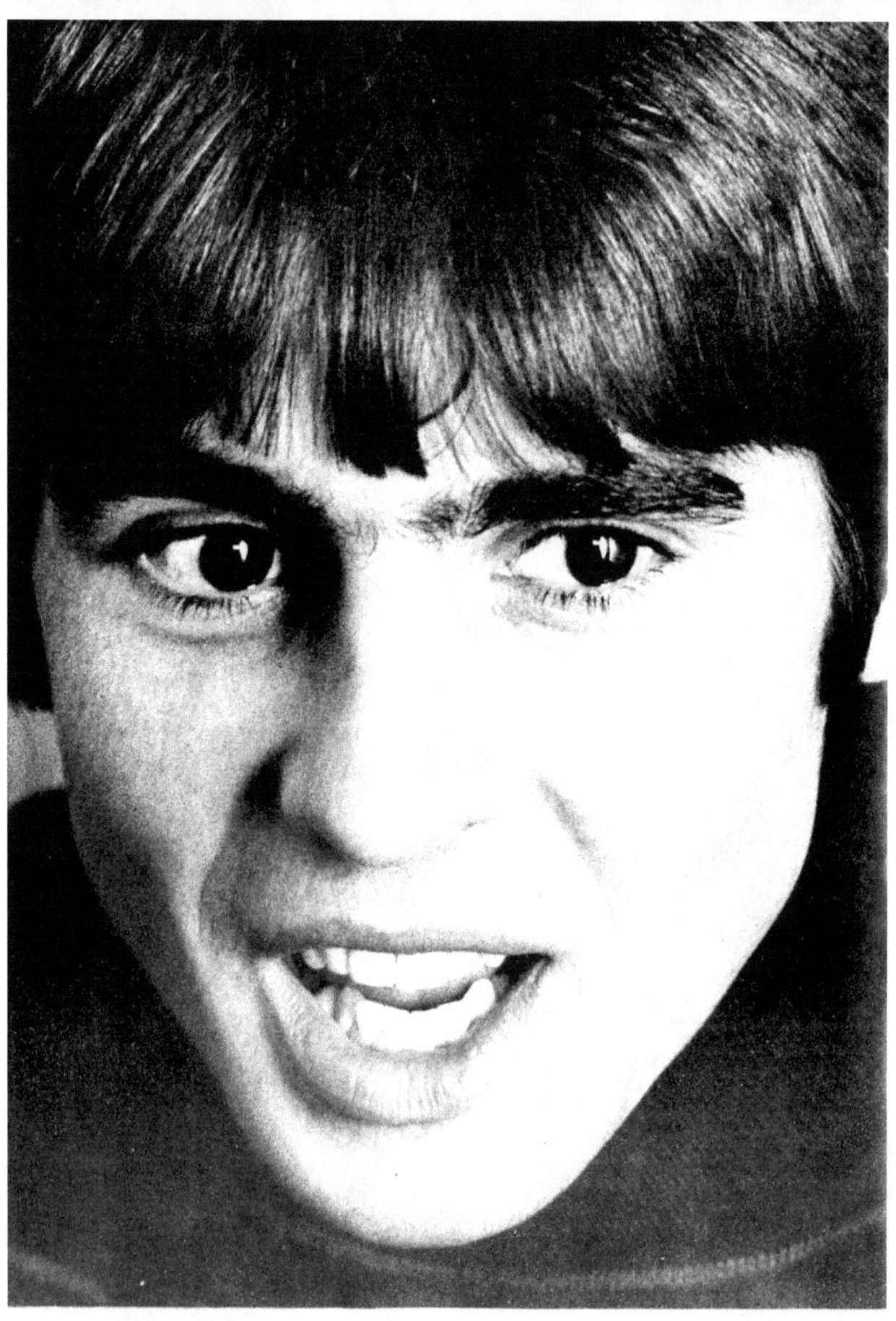

DAVY

Special Report by Jackie Richmond

OH, Davy, you should have told us! Davy, love, why did you have to leave us to find out about your marriage and your baby in the most soul-shocking way of all . . . through blown-up headlines in the national newspapers? Why didn't you let us, your fans, into the secret?

Since the news broke that you married Linda some 18 months ago, our phones have never stopped ringing. So many stories about the Monkees have appeared in the national press and so many have been downright untrue, that lots of your most loyal fans felt there was just a chance that this story, too, was inaccurate.

But, of course, it wasn't. You are married and you are a dad and a lot of fans still feel numb about the way they heard the news. So now all the Monkees are married. But, that's not half the tragedy that some of the Fleet Street newsmen have made it. That's not why I ask again; Oh, Davy, why did you do it?

Remember your last visit to Britain? You sat, legs swinging, in your publicist's office chatting away merrily to all of us? Remember being asked pointblank; "Any plans for marriage . . .?" Remember, most important, saying, and I quote; "There are so many beautiful girls in the world and I've only seen some of them. There's plenty of time for marriage but, right now, it's just not my scene"?

You were actually married at that time, Davy.

Remember telling me on the phone from America; "I would have proposed, maybe, to Lulu—she's a great girl. But I feel marriage at this stage would tie me down. There's so much for me yet to do in my career."

You were actually married at that time.

Now you have said, and I respect your feelings, that you feel you give a lot of yourself through your career. That you have the glare of publicity upon you most of the time and that you simply have to keep your personal life to yourself. That is fair enough. We, the fans, appreciate that you must be able to lead your own life with the prying eyes of cameras and the loaded questions of reporters.

But why DO pop stars sometimes feel that if they get married it has to be kept completely quiet? One theory is that they, or their advisers, feel that the fans would depart. The star is no longer "available". Perhaps there was some truth in that in the early days of the pop boom. Even so, John Lennon didn't

MONKEES ARCHIVES 1

hide away his first wife, Cynthia . . . it was just that nobody ever asked him about her.

DIGNITY

To stay on a Beatle kick, Ringo, George and Paul all got married . . . quietly and with dignity, but we knew about it. Elvis, too. So many others. Now the fans take a great interest in the wives and the children—remembering their birthdays and sending presents.

Most of us don't "go off" somebody because they find personal happiness through marriage. We admire, love, and respect our favourites; want to help them; want to see them find a life of bliss in return for the joy and the entertainment they provide for us through records, television and so on.

But we like to feel that we can share things with our idols. We want to know about the bad things, the good things . . . everything. And when we find that some very important things aren't told us . . . well, we get to think that maybe it is because we are somehow not trusted. All I can say is that a TRUE Monkee fan remains true; isn't somebody who grows hot and cold.

DELIGHTED

Believe me, Davy, we're delighted that you have found happiness with Linda and the baby. We're delighted, too, for Micky and Sammy . . . . for the Nesmith family. You all work hard for us and you deserve all the joys in the world.

We also like to feel that, though some of us may never get to meet you, you are our friends—and we are your friends. And what are friends for but to share confidences together and work together for the same end.

Alas, the way the news was broken . . . some 18 months late . . . has merely given some more ammunition to those who keep on knocking the Monkees. Sample quote: "Now the last Bachelor Monkee has gone, the group is in trouble". It's wrong. We all love you and will go on supporting you. There are millions of us, round the world.

LET DOWN

But we feel, right now, a bit let down. Only because we weren't taken into a really important confidence.

It's not really "Oh, Davy, why did you do it?" It's more "Oh, Davy, why did you do it THAT way?".

"Hey you! I thought I paid you to get rid of these flies!"

"Okay man, I'm ready. Bring 'em over here!"

MONKEES ARCHIVES 1

STOP PRESS...STOP PRESS...STOP

MIKE'S PARTY

Mike and Phyllis held a big Hallowe'en party at their house. They invited about 100 guests. Amongst them were our own folk-singing Donovan and the rest of the Monkees.

Mike dressed as a cowboy, Phyllis as a ballerina, Micky and Samantha as a Priest and Nun, Peter as a pioneer and Davy as a prince.

MIXED REVIEWS

As we reported last month, the boys' first full-length film received somewhat mixed reviews when it was premiered in New York on November 6th.

All the boys travelled to New York for the first major public showing of "Head" Their own personal verdict was "We didn't expect most of the film critics to like the film. But, we feel that it will have rather a different reception from the young-minded people everywhere when it goes on general release"

A second premiere was held in Los Angeles on November 20th.

NEXT ALBUM

We have already reported that the boys' new L.P which is being released now in America, will feature numbers from their film.

We now find that there are six new songs from the film on the album. There is also quite a lot of dialogue as well.

This must make it one of the most unusual L.P.s on the market now.

SINGLE OUT

The head of Screen Gems in London, Jack McGraw, recently returned from a trip to Hollywood and he told me that the boys have a big selection of tracks already recorded. It is hoped a new single will be released in time for your Christmas shopping.

Unfortunately, we had to go to press early last month and all the issues of the Monkees Monthly were printed before we learned that Davy's father had died and that Davy and David Pearl had flown in for the funeral.

NEW ARRIVALS

We have already shown you lots of pictures of the Monkees' pets in the Monkees Monthly.

In this issue you can see Davy with his rabbits.

Whilst Micky was on tour in Australia, one of his dogs had puppies. And just to make his house really over-full, one of his cats turned up with kittens. Samantha and Micky are very busy right now trying to find homes for all of the new arrivals. Incidentally, they can't send them to anyone in this country, so there's no point in writing to Micky asking for one of his puppies or kittens.

WHERE THEY WENT

After their 'down-under' tour ended, Mike and Phyllis took off on a holiday trip to Texas. As you know, this is his favourite American state which he visits whenever he is able to get away from Monkees business.

Peter travelled to Massachusetts and Micky took Samantha to Los Gatos to spend some time with his family

Davy gives a double V sign as he boards the plane for one of their frequent flights during the boys' Australian tour.

MONKEES ARCHIVES 1

THE MONKEES NEVER RELAX

Says' 'Going Down' co-songwriter Diane H.Iderbrand

Diane Hilderbrand is 22, a songwriter and singer—and a talented girl. A lucky girl, too. For she has written songs for the Monkees. She's known the boys for more than a year . . . and has been DATED by Peter Tork.

Which is where we come in. We met Diane, who wore white jeans, boots and a marvellous matey air, to talk about HER view of the boys. And let's say from the start that she rates them "great guys".

Diane's been writing songs for about nine years. She wrote music for the "Flying Nun" television series, soon out on BBC-TV. And lyrics to a film "The Tiger Makes Out", starring Eli Wallach. Now she's under contract to Screen Gems. Much of her writing is for new groups, like the Stone Country.

BUT . . . it's the Monkees we're concerned about. Diane wrote "Early Morning Blues And Greens", which Davy sings on the Monkees' third album. She also wrote, with Jack Keller, "Auntie Grizelda", often featured in the TV series. And with some blokes named Dolenz, Jones, Tork and Nesmith, "Going Down", the 'B' side of their last record.

MET IN TV STUDIOS

Here's something else. Diane has recorded "Early Morning Blues and Greens" herself . . . it comes out in the States around now and is expected to be released in Britain soon. But let's get on with the Monkee side of her career. Diane tells you in her own words . . .

"It was October, last year that I met them at the TV studios. They'd just seen 'Early Morning Blues' and it was Peter who asked me over to meet everybody. I know it sounds crazy but I'd met Peter before somewhere and for the life of me I couldn't remember just where it was. Lester Sill, the company boss, took me over there.

"Anyway I just watched things progress. I had only the simple one-note music, of the song written down. But the boys wanted to do it. Only problem was that they didn't know where or when.

"What I noticed first about the way they work is that they're always being hassled by people. They really do lead very busy lives and everybody pulls and pokes at them when they're out anywhere. So it's pretty strict security on the set. But they're real exuberant when they're working. Actually, I must tell you that Peter came up to my office in the Screen Gems' Building and we wrote a song together after work one day. Oh, it has these broken-down merry-go-round lyrics . . . guess we'll call it 'The Merry-Go-Round'. Peter had a couple of bars of the song going round in his head, so I got with him to finish it off.

"So it was Peter I got to know best. You know how people say Mike is a bit moody. Well, I went to Nashville where he was doing some sessions and I really got to know him well. And he's great. You know he's a boy from the South. Well, he told me: 'It's funny but everytime I come back to the South my I.Q. drops about twenty degrees'.

"Getting a Monkee to really relax is something else. Okay, it's been said before, but they really are always in the TV studios, or recording. Or off on a tour somewheres. Of course they DO have some time to themselves, but there are always so many people around. They're never left alone. They are on show all the time.

"Anyway, let's get on. I know Davy to speak to, that's about all. I like him in particular, as of the Monkees, but I don't really know him. Get it? As for Micky, well—he's on the go all the time. He burns up energy.

Mike's a determined fly killer **(TURN OVER)**

"But let's talk about Peter a little longer. I'm not going to talk about his personal life because I feel that's wrong. These guys have to work darned hard and they deserve some privacy...

"But I'll say this—Peter is very deep. Moody. But whether he enjoys something or not depends a lot on how he feels. Like we went sometimes to places in Hollywood where you can get Southern grits, and ham hocks and food like that. Or we'd go to teen clubs, to watch some real teenage talent. One club was a coloured place. But somebody always wants an autograph. Peter's great, though, for joining in things if he's in the right mood.

"You know, I play guitar and he plays guitar and banjo. Well, you go to some of these clubs and there are always instruments lying around. So he'll get up and start jamming. Like he'll meet a guy from the Modern Folk Quartet and soon everybody's joining in a session.

DATED PETER

"I dated Peter several times. But really when you go into it, the Monkees aren't so much for going out. They just get some friends around them and have conversation and maybe a little jamming. I don't want to sound all tied up with the Monkees because I'm under contract to the whole company. But I hear these criticisms of the Monkees and I shiver. You see when you're successful, there's always someone finding something wrong with you. They now know this. Especially as they are the MOST successful... phenomenal. That's my personal comment. It always happens...

"You probably heard about the Hollywood Bowl. I went to see them in a show there. They have this big pool right in front of the stage. Normally they cover it up. So this time they didn't figuring it'd keep the fans back. Anyway Micky does his James Brown bit and in rehearsal said he'd dive into the pool. Which he did. And immediately loads of fans started diving in after him... What a scene!!!

"Oh, gosh—back to Peter. He's just got this Mercedes Sedan. But really he doesn't spend much on himself—though he spends a whole lot on his friends. This guy is just TOO generous. Take clothes. He's got a closet full of them that he doesn't wear. But fans send him a lot of new clothes. His attitude is that if it suits him, he'll wear it. Probably for ever. He thinks a lot of fans who go to all this trouble on his behalf.

"You know they were terribly impressed with meeting the Beatles when they were in London. I told Peter I was going to London and he said to send the Beatles his love. And really Peter, and the others, are interested in meditation—as from the Maharishi. I guess we see basic truth in his work and in his word... so we're meditators.

"But when you meet the Monkees the big thing is their generosity. Like they bought a Mercedes for one of the secretaries on a recent tour. And Mike, at one date, sent out new cars to pick up lots of his relatives and he put them all up at a hotel for the night so they could see the show. Like he says: 'If I don't spend my money fast, I'll be broke in five years'. That's the way they all are. I could tell you about Mike buying a motor-bike for a friend and having it put there, all wrapped up, on this friend's desk in his office. Only I couldn't tell you EXACTLY what Mike wrote in the message—you couldn't print it! But Mike is like that. He gets right to the point when he's talking.

HELPS FRIENDS

"And Peter has helped out friends all over the place. Sure he gets depressed, sometimes, but who wouldn't in his position You can't keep on at full pelt all the time.

"They're all different individuals. I mean, Micky has his house in Laurel Canyon, which is a very popular area. He's a fanatic over improving everything and making it into a show place. But Peter doesn't seem concerned about his home at all. It's somewhere to live and to entertain friends and that's about the total of it.

"I adore the Monkees as characters and people. I only hope I write some more songs which suit their style. But I want to try all things. In London, I wrote some material with Colin Forcey of the Spectrum..."

Which is where the so-friendly Diane went right after our chat. A good songwriter herself, she knows what a tough business it can be—especially for those at the top.

A girl in a million—that about sums her up. After all, she's not just a business acquaintance of the Monkees. She's also a mate!   ENDS

... except when they're poor hungry flies!

MONKEES ARCHIVES 1

FIRST MONKEES SPECTACULAR

by our HOLLYWOOD REPORTER

Darwin was the man who thought up the theory of evolution and proved that man had descended from monkeys. Producer Jack Good made this his basic theme for the first Monkees TV Spectacular. He didn't stick very close to the original theme, though. It became more of a Jack Good looks at the Rock and Roll scene and compares it with today's music and today's stars TV show.

Davy, Micky, Mike and Peter helped, of course, with the planning of the whole special and after several weeks of hectic preparation, everyone finally gathered on one of Paramount Pictures big sound stages in Culver City, Los Angeles, at the end of November. Three whole days were to be devoted to the recording of this very special Pop show.

THE CAST

The all-star cast was made up by Little Richard, Fats Domino, Jerry Lee Lewis, the Buddy Miles Express, Julie Driscoll and the Brian Auger Trinity and, of course, the Monkees.

Brian Auger started the whole thing going as a sort of souped-up, rock-like Professor Darwin and his Trinity became a contemporary rock group. Then the Monkees rapidly come into the spotlight with Julie Driscoll trying to influence them to think modern

The whole show is a build-up for the high spot solos and group efforts by its stars.

There are some really great sequences. The boys appear as mechanical dolls in the "Wind-Up-Man" sequence. This is a new twist on the old mechanical toy skit and the Monkees did it really well, acting as though they were no longer made of flesh and blood but bits of tin and metal, moving jerkily to the strains of a clockwork motor inside their tummies.

All Davy fans will be knocked out with his "Buster Brown" outfit—short pants, big collar and the rest.

Mike does a marvellous solo with his guitar dressed in a really fabulous cowboy outfit. Here Jack Good thought up the great idea of splitting the screen, so that half of it contains Mike as a cowboy and the other half Mike dressed as he normally is. Mike the cowboy sings to Mike the Nesmith, if you like. A marvellous bit of television.

Micky sings "I'm A Believer" with Britain's Queen Jools of Pop, Julie Driscoll, bringing back memories of those months not so very long ago when the tune was constantly on our minds.

Peter does a great performance of "Prithee" in his usual characteristic manner.

But right through the Show the emphasis is on Rock and Roll and Jack Good who, as some of you may have read was responsible for the famous 'Oh Boy!' shows which introduced Cliff Richards, the Shadows, Marty Wilde and so many others to the British Pop scene in the late fifties, never lets us forget it, and you will all love the Monkees doing their Rock and Roll bit.

They all dressed for the part with typical rock hair styles, black shirts, silver ties, black pants, black winkle-picker shoes —the lot! The amazing thing is that they're just as good doing their rock-type stuff as they are with their normal Monkee material.

The whole show ends with a typical Jack Good rave-up, with all the artists going absolutely wild.

Both Brian Auger and Julie Driscoll said afterwards that they were very impressed with the Monkees and felt that many people in Britain don't give them credit for their talent.

RAVE-UP

The whole show was filmed in colour, and this immediately raises the question as to whether it will be shown on BBC-2, BBC-1 or even bought by ITV, which would mean that it could only appear in black and white. This has always been a sore point with the boys because their show was recorded in colour and, as you know only too well, when a colour film is shown in black and white, a lot of the impact must be lost through no fault of the artist at all.

On the other hand, I sincerely hope that it is shown in black and white so that every Monkee fan is able to see the boys' first TV Spectacular. Then, afterwards, for all those lucky Monkee people who have BBC-2, let's all try and persuade the BBC to show it on their colour channel as well.

We'll be showing you lots of great pics from the show in next month's issue. Don't miss it!

Mike has found the answer to having a quick kip when there are bright lights around—use an eye mask.

INSTANT REPLAY
REVIEWED BY TERRY SYLVESTER

Terry Sylvester is the most recent member of the Hollies, a group highly rated for their consistency, their musicianship and their know-how in the involved world of pop. Terry, from Liverpool, was once with the Swinging Blue Jeans and the Escorts, then hit the big-time when he took over from Graham Nash on rhythm guitar.

I presented him with a copy of the Monkees' latest album. We played it over—not once, but several times. And we talked about it. I won't hide his criticisms, because the Monkees themselves can take constructive criticism . . . so why shouldn't we! First a few general quotes:

"I've never seen the Monkees on stage, but those who have, say they're fantastic. I believe 'em, because their television shows were so very good. And I must say that they are all obviously darned fine actors. That's more than you can say for any other hit-record group in the world—including the Beatles. So they're off to a very good start. And their records are generally very commercial, which is a good thing. Some of the groups seem to despise that, but I wonder if it isn't because they don't know how to be commercial themselves, can't find the right direction—and therefore are jealous of the hits the Monkees have had.

"I like the Monkees because they are good at what they aim to do. Which brings me to their album, Instant Replay.

"First, I thought side one was easily the stronger. I was knocked out by the work of Mike and Davy rather more than that of Micky. Purely a matter of opinion, of course—but let's get into the record deeper.

"Take 'Through The Looking Glass'. Now I thought this was a bit disappointing as an opening track. Where it went wrong, I think, is that the three-part vocal harmony was great but they didn't keep it going—should have been there all the way instead of the one voice most of the time.

STRONG

"On 'Don't Listen To Linda', I realised just how strong Davy's voice has become. It's a Boyce-Hart song, with a good melody, and a nice string arrangement—everything in place, but the eye-opener was the way Davy handled the song out front. Yes, very good stuff.

"Then came 'Won't Be The Same Without Her', a Goffin-King song, which is a very good recommendation anyway. Again, the vocal side was excellent—rather like the Association. No I'm not suggesting they're copying, but I like the Association so that's a big compliment from me, believe me. On 'Just A Game', though, it was a Micky feature and I felt it was a bit ordinary.

"'Me Without You', another Boyce-Hart song, has good piano, good guitar, really excellent commercial stuff. And finally the Mike feature 'Don't Wait For Me' —the Nesmith voice very relaxing and good. Country-style steel guitar was used so well. Liked this a lot—as I liked all Mike's material and performances."

We gave another spin to side two, just to see if it registered any stronger. "You And I" didn't, for a start—Terry thought it was a pretty weak song. But he really perked up on "While I Cry", again with Mike singing—he thought this one had some great lyrics. "Ordinary Monkees" was the verdict on "Teardrop City"—but he went on a bit about how good Davy was on "The Girl I Left Behind Me". He could see the strength, as a dance piece, of "A Man Without A Dream", too. But again he expressed disappointment over a Micky side-closer "Shorty Blackwell"—"Just say I didn't like it very much".

And now some final quotes. "I'm sure they should have brought out 'I Won't Be The Same Without Her' as a single—must have been a hit. On side one, my favourite track was definitely 'Don't Listen To Linda' and on side two 'Man Without A Dream'.

"What else can I say. Only that I'd say it is easily the best album they've ever made."

MONKEES ARCHIVES 1

MONKEES ARCHIVES 1

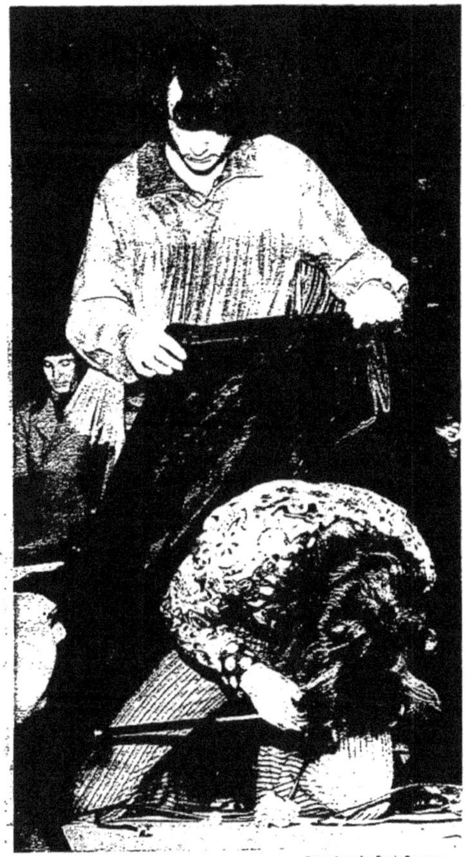

—Star photo by Boris Spremo

MIKE NESMITH TRIES to drag fellow Monkee Mickey Dolenz from stage as Mickey, on hands and knees, sobs and screams into microphone in midst of I Got a Woman. His elaborate histrionics were drowned out by crowd's shrieks.

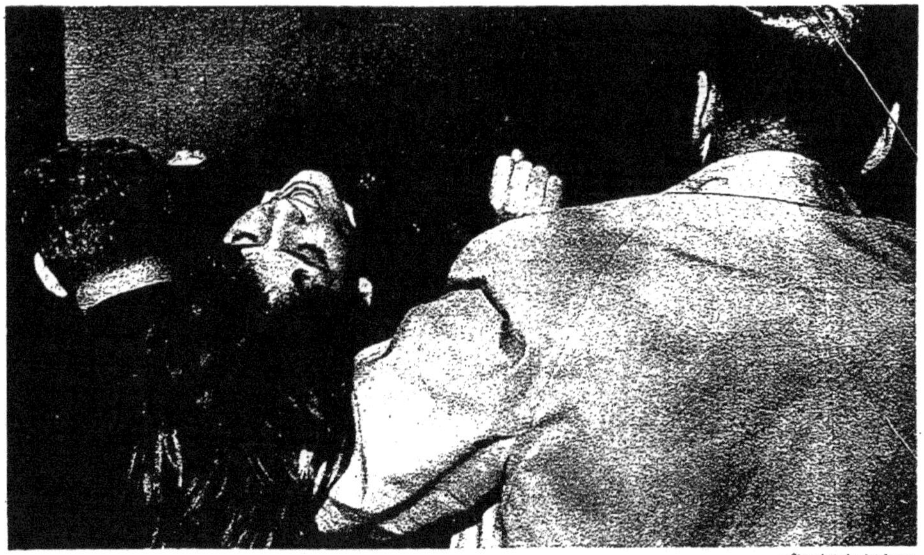

—Star photo by Art Jemes

HYSTERICAL GIRL is carried out of Maple Leaf Gardens after she'd climbed down to stage to get closer look at the Monkees. Arena was sold out weeks ago for $82,000 and 18,200 fans, most of them under 10, squealed and shrieked ecstatically, partly "to keep people from saying the Monkees aren't as good as they really are." Only 54 Monkees' fans needed first aid and only 2 required hospitalization, compared with 167 and 12 when Beatles played two concerts in Gardens.

Pre-teens give the word: Monkees beat the Beatles

The Monkees slipped quietly into town early yesterday, drove 18,200 youngsters into a frenzy at Maple Leaf Gardens and then left with about $75,000—all within 14 hours.

The Hollywood rock 'n' roll group also tied up more than 300 policemen most of the day.

Metro police aren't saying how much the concert affected regular duties, but one constable at the concert said there was only a desk sergeant and two cadets left in No. 33 division—the area bounded by Victoria Park, Bayview, Steeles and Eglinton Aves.

All top Metro police — Chief James Mackey and three of his deputy chiefs—were at the concert.

The $75,000 the Monkees took home made them the highest paid group ever to play the Gardens. The Beatles last year earned about $90,000, but had to work two performances for it. The Monkees played only one.

HYSTERIA RECORD

Where the Beatles still hold a Gardens record, however, is in hysteria. During last year's shows, 167 girls needed treatment at the St. John Ambulance first aid stations. Of these, 12 had to be sent to hospital.

The Monkees sent only 54 to first aid and two to hospital.

But their fans screamed, shrieked and thrashed in Their seats just as vigorously as any Beatle crowd.

From the moment the group walked on, it was almost impossible to hear anything on stage.

LITTLE PROBLEMS

The Monkee crowd was by far the youngest to attend a Gardens rock 'n' roll blast. The average age was about 10. And at least one parent brought along a four-year-old. He was an exception, though. Most parents waited outside in their cars, instead of venturing into the din of the Gardens. Most of those who did attend, spent the afternoon with their fingers in their ears.

The young crowd caused little problem for police—unlike the 12,000 that turned the Monkees' Winnipeg concert Saturday night into a near-riot.

In Toronto, one girl managed to clamber down over the chicken-wire fence surrounding the balcony above the stage. But she never made it. She was caught in mid-air and carried out of the building kicking and screaming. She spent the rest of the afternoon, sobbing on a step outside the building.

The Monkees arrived in Toronto from Winnipeg at 3 a.m. Even at that hour, there were 200 fans on hand to welcome them. But they never saw their heroes.

The group's chartered plane taxied into an out-of-the-way terminal at Toronto International Airport. From there, they were taken to the King Edward hotel, where they stayed locked-in until concert time.

Few youngsters guessed what hotel the Monkees were staying in, so only about 40 camped on its steps throughout the day. But more than 1,000 waited hours in the rain to see the group pull into the Gardens.

They left in their wake thousands of sobbing girls—some of whom ended up in the Gardens' first aid stations being held down by nurses while they screamed their idols' names.

Downsview base tragedy

Mother, 2 girls die in fire father's rescue efforts fail

An anguished father lies seriously burned in Sunnybrook hospital today after he failed to save his wife and two daughters from burning to death in their home on the Canadian Forces base, Downsview.

Mrs. Jean Anyan, 39, her daughters Shelly, 6, and Linda, 13, died in the fire which swept their two-storey row house early Sunday.

In hospital suffering from burns to his lungs, hands, feet and face is S/Sgt. Stanley Anyan, 41, a vehicle mechanic in the Canadian Army.

AFTER DANCE

Anyan did manage to rescue his son, Clarke, 15, by pulling him through a basement window. Another son, Stanley, 17, was away at camp for the weekend.

Sgt. Anyan and his wife had returned from a dance where they were celebrating their 21st wedding anniversary and had gone to bed when Anyan smelled smoke.

He went downstairs and found the living room an inferno and discovered that Clarke was trapped in the basement bedroom. He ran outside, kicked in a basement window and dragged the boy to safety.

Cut and bleeding from the broken glass, Anyan ran back into the house in his bare feet and found the stairway to the second floor engulfed in flames.

He tried to climb the stairs but his hands, face and feet were burning. Finally, choking with the smoke and fumes, he staggered back outside and climbed to the roof where he tried to break through to the burning interior.

The Ontario Fire Marshal's office, the Department of National Defence, North York fire department and the Metro police arson squad are all investigating.

North York firemen said the blaze apparently started in the living room but the cause is unknown.

Reports that neighbors heard an explosion are being investigated, Warrant Officer J.R. Johnson, base fire chief, said.

The fire was discovered by Paul Mellor, 24, of Jedburgh Rd., who was visiting Wayne Brownrigg, 24, next door to the Anyans.

The two men pulled the street alarm box and raced to rouse neighbors.

GIRL IN WINDOW

Mellor saw the oldest girl, Linda, pounding on the glass of the upstairs bedroom window and screaming: "Help! Please get me out of here."

Mellor and Brownrigg tried to get in both the front and back doors and climbed to a small porch roof but the heat and smoke drove them back.

"It was hopeless to try and reach her," Mellor said. "Flames were shooting out of the ground floor windows and it was so hot we couldn't even reach the door."

Steinberg's says 890 items reduced since stamps went

Steinberg's supermarkets have cut prices on 890 items since the company dropped trading stamps in its 44 Ontario stores, according to advertising manager Steve Bakowsky.

He said the rest of 900 scheduled price cuts will be made today.

"Our people could not get caught up with the amount of work. We had hopes that they would be able to complete the pricing last week," Bakowsky said.

Steinberg's announced last week it was dropping its Pinky stamps in order to cut food prices.

Mrs. Margaret Rouble, chairman of Women Against Soaring Prices, said a WASP affiliate, the Canadian Consumers Protest Association, has recently gathered evidence to indicate consumers don't want stamps at all. The evidence, collected in the Barrie-Camp Borden area, is part of a nationwide stamp survey the association is carrying out.

Of 200 women answering a questionnaire in the Barrie-Camp Borden area, 72 per cent favored cutting prices by two per cent rather than keeping trading stamp or cashier tape plans, only two per cent wanted to keep stamps, and 26 per cent were undecided.

FULTON'S THE CHOICE OF TORY LAWYERS

Former justice minister E. Davie Fulton would be the next Tory party leader if Ontario's Conservative lawyers had their way.

In a mail ballot organized by the Osgoode Hall Progressive Conservative Association, Fulton received 23 per cent of the votes. He was followed by national party president Dalton Camp with 25 per cent, and Ontario Premier John Robarts with 17 per cent.

Senator Wallace McCutcheon, former federal agriculture minister Alvin Hamilton and Ontario Education Minister William Davis got 8 per cent each.

THEIR PIONEER DAY JUST GREW AND GREW

Principal Don Newman didn't expect anything grand when he asked pupils at his North York school for artifacts for a "Pioneer Day" centennial project.

But before they were through he had to borrow two guards from the board of education to watch the collection.

Sloane Ave. public school was swamped with an expensive array of pioneer relics including a brass coffee urn, a 150-year old quilt valued at $250, a mahogany spinning wheel, yellowed photos of long forgotten relatives, bearskins, racoon skins and one kangaroo skin.

The gymnasium was converted into a miniature Ponderosa quaintly cluttered with the relics and with boys and girls in costumes from Canada's past.

And it was flavored with the aroma of chuckwagon stew, buttered johnnycake and fudge.

The program was so successful it was held over an extra day at the request of parents and principals from other schools who were gathering pointers for their own centennial projects.

More than 1,500 pioneer buffs roamed the settlement in the two days including Dr. Hugh Partlow, superintendent of public schools who was seen cutting a mean bearskin rug.

"They even wanted us to keep the thing on all week," says Newman, who explained that two days was all the teachers and pupils could take.

It was two days the pupils will never forget.

"You can't learn anything from words in a book," said 13-year-old blacksmith Gary Sweeney. "You can only learn from experience and ours taught us just how hard our forefathers worked to make Canada. They nearly broke their backs."

"Right," added woodcarver Eric Hatashita, 13: "A picture is worth a thousand words but an experience is worth a thousand pictures."

History teacher Marshall Geer spent two months with the pupils preparing the big show. They visited libraries, museums, Black Creek Pioneer Village and Albion Hills Conservation School, where they were taught bygone crafts.

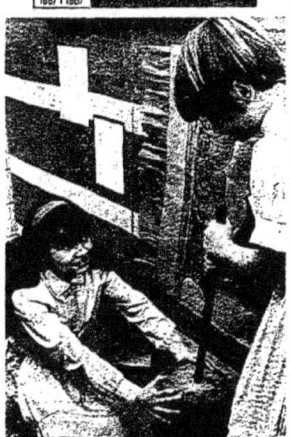

1867 | 1967 *THE CENTENNIAL in our schools*

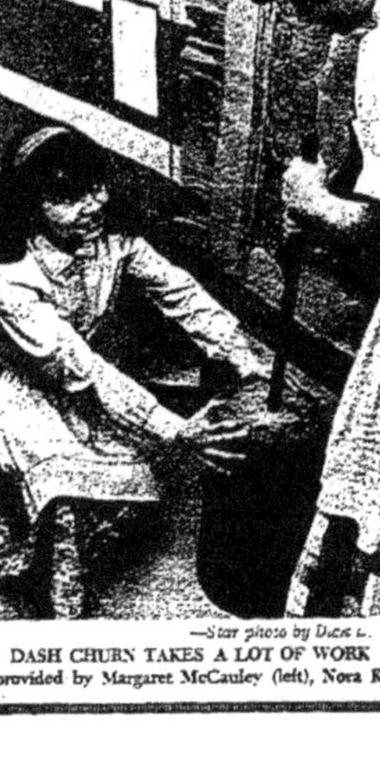

—Star photo by Dick L.

DASH CHURN TAKES A LOT OF WORK

It's provided by Margaret McCauley (left), Nora Kelly

DATELINE METRO

50 led to surface after subway fire

More than 50 passengers were evacuated from a northbound Yonge subway train at noon Sunday when fire broke out in the front car.

There were "several explosions—real blasts—and 20 or 30 electric flashes lit up the tunnel," said Stuart Wearne, 19, of Charles St., a newly-arrived Australian taking his first subway ride.

"Women screamed," he said. "Some of them were closer to the fire than I. The conductor came in and said 'don't panic'."

Firemen with gas masks put out the blaze as passengers were led along the tracks, under a bridge and up the steps to Yonge St.

Subway service was delayed for 50 minutes and those inconvenienced were rerouted via surface facilities. The TTC is investigating cause of the blaze.

Coleman strikers reject offer

Canadian Coleman Co. strikers have turned down a return-to-work offer by a 95 per cent vote, Alec Munro, president of the local CLC union, reports.

A negotiating team has been working with management officials for two weeks trying to settle the five-month-old strike. Meetings were arranged by William Dickie, chief labor department conciliator.

Munro says the company would take back 50 workers within four weeks of a new agreement being signed, another 50 within 10 weeks and the remainder, about 150, by October. He claims the company has hired 200 new workers since the strike began.

Frank Shaw, Coleman administrative vice president, said the firm offered a pay increase of 41 cents over 2½ years. The present labor rate is $2 an hour.

Shaw said 65 workers who went on strike last October have returned to work and 170 others have been hired.

'Unsafe' site picketed

Sixty Laborers' Union members set up a picket line at a sewer construction site in Etobicoke today to protest "unsafe and unsanitary" working conditions.

The open-cut project, at Islington Ave. and Rexdale Blvd., is being built by Donegal Construction Co.

Norbert Pike, Local 183 safety director, said the work stoppage was decided at a union meeting yesterday after the company had refused repeated requests to improve conditions.

Pike said the company stacks material at the edge of a trench, endangering the men below and has improper shoring in the trenches.

Hartley McCallum, Donegal president, denied the job is unsafe. "We have an Etobicoke safety inspector on the job every day," he said.

Please die in scheduled hours

Just be careful when you die in Metro.

Pick the wrong time and your undertaker might have trouble getting a burial permit.

Permits are issued by city clerks.

When the clerk's office is closed, police take over the job—but, police are notifying all undertakers that permits will be available only at designated stations and only for limited hours.

QUOTE OF THE DAY

Commenting on how some Swansea and Forest Hill residents are looking for something to criticize since their villages joined Toronto, Controller Margaret Campbell last week told Forest Hill businessmen one homeowner, who reported a water main leak, had this retort when he was told it would be fixed immediately:

"Ah, but it's not like the old days. They would have warned us in advance then."

MONKEES ARCHIVES 1

The inside story on

It was, as the Monkees themselves say, one tremendous, memorable, fascinating trip. The boys, plus their entourage, went to Australia, then Japan... breaking new ground and bringing great joy to a few more million fans. One could write a book about what the Monkees saw and did, even though it was a fairly shortish tour.

But we haven't got a whole book to spare. So here are some of the highlights, compiled by the boys themselves... and passed on to readers of Monkees Monthly with love from Davy and Mike and Peter and Micky. Ready? Off we go...

They flew from San Francisco, by Quantas Airways, and stopped off in Fiji for a short while before arriving in Sydney, Australia. And at Fiji were the national drill team colourful characters who wear navy blue skirts. Maybe you can remember them from State occasions when they've often been in the news.

Well, Peter got them all to do the "V"-for-peace sign. He started it off and they followed on. That was quite a sight, believe us. But on to Sydney, a city literally afire with enthusiasm for the Monkees. Literally afire? Well, the boys were greeted with fireworks and sparklers, as well as banners and flags... and that despite the fact that it was shortly before breakfast-time when they actually arrived!

A short flight to Melbourne and there they were, ready for the first two evening concerts at the 6,700-seater Festival Hall. But getting to the centre of Melbourne from the airport was a pretty amazing scene. An eight-mile journey, yet there were people lining the route at every part of it. Not exactly ten deep, mind you, because Australia has a comparatively small population... but at every point there was SOMEBODY.

Mechanics in overalls poured out of the garages and workshops, to give the Monkees the thumbs-up sign as the motorcade moved past. And 2,000 pupils from the convent came out, all in special uniform, to wave to the boys and cheer them on. The nuns came out too, to add to a very colourful occasion.

Press conferences all the way, of course. Wherever the boys go, journalists gather to tempt them into talking about world affairs as well as show business. But the Aussie conferences are, by common agreement, rather tougher than in other countries

So the boys had to take turns talking about such subjects as drugs and Vietnam and world peace and the like. As ever, they came out of the ordeal well... ad-libbing among themselves and obviously making a lot of sense to the assembled newspapermen.

But a word or two here about the actual concerts. Australian teenagers like pretty much the same Monkee music as fans in America or Britain. Where they are different, though, is in what they throw on stage to the boys during shows. Most other places they throw rings, or autograph books or sweets. But the Aussie fans threw up paper streamers and lots of beads—love-beads, I mean —made up in rows and rings.

On stage, it goes without saying, the boys were in tremendous form. They all had suits specially made for the tour, with Mike the most colourful in a jacket made out of the United States flag which he wore for his special solo spot.

Those shows were triumphs and then it was back to Sydney, with a bit of time to spare before the shows at the 11,000-seater Sydney Stadium. Most of the party went out shopping... to a place where they sold "antique clothes". Weird stuff but the boys were specially sold on some incense and candles, which they carted back to the hotel... the Sheraton Motor Hotel, a plush establishment in Sydney.

This meant that the hotels had lower-than-usual electricity bills for a while because the boys lit the candles in their rooms and relaxed in an aura of incense. Trust them to come up with something a bit off-beat to greet all the visitors to their suites.

Funny things happened too at the shows. This Sydney Stadium, a super-massive place, has a revolving stage, which is one of the highlights of most shows there. But there was such a shower of paper streamers for the boys that the paper gummed up the works and it took a posse of technicians to free the stage and let the show go on.

Pause here to explain that the Cherokees, a five-piece Aussie group with hit records of their own, did the backing for the Monkees on stage... and earned high praise and thanks from the boys. The other group on the bill were Marcy Jones and the Cookies, four Australian girls who also went down well with the huge audiences.

Right near the Hotel Sheraton was what the Americans call an

MONKEES ARCHIVES 1

MONKEES ARCHIVES 1

At Hong Kong, knocked out to be on Chinese soil as it were, they sent postcards home. And then on to Tokyo, where ten thousand fans were massed at the airport . . . on the roof, out of every window, just a mass of Japanese faces which lit up with pleasure at the first sight of the boys. The concerts also were in 10,000-seater halls, and later on to Osaka from Kyoto on that amazing 150-mile "bullet" train developed in Japan.

THREATS

Only problem in Japan is that the left-wing element politically are very anti-American. In fact, there were threats uttered that somebody would kill the Monkees . . . but the boys kept plugging on and didn't let it worry them. Because of crowd problems, however, most of their shopping was done in the hotel rooms . . . local stores sent big selections of goods, like silks and fans, up to their rooms. But some of the party also went on shopping trips to the ginza (like a trade arcade) and Rick Klein went to the schinjuku, the local beatnik area — not exactly the most pleasant place in the world.

Tours were arranged round the Nikon camera factory and round the Honda motor (car and cycle) organisation. Incidentally Micky bought a very powerful microscope and he and Mike spent the rest of that evening looking at slides of bugs and hairs and droplets of blood which they got by pricking their own fingers.

FLORAL

In Japan, they were backed on stage by five Japanese boys known as the Floral, and one of the concerts was televised for future showing. There was plenty to see in Japan. And plenty of fans to make it a truly memorable visit.

But all good things have to end. The boys and their entourage left Japan on a Tuesday at 8.30 a.m. And arrived back in Los Angeles at 7.30 a.m. the SAME DAY! Funny how time differences work out . . . half-way round the world and yet you get home earlier than you left!

'Oh no you don't, I'm not falling for that old trick.

DID YOU MISS ANY OF THESE ISSUES?

| 9 | 10 | 11 | 12 | 13 | 14 |

If you did and you'd like to make-up your collection just send us a 2/6d. Postal Order for each copy that you are missing and we'll get them off to you straight away. Make your P.O. payable to Beat Publications Ltd., and send it with details of which issues you want, to: Monkees Monthly, Back Issues, 58 Parker Street, London, W.C.2.

PLEASE NOTE THAT ISSUES No. 2 (MARCH 67) AND No. 4 (MAY 67) ARE COMPLETELY OUT OF PRINT AND CANNOT BE SUPPLIED

MONKEES ARCHIVES 1

MONKEES ARCHIVES 1

WHY DIDN'T D. W. WASHBURN MAKE THE TOP TEN?

asks Jackie Richmond

Just because we're all such keen Monkee fans doesn't mean that we've got to bury our heads in the sand like a gang of tame ostriches. We've got to own up when things go wrong for the boys, even when it means being ribbed by our mates who perhaps aren't so devoted to Micky, Davy, Pete and Mike.

One case in point is the comparative failure of "D. W. Washburn" in the British charts. I expect somebody has had a go at you about this. "Hello, what about the Monkees then! Slipping, aren't they! Told you they would...!" Really annoying, isn't it! But facts are facts, no matter how you try to twist them, and after "Valleri" it WAS disappointing that "D. W. Washburn" got no higher than number twenty in one of our charts...

RELAXED

It's really rather strange. The disc reviewers all liked it—one said it was "a lazily relaxed number that's a cross between razzamatazz, Good Time, vaudeville and Dixie. You'll be singing along with it from the very first time you hear it. This is a disc with immediate commercial impact."

And the others tended to agree. BUT not enough people found it commercial enough to nip out and buy it in large enough numbers to make the Top Ten. W-e-l-l... let's look at the problem a little more closely.

First of all, we know that time, a precious thing, has not always been on the side of the Monkees. The boys have been so darned busy that some aspects of their career have to be carried through in a tremendous rush. From now on, though, they are MAKING more time to pick out a likely single—and having a whole lot more to do with the actual production side.

But they've also got a never-ending problem. If they pick a single which is aimed specially at the massive Monkee market in America, it simply has to be a bit of a gamble as to whether it will take off here. Perhaps "D. W. Washburn" was just not quite right for the British buyers. Trouble is that if a mistake is made, it can't suddenly be put right.

A slipped disc, no matter by who, sticks on the evidence of the charts. Which, in turn, leads to the knockers having their little knocks... and so making all of us hopping mad! You can't really just try out a new single for a week or so, then withdraw it or forget all about it and leap into the lists with an instant follow-

continued on page 39

'They were easy! I only ever had trouble with one...'

...this one!'

MONKEES ARCHIVES 1

continued from page 34

up. That would REALLY give the knockers something to talk about, wouldn't it?

Even so, it has to be admitted that it seems that fewer people were attracted by "D. W. Washburn" so, the proof as to why, could simply be that it WAS the wrong song. Or the wrong time to release it...

But let's not get too carried away about the charts anyway. In themselves, they're as accurate as possible considering the speed of doing them every single week of the year. But they show, roughly, who is selling the most records in that particular week.

DIFFERENT

Now where you actually end up in the charts depends on a lot of different things. Is there a boom or a slump in record sales generally?—that's an important point. In a slump, you could get to number one spot and yet sell only half as many copies as would be needed in a boom spell. So you get the same honour of being right at the top... but perhaps only half the money from royalties.

Another thing: If all the fans go out and buy a new single in the first couple of weeks on sale, the record could hurtle up and then hurtle out again in a short space of time. But if the spending is spread over a couple of months, the record could stick around the ten-to-twenty mark all that time ... and actually SELL MORE than a record which gets to number one.

Get it? It's a bit complicated, I know, but it points how sometimes chart positions are not entirely right in proving just how many fans bought any particular record.

Let's get off that subject for a while... and consider what has been happening to other top-rated groups during the time that the Monkees' last couple of singles haven't zoomed as high as we'd like. Because the fact is that there's a whole change come over the chart scene in any case. The Who, Traffic, and many others have found that their terrific popularity among fans is not always shown by the places they get to in the charts. Because you get to the top five with one record, there's no guarantee that the next one will do even half as well.

It all depends on the actual material and performance on the "follow-up". And there are ever so many groups who get one hit record and then are never heard of again. No chance of that happening to the Monkees, of course—they've already become almost "veterans" of the hit-making stakes.

MASSIVE

And getting to number twenty really isn't so bad—not with the massive number of records released each week of the year.

Still, we mustn't make like ostriches. It's NOT so good that the Monkees didn't make at least the Top Ten with their last single. It's up to us all to help ensure the next one is a chart-smasher of a success. If you think there IS something wrong with the actual choice of songs for recent singles... well, why not drop me a line about it! Let's get together on this thing.

JACKIE RICHMOND

MONKEES ARCHIVES 1

ON THE ROAD WITH THE MONKEES

MONKEES ARCHIVES 1

HANG ON to your hair-ribbons, sweeties, cos it's Monkees' travel-time again—and now the destination is Birmingham, Alabama! The on-the-go trio went down South recently, making two appearances for radio station WSGN in Birmingham—one musical and one conversational! Davy, Mike and Micky were asked to be the special guests at a giant youth rally held at the Alabama State Fairgrounds. Davy was unable to get to Birmingham until late at night and until he got there Mike and Micky "rallied" to the occasion and kept the talk going in their usual madcap fashion! The Monkees' second day in Birmingham was devoted to making music—deejay-wise at the WSGN studios and live at City Auditorium. Davy, Mike and Micky captivated thousands of Birmingham teeners who came to see and sigh over their adorable favs. Now—let's go and spend some time with the Monkees in Birmingham!

The fun-filled two days began when Micky and Mike arrived at Birmingham's airport and were greeted by WSGN Program Director Walt Williams and thousands of Monkee-lovers.

Davy arrived later with (left) Colgems Records' executive Danny Davis. Throngs of fans were on hand to welcome Davy with love beads, flowers and warm smiles.

WSGN deejay Dave Roddy seems amused while Mike takes another of Micky's jokes in stride! The zany pair made a special talk appearance at the youth rally—and they were super!

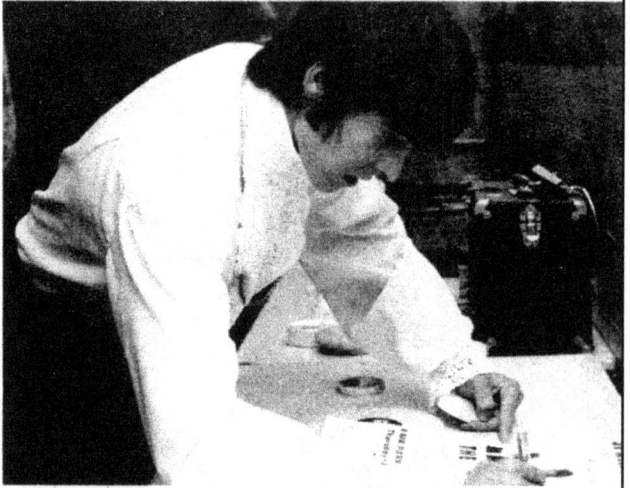

When Davy wasn't signing posters, he was Monkeeing it up with Mike and Micky—and mesmerizing audiences (radio and live) with the magic of Mommy and Daddy and Good Clean Fun—just great!

MONKEES ARCHIVES 1

MONKEES ARCHIVES 1

THEIR VERY FIRST PRESS CONFERENCE

Part 2

In the huge Buckingham Suite of Kensington's Royal Garden Hotel THE MONKEES held their first ever Press Conference when they visited London for their series of Wembley concerts. Every word spoken by Micky, Davy, Peter and Mike as they faced a battery of questions from 300 reporters and magazine writers was recorded for THE MONKEES BOOK. This month you can read the second and final section of the Press Conference questions and answers.

Q.: I UNDERSTAND, DAVY, THAT YOU HAVE BEEN CALLED UP. IS THAT RIGHT?
DAVY: Yes, I got my classification papers and I am appealing, I will be classified 3A, I think. I'm not sure. I really don't know any more than you do about it.
Q.: HAVE YOU HAD YOUR MEDICAL TEST YET?
DAVY: No. If you have your medical test you're in the army!
Q.: DAVY, DO YOU HAVE AN INDEPENDENT RECORD LABEL?
DAVY: Yes. At the moment it's owned by Davy Jones Enterprises but it doesn't have a label yet. I intend to record new talent. I've already had a group of Texans called The Children in the studio.
Q.: SOME OF THE BEATLES HAVE ADMITTED TAKING L.S.D....
MICKY: (Breaking in) Ah! There it is! That one we were waiting for!
Q.: (Continuing) ... also two of the Rolling Stones who are on drug charges claim drugs help them in their work. Do you think it is necessary for pop groups to take drugs?
MICKY: Do you like The Beatles' album?
Q.: Yes.
MICKY: Well?
Q.: BUT DO YOU THINK IT'S NECESSARY?
MICKY: No. I drink coffee. That's about the worst drug I take.
PETER: I took asprin once. It destroyed my head and it provided me with a lot of inspiration. I'm gonna write a song.
MIKE: I have a real problem. I get high on one-a-day vitamins. Anything else really wastes me.
MICKY: I drink chlorine with ...
DAVY: (Breaking in) Ex-Lax does it to me. It keeps me going all the time. No? O.K.!
MICKY: I don't think anybody needs anything. It's just whatever is right for whoever is involved.

Q.: I'VE HEARD IT SAID, MIKE, THAT YOU'RE DIFFICULT TO GET ON WITH. WOULD YOU AGREE WITH THIS?
MIKE: Yes.
Q.: WHY?
DAVY: Nobody's been able to ask him enough questions to find out!
Q.: IS IT SOMETHING YOU ACT OR DO YOU REALLY HATE PEOPLE?
MIKE: Well, it really depends on you doesn't it.
Q.: WELL, I'M VERY LIKEABLE!!!

Micky—Writing a drum solo!

MONKEES ARCHIVES 1

MIKE: Then I'd probably get along with you famously!!!

Q.: I'D LIKE TO ASK DAVY WHAT HE THINKS OF THE RE-RELEASE OF HIS OLD ALBUM.

DAVY: Oh, yes, Nice, isn't it. Lovely isn't it. My father likes it. And my sisters. And Micky likes it too because we're friends. I don't particularly like it. I tried to stop it coming out because I thought it was a bad album.

PETER: Micky likes it because he wants to put an album out himself!

Q.: HAVE YOU ANY PLANS TO GROW ANY FACIAL HAIR IN THE NEAR FUTURE?

PETER: I can't stop myself!!! Mike's got boards there as you call them here. I'd like to grow a beard one of these years.

MICKY: We can't. The Beatles did it already.

PETER: We'd be accused of imitating. Ha! Ha!

Q.: IS THERE ANY CHANCE OF YOU GOING TO BELGIUM OR HOLLAND IN THE NEAR FUTURE?

PETER: There's a chance of anything, you know, really.

Q.: TALKING ABOUT THE BEATLES. WHAT IS YOUR PERSONAL RELATIONSHIP, YOUR ARTISTIC RELATIONSHIP TO THEM?

MICKY: I like them very, very, very, very much.

PETER: I don't know them yet at all.

MIKE: Artistically we all feel the same way about them.

PETER: Except Davy who doesn't understand their new album!

Q.: MIKE, IS YOUR WIFE WITH YOU THIS TIME?

MIKE: No (Editor's note: Mike's wife flew into London to join him three days later).

Q.: DO THE REST OF THE GROUP THINK IT'S A GOOD THING FOR YOU TO TAKE YOUR WIFE ON TOURS?

MIKE: Well, it's kinda dangerous.

Q.: WHY?

MIKE: I'll let you figure that out!

Q.: FIRST OF ALL NOBODY'S SAID "WELCOME TO LONDON"...

MONKEES (Together): Thank you. Thank you very much. We're glad to be here.

PETER: And welcome to the Press Conference, sir!

Q. (Continuing): ...WE'VE HAD THREE OF YOU OVER HERE BEFORE AND WE'RE VERY GLAD THAT YOU CAME. THANK YOU FOR YOUR CO-OPERATION. PETER, YOU'RE HERE FOR THE FIRST TIME AND WE HOPE YOU LIKE IT. IS THERE ANY FOLK SINGER THAT YOU WOULD LIKE TO SEE IN THIS COUNTRY? I KNOW YOU'RE VERY KEEN ON FOLK.

PETER: All of them.

Q.: DAVY, THERE HAVE BEEN REPORTS THAT YOU'RE UNHAPPY ABOUT BEING A MONKEE, THAT YOU'RE RESTLESS AND THAT YOU FEEL YOU COULD NOW AFFORD TO GO SOLO. HAVE YOU ANY PLANS TO DO THAT THIS YEAR?

DAVY: No I don't. I might as well clear it up now by saying I am not leaving The Monkees and I'll be with them as long as they're Monkees.

Q.: PETER, HOW'S YOUR FRENCH?...

PETER: Is that your question? It's pretty bad. Not your question. My French.

Q. (Continuing): I LEARN FROM PARIS THAT SOME OF YOU DESIGNED SOME CLOTHES. DO YOU ALL DESIGN YOUR OWN CLOTHES OR JUST MICKY?

MICKY: I just designed my first clothes about two weeks ago and I haven't worn them. I don't do a whole lot of that.

PETER: I designed one clothe!

Q.: YOU GET A WEEKLY SALARY. COULD YOU TELL US HOW MUCH AFTER EVERYBODY HAS TAKEN A CUT?

PETER: We get a salary for doing the TV show and we get residuals from the TV show when it's played again and record royalties, money from concerts and so on. It all comes to us in different forms through different organisations and only my book-keeper knows for sure how much I get.

Q.: YOU THINK IT'S QUITE REASONABLE ANYWAY?

PETER: Well, you know, it could be less and it could be more!

Q.: YOU DON'T THINK YOU'RE BEING BLED?

PETER: No, Do you?

Q.: DAVY, HOW LONG WERE YOU PLAYING IN "OLIVER!"?

DAVY: In London in the West End at the New Theatre for 7 months. I spent three years on Broadway and then I did 4 months on the road. Then I went to Hollywood and met The Monkees.

THE END

Micky obviously got a big kick out of this sign!

MONKEES ARCHIVES 1

MONKEES ARCHIVES 1

MONKEES DO SHOWS FASTER

Not puppet!

FIRSTLY, we dealt with the subject which most people appear to be ducking — the resentment felt very strongly in some show business quarters that the Monkees are really non-playing puppets and have no right to their success as a pop group. (Before I get swamped with letters, may I say that the Monkees in my opinion are 'what's next' and I go happily around with the wheel.)

"I can only speak for myself," said Davy. "I am an actor and I have never pretended to be anything else—the public have made me into a rock'n'roll singer. No one is trying to fool anyone!

"People have tried to put us down by saying we copy the Beatles. So all right, maybe 'The Monkees' is a half-hour 'Hard Days Night!' But now we read that the Who are working on a TV series around a group. Now who's copying who?

"In our show we all play ourselves with the exception of Peter Tork, who plays a 'thick' and he's not. Pete doesn't really dig the teeny-boppers scene. Some fans wrote to him that they were watching his house through high-powered binoculars and now he has the curtains drawn all day!

"There are 32 Monkee programmes now completed and in about two programmes' time you should notice about 180 per cent improvement. We really began to get on top of it—ad libbing and taking the script from the top.

"Originally the show took five days to film. Now we've got it down to two-and-a-half. But people still have no idea how hard we work or they'd never put us down."

There has also been considerable speculation over how much the Monkees are masters of their own destinies. How much say does the group have? Or are they completely controlled by management? Davy side-stepped this one and, bearing in mind our company, it was forgiveable.

"Look," he went on, "we're just out to make people happy and enjoy ourselves at the same time!"

NEXT WEEK — Davy talks about the big subject — BEATLES v. MONKEES! Don't miss it!

DAVY & Mrs. SHARPLES

IT was a sentimental journey for Davy Jones when he visited the set of Granada's "Coronation Street" in Manchester recently. Waiting to greet him was his "grandmother," Ena Sharples, actress Violet Carson.

In March, 1961, soon after the TV series started, Davy was brought into the programme to play 11-year-old Colin Lomax, Ena Sharples' grandson.

Davy was in Manchester to visit his relatives, and his father went with him to the studio, where Davy introduced him to the "Coronation Street" cast.

Little Lucille Hewitt—actress Jennifer Moss—renewed her acquaintance with Davy.

"You've grown," she cracked.

"Grown?" said Davy. "Why, even you used to be taller than me."

In the bar of the Rover's Return, the street's fictitious pub, grandma Sharples told Davy: "You've done very well for yourself.

"But make the most of it while it lasts. The public can be very fickle."

Last week: A big hug for DAVY JONES from Mrs. Sharples (VIOLET CARSON).

MONKEES ARCHIVES 1

DAVY JONES looks pleased with life during his interview with Keith Altham in London recently. The interview continues next week when Davy talks about the Beatles, religion and many other things. And more pics, too!!

In 1961; when DAVY JONES acted in "Coronation Street" with VIOLET CARSON, as Mrs. Sharples.

MONKEES ARCHIVES 1

"Where do you think you're going?" Mike's voice stopped me cold for all of about one third of a second.

"Out fastest!" I replied and proceeded to finish my eighty yard dash.

"I'm sorry you couldn't find the recipes this time," Davy called out to me.

"Thanks, but I have them with me, bye!" I panted while dashing through the front hall.

Davy yelped, "THE TEAPOT!" I flew out the front door leaving chaos behind me as all of them tore for said teapot.

"IT'S EMPTY!" wailed Peter, "All the recipes are gone."

"Hey, here's a note," said Mike.

"What does it say?" asked Davy.

"It says, 'Dear fellas and groovy hosts' now isn't that sweet, thank you multimillions of times for your flash recipes and all that delish food. Better hiding places to you all, sorry about the teapot not working. See you all next month and try again Davy. Actually teapot was a great idea. I'd never have found the recipes if the paper hadn't settled in my cup; love to you all...always your faithful tag along...recipe thief."

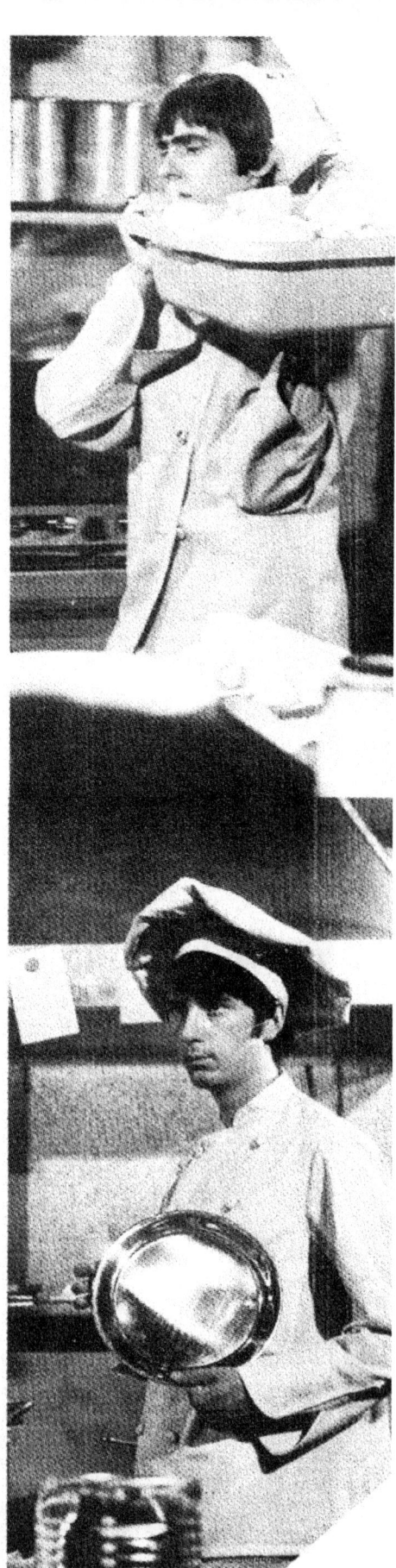

MICKY'S MARVELOUS MOCHA FROST

1 gallon mocha ice cream
1 gallon coffee ice cream
2 gallons whole milk
4 tablespoons coffee mix
2 eggs

Combine eggs and coffee mix together and whip until foamy. Combine the rest of the ingredients and mix everything together until thick. Pour into big glasses and sprinkle with nutmeg. Serves 10.

DAVY'S HEAVENLY DEVONSHIRE TARTLETTS

½ pound cream cheese
½ cup sugar
¼ cup butter
2 egg yolks
2 cups thick cream, sweet
½ teaspoon salt
¼ teaspoon nutmeg
1 tablespoon orange juice
1 box of pastry mix

Mix up the pastry and line muffin or tart pans with it. Mix the cheese with the sugar, butter, yolks, salt, nutmeg, and orange juice. Prick the pastry and fill it with the cheese mixture. Bake in a hot oven (450 degrees) for ten minutes and then reduce the heat to 325° F. and bake 15 minutes longer or until brown and firm. When done, turn upside down on a sheet of paper to cool. Spread each tartlett with your favorite jelly or jam and top with the heavy, thick cream. Serves 12.

MIKE'S TEA CAKES

1⅔ cups cups sifted cake flour
1½ teaspoons baking powder
¼ teaspoon salt
⅓ cup shortening
1 can of fudge frosting
1 cup sugar
2 eggs, well beaten
⅔ cups milk
1 teaspoon vanilla

Mix flour, baking powder and salt together. Combine shortening with sugar until fluffy and add eggs. Add flour mixture alternately with milk in small amounts to shortening and sugar. Add flavoring. Fill greased cup cake pan ⅔ full. Bake in a hot oven (350° F.) 15 to 18 minutes. Makes two dozen. When cooled spread frosting on top and decorate.

PETER'S PERFECT WATERCRESS TOASTIES

2 loaves of bread
1 cup milk
2 packages of cream cheese
3 bunches of watercress

Combine the milk and the cheese and blend until smooth and creamy. Cut the bread into slices and spread with cream cheese mix. Top each slice of bread with watercress and roll the bread from the top right corner to the bottom left and hold it together with a toothpick. Put in the oven and heat at 350° F. for five minutes.

MONKEES ARCHIVES 1

The Monkees clown for the photographer. They are (from left): Mickey Dolenz, Davy Jones, Mike Nesmith and Peter Tork.

Monkees' Antics Are A Screaming Success

By TOM STITES
Of the Post-Dispatch Staff

WHEN THE MUSIC ENDED at the Monkees show Saturday night and the squeals and screams died away, imaginary whistles sounded and bells rang in the ears of several thousand St. Louis teenagers.

Mike Nesmith, eldest of the four singers, knows the roar of delirious fans and is acquainted with the bells and whistles the roar causes.

"I wear earplugs," Nesmith said at a lunch the day before the concert. "You know what happens when a gun goes off right beside your ear? You can't hear for a little while.

"Well, my doctor says that every time we give a concert, it's the same as a gun going off, only it lasts for an hour. I've lost 12 per cent of my hearing."

The Monkees have four 200-watt amplifiers and 18 large speakers, but the fans at Kiel Auditorium Convention Hall outyell the amplifiers 50 to 1. It's not the sound system that does the damage, it's the screams.

"It's frightening," Nesmith said. "You step out there sometimes and wish you could go back. It's really enough to shake you. We can barely hear ourselves."

After the Monkees get accustomed to the noise, they have to contend with flashbulbs. Hundreds of bulbs went off almost continuously, creating an impromptu psychedelic light show. When Davy Jones, the handsomest Monkee, was singing a solo, he had to turn away and shut his eyes.

Then there's physical assault. Eighteen ushers deployed across the front of the stage were not enough to prevent a few girls from lunging onto part of the stage.

Someone is always bugging the Monkees. For example, some industrious fans penetrated the security that surrounded the group and learned

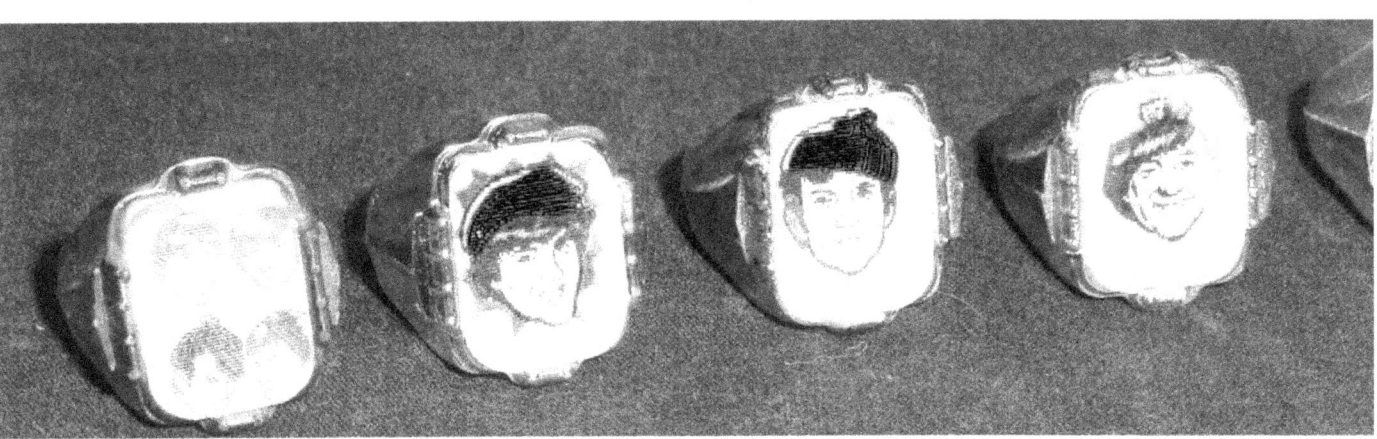

Monkees Find Success Can Be Frightening

FROM PAGE ONE

that they were staying at the Hilton Inn. Word spread, and soon there was a large crowd of teen-agers with cameras and autograph books.

Elaborate logistics are required to keep the fans away long enough for the Monkees to rest, and on the tour there are 32 persons and $500,000 worth of equipment to be moved efficiently in two planes.

"It's just like an Air Force operation," said Nesmith, who is an Air Force veteran. "We come in like a big black bird."

As Nesmith ate chili, hamburger steak and french fries in the hotel restaurant, teen-age noses pressed against the window. Hotel employees kept a large crowd of teen-agers well out of range.

Nesmith had been the last Monkee to leave his room, because he wanted to avoid the crush as long as possible. When he left for lunch at 2 p.m., Davy Jones was sunning himself by the pool, guarded by a policeman, and Mickey Dolenz and Peter Tork had eaten and left the hotel.

Because he is shy, Nesmith prefers seclusion to adulation. "Fame was groovy at first," he said, "but now it's kind of a drag. I just sit in my hotel room and wish I could go outside.

"At home (Los Angeles), it's not so bad. All my cars have black windows in them. I can see out but no one can see in. And my home is kind of a fortress. But I can't go anywhere without being recognized, and here they come. I've tried every disguise, even face putty."

A WOMAN who had finished lunch infiltrated the guards and asked Nesmith to autograph two napkins for her daughter, which have become his trademark.

He and the others were chosen and, despite musical inexperience on the part of one of them, were trained and molded into the Monkees.

When the show appeared on group will go back to making records and filming their television show, which sometimes takes up to 20 hours a day.

THE SHOW is zany. The Monkees do whatever they want sometimes, and at other times

MONKEES ARCHIVES 1

He complied. Another, a grandmother type, smiled as she walked by and said, "Hi Mike." He smiled back.

"Some girls would know me," he went on, "if all they could see was the corner of my eye."

They know your gait, the way you are disposed to hold your hands when you walk, the curvature of your back."

Nesmith has seven cars, a Pontiac GTO, a station wagon, a jeep, a truck, a Mercedes-Benz limousine, a Mini-Cooper racing car and a Buick Riviera. He also has two motorcycles.

His house, high on Mulholland drive, has a 20-mile view in every direction. He has another house in Tahiti, where he goes when he can get away from the crush. He says he can't go to Europe to relax any more than the Beatles can come to the United States.

"Remember how big the Beatles made it when they came to the states?" Nesmith asked. "Well, multiply by four. That's how we hit Europe.

"We've made more money in a year than the Beatles have made in their entire career. And how long has that been? Five years, I guess." From television, records, products and concerts, from all sources, we've grossed millions of dollars."

But the Beatles didn't have a television show. Nineteen months ago the Monkees, without even knowing one another, stumbled into independent wealth.

They were among 437 young men who answered an advertisement in Variety that sought, vaguely, "a quartet of hip, insane, folk-oriented rock 'n' rollers, 17 to 21, with the courage to work."

They were interviewed by two television producers who wanted to create a show featuring an American version of the Beatles.

Nesmith was a folk singer who had had some success on the West Coast and liked to write songs. He showed up for NBC last Sept. 10 the Monkees were so green that they had to sing silently along with a recording of their voices. For their first records, several "supplementary musicians" helped out.

But 99,000 teen-agers in the St. Louis area watched the first show, rating service figures indicate, and they didn't mind. Success came immediately, and grew as more and more teen-agers overpowered their parents' taste for programs and turned the dial to the Monkees every Monday night.

Their record, "Last Train to Clarksville," which had been released before the show went on the air, started selling so fast that it shot to No. 1 in the nation. It has sold 5,000,000 copies.

LUNCH PAILS, vacuum bottles and other objects bearing the Monkees' pictures and names became popular.

Their concerts almost always sell out. Their fans here had bought all 10,500 seats in the Convention Hall more than 30 hours before the show began, and the cheapest tickets cost $5. The last time the hall had sold out for such an event was for Elvis Presley, the first rock 'n' roll idol, more than 10 years ago.

The concert tour is covering 30 cities in the United States and Europe in 58 days. One of the European stops was London, where Nesmith stayed with John Lennon of the Beatles.

"John is always happy to see me," he said. "He says the Monkees have made it possible for him to do what I wish I could do. Now that we have come along, he can go most anywhere he pleases."

When the tour is over, the work from a suggestion. There are fast cuts, effects from hand-held cameras and a lot of kidding.

"Television is a vast wasteland," Nesmith said. "So we went in and said, let's waste it.

"Even so, I think what we do is pretty important for the kids because it takes a little edge off the pain of having to grow up. From the way they react to us, it's obvious that they have something to let out, and we're the outlet.

"The identity we have is the identity they have in their own minds. They're not screaming for me, they're screaming for what they think I am. They don't really know what I am. How could they? In a concert, we're just four little spots down there on the stage, a hundred feet away."

He acknowledged that the screaming could not last forever. If the television show ended now," he said, "it would take a year or two for the furor to die down. But the show will be on again this season, and with all that exposure, who knows? We might last five years, maybe longer, it's hard to say."

BUT WHILE the screaming lasts, Nesmith said, he and the other Monkees have a responsibility to their fans. "I have one of every product that has my name on it sent to me before it is put on the market," Nesmith said.

"When they start selling a little piece of plastic that says Pe-

Mike Nesmith, who began as a folk singer, says the Monkees made more money last year than the Beatles have made in their entire career.

ter, Mickey, Davy and Mike on it for $1, that's greed, not a service. And I made them use a better thermos bottle. If my name's on it, I'm going to see that they get their money's worth."

Nesmith said he thought that the group had absolutely no social significance.

"We just say we've got a date with the younger generation. We say we'll pick you up at 7:30, we don't know what we'll do, but we'll have fun.

"When a 13-year-old gets to be 20, all he'll remember was that he had a little fun. And he might remember seeing us walk up to get our Emmy (for best comedy show of 1967) and smirking at his parents and saying I told you so."

MONKEES ARCHIVES 1

MONKEES ARCHIVES 1

MONKEES: AFTER THE TOUR... WHAT NOW?

Davy sat alone in his English Cottage high up over the Sunset Strip. It was quiet because that was the way Davy wanted it to be. There would be no friends dropping in unexpectedly and no phone calls from various business associates. He had notified his answering service to take all incoming calls. Even Linda would not be there that afternoon because she had personal business of her own to take care of.

Davy felt tired and he also was down. That was the way he always felt after a tour had ended. The noise, the crowds, the pressure, and the fun were all behind him now. He thought back over the past few months almost as if it were some kind of a dream. Some parts of it were very exciting, but others seemed to have lost that special magic the previous Monkee tours held. Things had changed, but this is the way the Monkees wanted it. Now Davy wondered about what would happen from now on.

Over the past year Davy has been offered many, many special acting and performing jobs that he had to turn down because Micky, Mike and he had decided to stick together as a team and make the Monkees greater than ever. In some ways they succeeded. Their music, Davy believes, has improved, as have their performing skills. But it has been many long months since a Monkee recording has hit any of the charts. The Monkees want to do new things with their recordings but so far these sounds have not been accepted by their former fans.

Davy, basically, has never considered himself a singer. He's an actor who can sing and dance. Now the choice facing Davy is whether to continue as a part of the Monkees and try to put Micky, Mike and himself back on top, or to chuck the whole scene and strike out on his own as an actor.

Now that the tour is behind him, Davy may make this choice. Up to now he's refused all offers, preferring to stick with his friends. But with the results of the tour still fresh in his mind, Davy has some strong thinking to do. What do you think he should do?

> FaVE PREDICTION: DAVY TO STAR IN TWO BIG FILMS THAT WILL MAKE HIM MORE POPULAR. HIS ENERGIES WILL BE SPENT ON MOTION PICTURES AND TV.

Micky tossed Ami Bluebell into the air and gave Sam one of his long, wide smiles. He was glad to be home and glad to be with his wife and daughter once again. Micky, the most energetic of all the Monkees, wasn't even tired after the months of traveling. He was eager to get to work on various projects around the house that he hadn't had time to complete.

Sam told him how well the candles he makes were selling at her store and he was anxious to see the photos he'd taken on tour once they got developed. Micky had lost weight once again and Sam would have to fatten him up.

MONKEES ARCHIVES 1

Though he doesn't show it on the outside, Micky is perhaps the most serious of all the Monkees. He knew that things were changing for the group and that he'd better take on some additional projects of his own. Micky loves to act and he's tried on several occasions to get certain parts in films, but his time is so full that he's never been able to do this. Free time is very precious to Micky because he has so many interests that he wants to pursue.

He loves his giant white touring car that he now drives around town and his endless building projects could keep him busy for years to come even without any professional work.

But Micky is dependent upon people in many ways. He needs to have the excitement of a live audience. He needs to perform in front of people and to be well accepted. Before the Monkees hit, Micky sang with other groups and did live shows in front of small audiences whenever and wherever he could. Sam realizes this instinct in Micky is a great drive and she encourages him to continue his career no matter how hard he has to work.

Today Micky faces the biggest test in his career. If the Monkees keep on lessening their appearances and recordings, how will he function careerwise? Micky knows that Davy will act, but Davy's not a comic and Mick is. This makes it harder to get a strong role. For the time being Micky is happy to stay at home with his family and get it on with his hobbies. But how long will this last?

Mike and Phyllis Nesmith have been through a lot together. They worked hard sharing the lean years while Mike struggled to get to the top. Then, as suddenly as fame came, their happiness went out of the window. They've had to make a whole, new beginning, but today Mike and Phyllis seem contented. More than any of the other Monkees Mike knows where he's going.

The tour gave Mike more insight into what kinds of music he wants to produce in the future. He has a keen ear and eye for what is commercial and he plans to put this talent into effect on a more regular basis. As far as the Monkees go, Mike believes sincerely that they will capture a strong audience once again for their recordings. They have been passing through a transitory phase the past year, and the loss of Peter Tork was more of an adjustment than they had thought at first.

For Mike Nesmith the road is clear cut. He will continue to look for undiscovered talent, write music, and produce recordings that he feels will benefit himself and everyone concerned.

> FaVE PREDICTION: MICKY WILL SPEND MORE TIME AT HOME AND LESS TIME AS A MONKEE. HE WILL BEGIN DOING COMEDY ROLES IN VARIOUS TV SHOWS WITHIN A FEW SEASONS.

> FaVE PREDICTION: MIKE WILL PULL AWAY ENTIRELY FROM THE MONKEES AND CONCENTRATE ON HIS OWN RECORD PRODUCTION BUSINESS.

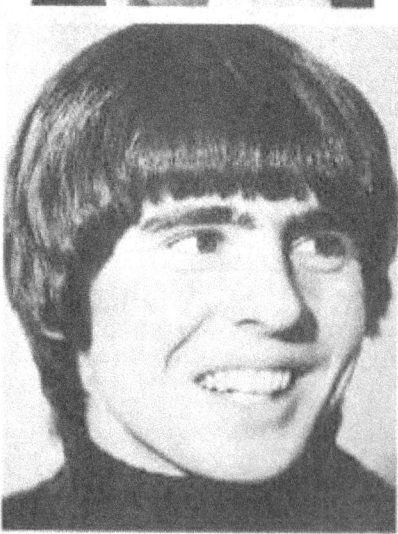

MONKEES ARCHIVES 1

MONKEES ARCHIVES 1

STOP PRESS...STOP PRESS...STOP

New Album a Smash!

The boys' second album, "More of the Monkees", is already in fantastic demand and could well turn out to be the biggest selling L.P. of '67, provided, of course, that the Monkees next L.P. doesn't beat it.

Titles of the songs on "More of the Monkees" are:— "She", "When Love Comes Knockin' (At Your Door)", "Mary, Mary", "Hold On Girl", "Your Auntie Grizelda", "(I'm Not Your) Steppin' Stone", "Look Out (Here Comes Tomorrow)", "I Love You Darling", "The Kind of Girl I Could Love", "Sometimes in the Morning", "Laugh", "The Day We Fall in Love", and "I'm a Believer".

TOP ALL OVER

The Monkees records are topping charts all over the world and at our last check they were still at number one in Australia, Eire and Finland, number two in Mexico and number six in the Philippines, number nine in Singapore and number ten in the U.S.A.

MIKE WRITES 'B' SIDE

Well-known songwriter and American folk singer, Neil Diamond, is the composer of the boys' new single release, "A Little Bit Me, A Little Bit You". B-side "The Girl I Knew Somewhere" was penned by none other than Mike Nesmith himself. As you know, he has been writing songs for a long time and, as he told us when he visited this country, several of his compositions would be appearing on future releases.

He also told us that the first song he ever wrote was called "Sleep". When asked if it had ever been released as a record, he replied, "No, for several reasons, the main one being it was no darn good!"

SOLO CONCERTS

On the first of this month—April Fools Day—the boys started a short Canadian tour. First stop was the prairie city of Winnipeg, and on the second they moved on to the Maple Leaf Gardens, Toronto, where they appeared before 17,000 fans. All the tickets for this show were sold out within four hours of going on sale on February 18th. The Boys have really made April Fools of all their critics with these performances, because there are no supporting acts and they alone performed from one end of the show to the other.

Recording

Davy, Mike, Micky and Pete are all back in Los Angeles and are busy recording numbers for their next album (as yet untitled) which will also be used in the next 26 weeks' series which they should start filming at the beginning of April.

FIRST FILM

The Monkees are due to start work on their first major feature film for Columbia Pictures this coming summer, but so far no definite plans have been finalised, and the script hasn't even been selected yet.

SAMMY DAVIS IN MONKEES SHOW

There is something rather exciting about one of the forthcoming Monkees Shows, Davy told me when he was in England. "One day when we were on the film set Sammy Davis Jnr. (who was in the studio above us filming 'I Dream of Jeannie') came into our studio to apologise for all the noise they were making and while he was with us stayed to do a skit for The Monkees Show." Normally Sammy Davis would have charged a fortune to appear but because of his good relations with the boys he did the skit for nothing!

MONKEES ARCHIVES 1

During their New York City press conference, when a reporter asked Micky Dolenz what he wanted to do if and when The Monkees decided to stop being The Monkees, he didn't even have to think about his answer!

"A disc jockey," he said, kind of cheerfully, looking kind of happy when he pictured himself in the role of a raving DJ!

What kind of a DJ would Micky or any of the other Monkees make? Porbably the greatest!

So, it wasn't surprising that when The Monkees visited radio station KRUX when they appeared in Phoenix, Arizona, they took over the studios!

FLIP was there the day The Monkees turned the turntables!

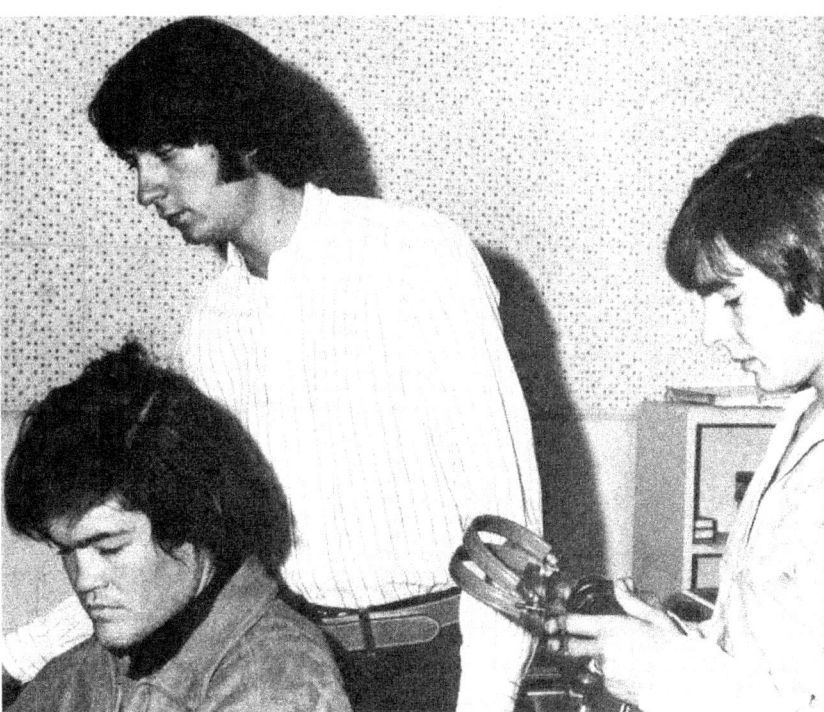

Here, Micky, Davy and Mike check over the equipment. All the guys dig electronic equipment.

Micky, as a matter of fact, has just bought a machine to help him work out electronic music at home.

the monkees turn the {turn} tables!

MICKY, DAVY, MIKE & PETER FIND OUT WHAT IT'S LIKE TO BE ON THE FLIP SIDE!

As Micky checks out the engineer's panel, Mike tries to help him discover what each of the switches can do. Somehow, Micky always managed to pull the right switch and press the right button!

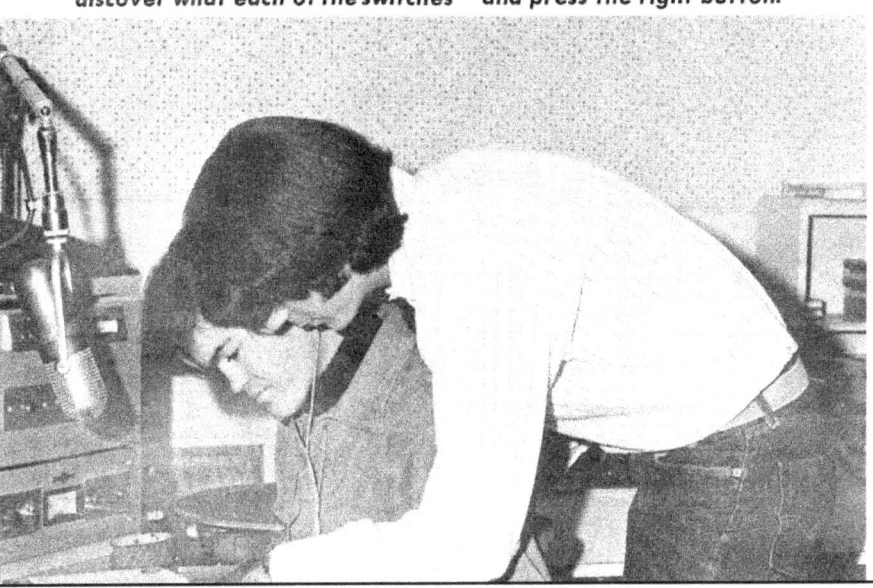

Now, Micky's on his own! Headset snapped on, one of their superhit albums ready to play, microphone in place, Micky is ready to go on the air!

MONKEES ARCHIVES 1

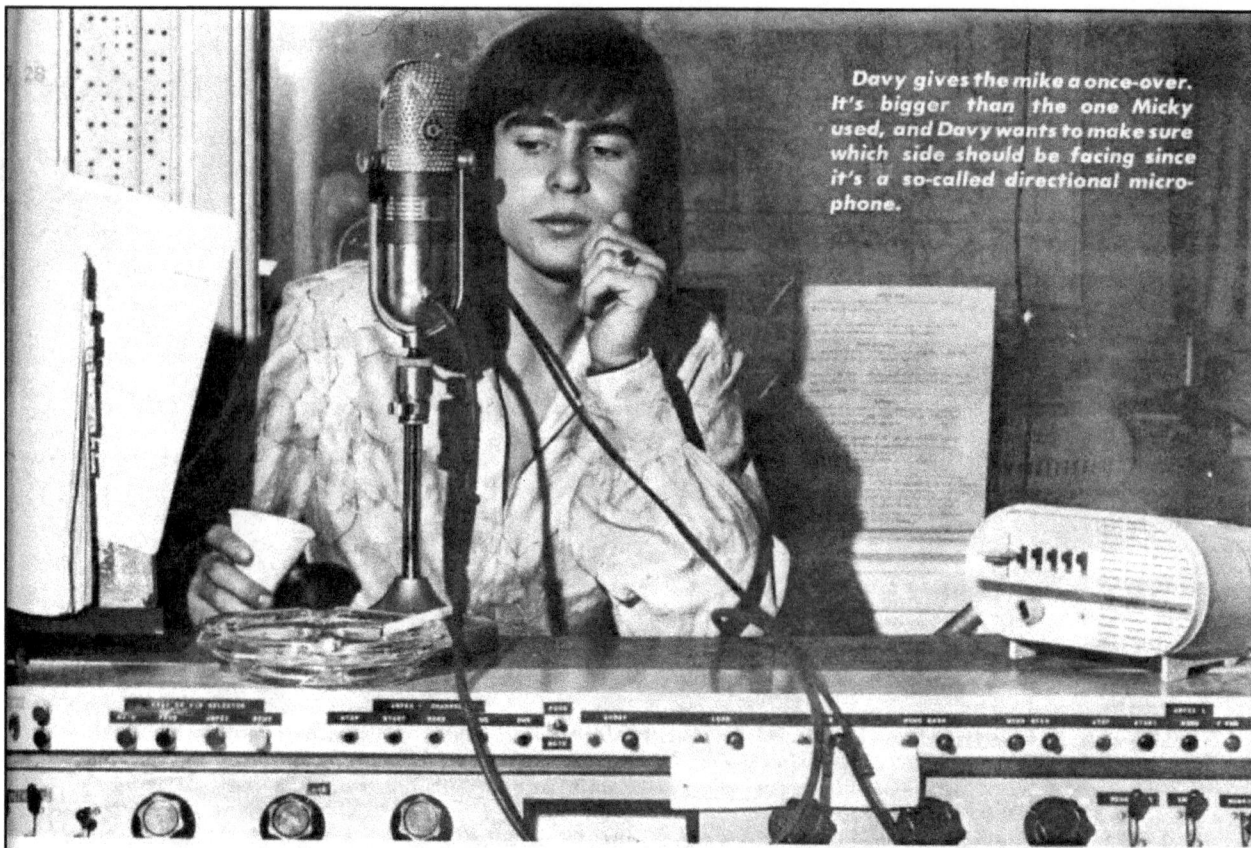

Davy gives the mike a once-over. It's bigger than the one Micky used, and Davy wants to make sure which side should be facing since it's a so-called directional microphone.

Quickly, Davy sizes it up and, cup of water in hand, is ready to rave on over KRUX. Davy makes a perfect DJ although, unlike Micky, he's never really thought of becoming a disc jockey. (At one press conference this summer a reporter asked Davy, "I understand that you were a disc jockey before you became a Monkee. Are you ever thinking of going back to it?" As everyone laughed, Davy gently answered, "No . . . I was a horse jockey!")

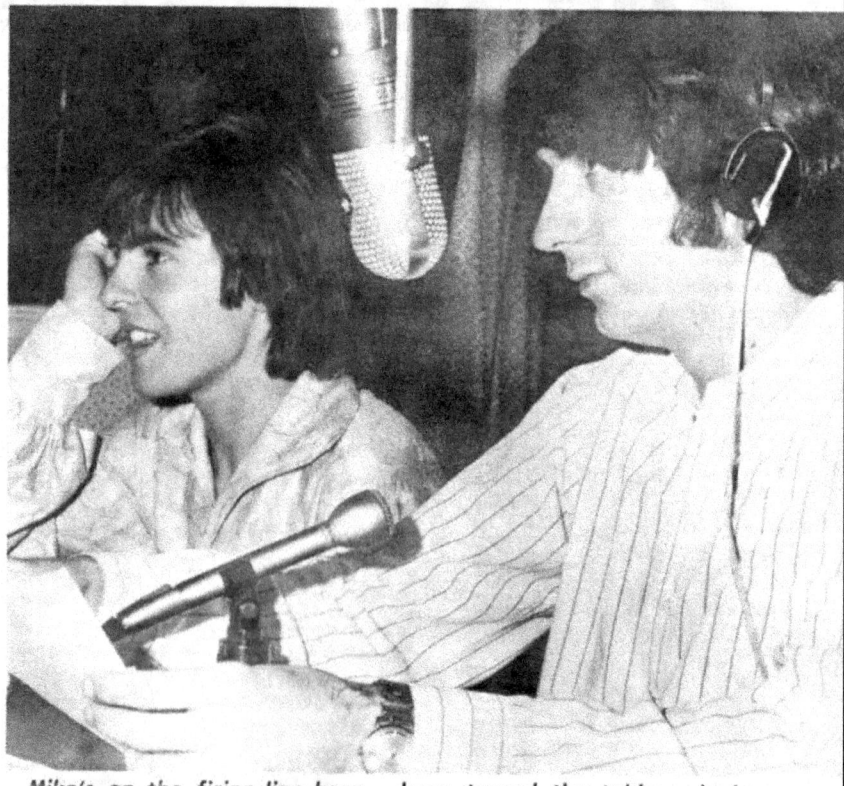

Mike's on the firing line here, and like the others, he enjoyed his day as a DJ—the day The Monkees turned the tables, playing their records instead of recording them!

The Monkees Tour Europe

BY DAVID PRICE

David Price was Davy Jones' stand-in during filming of the Monkees TV show and also cared for their equipment during the tour.

Everybody keeps asking me, "what's it like to really live with the Monkees?" Well, it's quite an experience in more ways than one. So, in this article I'm going to tell you some things that happened on the tour and then you can judge for yourselves!

PARIS

When we did the shooting of the Monkee show in Paris last July, I had a chance to get to know the boys better than ever. You see, in France, they're unknown and this made it easy for them to walk around the streets without any fans bothering them.

Mike was more cool than ever and got a great charge out of just roaming the streets and not signing any autographs. Mike's really interested in a lot of things and this three day spree gave him a chance to stroll around, look at different art objects, and study people. I remember he said how good it was to be able to look at everyone else for a change instead of having everyone staring at him.

PETER THE FRENCHMAN

Peter's the only Monkee who can speak French so he probably had a better time than the other three. He talked to everyone, and he got around a lot better because he could ask for directions

in the right language. Peter makes friends very easily. Some people have told me that they think Peter is very hard to get to know. This is only true if Peter doesn't dig the person. Actually, Peter is very friendly and open to people he likes being with.

Anyway, one day in Paris, Micky showed up for the day's shooting wearing a French policeman's hat. Nobody knew where he got it and Micky wouldn't tell. We knew he didn't buy it, though. To this day, it's still a secret, but it is one of his favorite hats.

DAVY AND CLOTHES

We filmed a whole day in the Flea Market in Paris. This is sort of an open place where they sell almost everything you can think of. Davy bought a fabulous black stovepipe hat for himself. When the director saw him in it, he asked Davy to wear it in the show. So when you see this segment next season on TV, you'll know that Davy's wearing his own hat.

He also bought a blue military jacket and he wore this in the show, too. Davy can't resist buying clothes ... for himself and any of his friends who might be along.

GIRLS IN PARIS

There were no actual dates for the Monkees in Paris. The boys did hang around with some of the French girls who worked on the TV segment we were filming. They tried to teach Micky, Davy and Mike French, but there just wasn't enough time to learn anything.

OPINIONS OF FRANCE

The Monkees really flipped over the beauty of Paris. But none of them really dug the French food. Everyone kept wanting a good, old fashioned steak dinner and in Paris the French put sauce on everything. One night Mike found a really groovy Hungarian restaurant and he thought the goulash was outasite.

The big news about England was the fact that there were more

people at the Monkees' press conference than had attended Winston Churchill's conference in World War II. Most of us don't remember back that far, but it really had been the most important press conference in the history of England and now the Monkees' had topped it.

It was really a groove being backstage with the Monkees before they went out before the 400 English newspapermen who were there to question them. In case you don't know, the English newsmen aren't known to be the world's friendliest. In fact, they love knocking American performers and it would have pleased them if the Monkees had been really stupid in their answers. Fortunately, I can tell you that all four Monkees responded well to the questions and were quite witty in their replies.

I won't bother repeating the questions they asked because you probably know all the right answers already. But I will tell you that the reporters tried to get the Monkees to say something controversial like John Lennon's statement about Christ or Paul McCartney's statement about drugs. The Monkees were all too smart for them. They just joked back at the questions and the reporters loved it.

Mike was asked more questions than any of the other Monkees because he seems to be the quietest and they were trying to get him to talk. Davy wound up doing most of the talking and you know Davy, he's a very groovy conversationalist. I think Davy was more at ease than the others because England is his home.

CONCERT GETAWAYS

The concerts were all groovy in England. They gave five and almost all of them were sell-outs. A funny thing happened at the Friday concert. One of our security men spotted a boy in the audience who resembled Davy. He had long hair and everything so the officer asked him to come back stage.

After the concert our security guards used this boy as a decoy. All the fans thought he was Davy so they mobbed him and let the other Monkees get away. This trick worked so well, we may use it at other concerts.

SHOPPING IN LONDON

East Indian clothes are very big in London right now. You know, the long Mandarin coats and things like that. Davy flipped over these and bought quite a few. Carnaby Street is really out now in England so Davy shopped at Dandy's Fashions and places like this.

Phyllis flew in to see Mike in London and the two of them ran off to Biba's to buy some new clothes for Phyllis. Mike also bought a new Mini (auto, this is) in London. Mike and Phyllis really dig buying things, but then, I guess we all do.

Speaking of buying things, Micky did the most outasite thing you've ever heard of in London. He arranged to buy one of these big two decker London buses. You know the ones I mean ... those where the people can sit on the top floor outside and then there's an enclosed bottom side. Well, his plan is this. He's going to have the bus shipped over to New York and then drive it from New York to California after the inside is decorated in a real groovy style. Who knows, Micky may be driving through your own town soon.

DATES IN LONDON

Micky didn't date anyone but Samantha in London. But Davy dated several different girls for various parties. Peter had little time for girls because Brian Jones of the Stones, who Peter met in Monterey, was busy showing Peter all the spots of interest around the city.

Davy did get a chance to have a quiet two day reunion with his father. Mr. Jones was feeling well when Davy visited him and this made Davy very happy because Davy has been worried about his father the past few months. When Davy got back from the visit, he was all smiles. The relationship between Davy and Mr. Jones is one of the finest I've ever seen between a father and son. ♥

MONKEES ARCHIVES 1

MONKEES ARCHIVES 1

MONKEES ARCHIVES 1

MONKEES ON TOUR

UNLIKE so many of our present day star groups, the Monkees are firm believers in personal contact with their fans. And that means appearing on stage as often as they can.

As every Monkee fan knows, the boys were faced with an awkward problem when Peter departed last year. But Davy, Micky and Mike were absolutely determined that all future shows would be even more impressive.

This is the main reason that they departed from the scene for several months. As Jackie Richmond has told you in recent issues, they have been working out a whole new and very exciting stage show.

They have concentrated on building up a top line group to provide the main musical backing for their act so that the boys are free to make as close a contact with the audience as possible and therefore entertain properly.

So the Goodtimers was formed. They had previously played together as Ike and Tina Turner's backing group so, as you can imagine, supporting two top line names like that, they are among the best instrumentalists on the scene. The Goodtimers consists of Sam Rhodes who handles a lot of the support vocals; Mac Johnson on trumpet; Willie on guitar; Thomas Norwood, drums; Lane on keyboard; Clifford Solomon on sax and Tony Burrell on bass.

But, as the old saying goes, the proof of the pudding is in the eating. No matter how good the Monkees have proved themselves on record, or were reported to be in rehearsals with the Goodtimers, they had to go on the stage and prove to an audience that the new Monkees trio plus the Goodtimers was much better than the old four Monkees.

One-nighters

At the end of March, Davy, Micky and Mike, plus the Goodtimers set out on a series of one-nighters—Vancouver on March 28th, Seattle on the 29th, through Birmingham, Augusta, Hawaii, Chicago, Alberta, with still more to come.

Okay, how did they do?

There is only one answer and that is—they knocked 'em cold! All the magic that British fans remember from the Monkees' appearances at the Empire Pool in the middle of 1967 has been retained and, incredibly, improved on!

Let's look at one of the very first concerts when they appeared in the Pacific Colisseum in Vancouver before 5,200 cheering fans. Right from the moment they stepped on stage they had the audience eating out of the palms of their hands.

Before the show, the Monkees said that "For quite a while we have been doing our own thing on their terms. Now it's our turn, our thing, our terms."

The first half was taken up by the 1910 Fruit Gum Co. who, you will remember, hit the charts in a big way with "Yummy, Yummy, Yummy" a few months back, and the Goodtimers with Sam Rhodes handling most of the vocal work in a soulful style.

When Davy and Micky stepped on stage they roared straight into one of their biggest hits, "Last Train to Clarksville", but the audience soon realised that the boys were taking them by the hand and introducing them to the new Monkees!

The truth is that the Monkees now have three stage acts — one called Davy Jones, one Micky Dolenz and the other Mike Nesmith.

Micky concentrates on rhythm and blues. We all know his tremendous ability with a rock number. Nobody can put them over with more power and drive

Davy on stage at the Pacific Coliseum in Vancouver during their current tour.

than our very own Dolenz. And on this tour he has proved his abilities over and over again.

Davy has a completely different approach, tending to concentrate on ballads and simple love songs, and no-one can be more appealing on stage with this type of music.

Mike sticks to his big love — country music. He plays the guitar beautifully and almost every critic has singled out his solo on acoustic guitar as one of the most moving parts of the show. To quote Brian McLeod of "The Province" . . . "Every note could be heard as Nesmith proved conclusively that he can write music and has a feel for meaningful words." This journalist also sums up the whole temper of the show when he quotes: "The Monkees first quieted, then entertained, and then seemed to educate their fans. This they were able to do by virtue of their diverging musical paths. Since the TV days the group seems to have expanded on its essential talents." The result is that Davy Jones now sings songs like "I Want To Be Free" in a way that would put many Las Vegas stylists to shame.

The Monkees have always been complete entertainers on stage. They would never stroll on stage in dirty outfits and fiddle around with their amplifiers and guitars for five minutes like some groups do before they start on their first number. Their sole aim is to entertain every individual person in the audience.

Part of this, of course, is their clothes. They never have just one suit for a show—they have dozens. And they switch clothes at a fantastic rate. Davy still favours velvet suits with elaborately frilled shirts. In fact, all the boys do.

When they are on stage together as a trio, they tend to dress alike, but when they are in the spotlight alone, then they quickly switch to more casual gear and so create a change of mood. In other words, they always try and fit the clothes to the song they are going to sing.

They have always been stylish dressers and spend thousands of pounds on getting clothes specially made for every new tour, and this one has been no exception. The boys spent a lot of time with designers in Hollywood working on new stage suits, shirts, trousers and shoes that they would wear.

All their usual back-room experts have been with them helping to create the same dynamic effects which have excited audiences right around the world.

Anyone who was in the Wembley audiences will remember the large screen which was erected behind the boys and on which their technicians threw a sort of light show. The scenes began with still shots of the boys interdispersed with amusing shots, photos of all sorts of events and people, and ended up with a dynamic and vibrating pattern of lights tuned exactly to what the boys were playing on stage.

Let's end with another report from a local critic who has also seen their show. This time it's Janine Gressel of the *Seattle Times* and, like all the other people that I have quoted, it's all word for word, exactly as she wrote it.

"The change in format has allowed each of the members to develop himself in his own direction. Since these aren't the restrictions of conforming to a group image, each is given the room to explore his own capabilities, interests and abilities in music. This has been a challenge to the trio. There is no chance to mask a lack of creativity by hiding behind the group facade. There is no one to blame but himself if his act fails; it is also far more rewarding if it succeeds. The Monkees are in the process of succeeding. But on the whole, their show is immensely interesting. It is exciting to see three performers who could have rested on their laurels have the nerve and artistic integrity to change a successful style. The new Monkees have risen to the challenge and are succeeding beautifully."

So now every one knows what a great show the boys are building up for their forthcoming Autumn tour.

It certainly is worth waiting for!

MONKEES ARCHIVES 1

MONKEES ARCHIVES 1

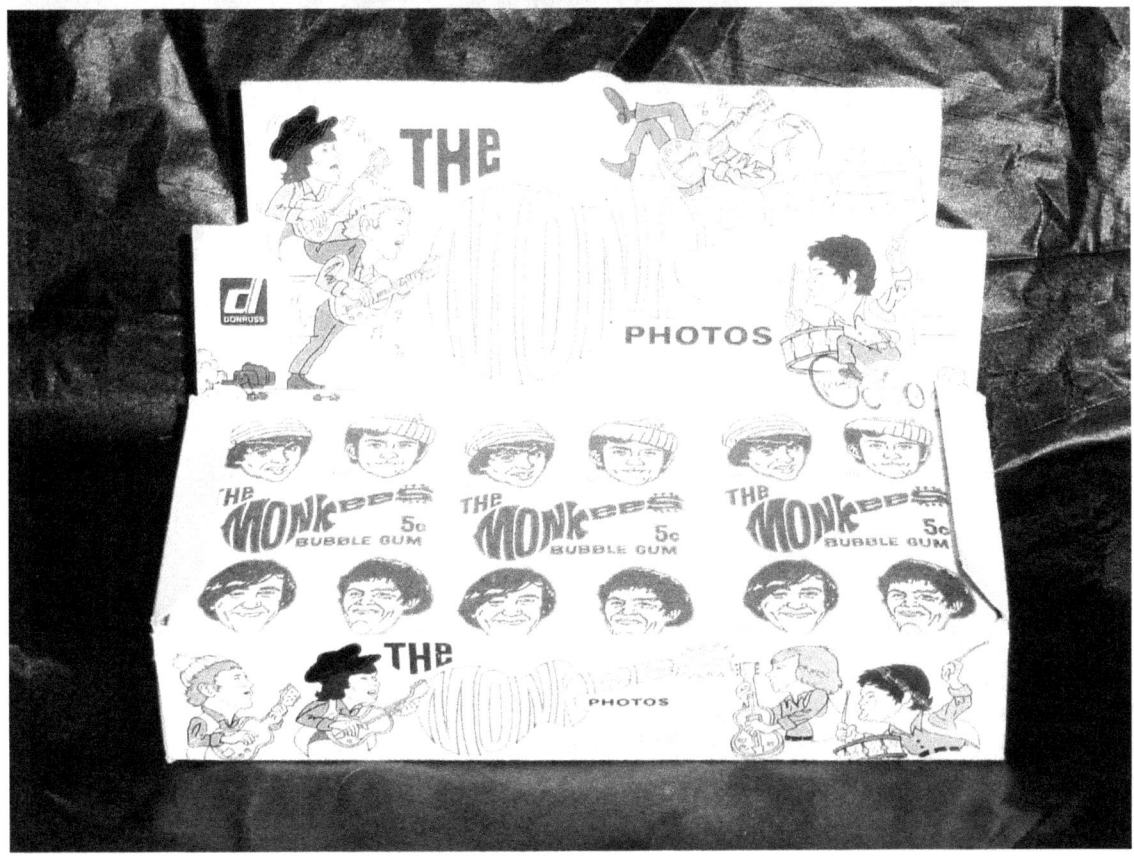

MONKEES ARCHIVES 1

DEC. 67   Monkees   No. 11

Monkees

2/-

MONKEES ARCHIVES 1

By Lee Sellers

I was one of the lucky girls chosen to answer fan mail for the Monkees at Screen Gems Studios, Hollywood, California; during Christmas vacation last year.

Before getting into the studio, on my first day the guard had to check with Frew Smallwood, who is head of Monkee Fan Mail. Each day afterwards I would write my name down on a chart and the guard would check my name and give me a studio pass.

The first day was a Monday morning, which meant that things were going to be pretty hectic. Marilyn Schlossberg, who is head of Monkee publicity, showed me what I was to do. Three rooms were being used for Fan Mail, one of the rooms was Frew's office, the other two were used for answering letters.

When the chairs became scarce the girls would sit on top of the mailbags. Around 10.30 a.m. we were introduced to our supervisor, Charlene "Charlie" Novak. The atmosphere was really groovy, kids were working hard, there were three or four transistor radios playing "mood" music and then one girl said "I just saw Peter walk in!" We asked Charlie if she could possibly get him to come in, so away she went.

We didn't think Peter would come in so we continued working. Then, all of a sudden, the door burst open and a voice said "Hi group!" Peter's unexpected entrance startled one girl so much she tossed a bundle of mail she had been sorting into the air! Peter exclaimed "You shouldn't be so nervous!" He asked the girl if she would forgive him for startling her, the girl gave a meek smile and nodded "Yes". Peter beamed a smile and before leaving he said jokingly "Work hard, slaves." I must admit it was a pleasant surprise to have a Monkee barge in on us while we were working.

After lunch, we came back onto the lot just as someone was going into Stage 7, where the Monkees film their show, all of us had the same idea. We didn't have any trouble getting in and as my eyes started roaming around they settled on a tall, slim, goodlooking young man who had just jumped down some stairs; as he came toward our group I said "Hi Micky!" he smiled brightly and said "Hi!" shaking my hand with a warm, friendly grip. Just then we heard Marilyn's voice, "O.K. you kids, back to work." Honestly I never ran so fast in all my life!!!

We got out of the studio just in time to catch up with Charlie, she said "I called to you girls not to go in there." We said we were sorry but we didn't hear her. As we approached the office we saw two men with cameras and tape recorders interviewing Mike Nesmith, who was lying in the back seat of his black, convertible, GTO Pontiac. Mike stopped talking

'For the last time Peter, there's NO SUCH PERSON AS.....!!'

MONKEES ARCHIVES 1

half feet high, Peter exclaimed "Tremendous, keep up the good work!"

Wednesday I will NEVER forget. On that day they were filming in Stage 10 which is OUTSIDE the gates. I waited with a couple of other girls for them to come into work; since they parked their cars INSIDE the lot they would have to walk right by us to get to Stage 10. Peter was the first to come along, he was dressed in a polka-dotted shirt, beige cord jeans, sheepskin jacket, moccasins and NO SOCKS! We said "Hi" and asked him how he was, he replied "Fine, and you?" "Pretty good, but how come Davy isn't here?" He told us that Davy had left early Monday morning to attend his sister's wedding in Manchester, England. Two other girls had heard this and they both started to cry, they had been waiting faithfully outside the gates for almost six hours to catch a glimpse of the delightful Davy Jones.

BLEW A KISS

Peter understood how the girls must have felt, but he turned to us and said "I'd better go now" he then blew us all a kiss and we waved good-bye. Micky came walking slowly along and we struck up a small conversation with him: "How are you, Micky?" "Just freezing, that's all" he told us between chattering teeth. No wonder he was cold, he was dressed in choc. brown bellbottoms, paisley shirt, suede boots and NO COAT. He said as he was leaving "I'll be up later, O.K.?" "Groovy!" we replied. And then, last but certainly not least, Mike passed us looking very pensive, so we just waved to each other. He was dressed very comfortably in faded blue jeans, checked shirt and his favourite old boots.

Micky kept his promise and came up to the office at about 3.00, he had come to pick up some mail and receive some presents. I caught Micky just as he was going out of the door, I presented him with "Spaniard in the Works" which I had wrapped in gold and green felt and paisley designed paper. He was so overwhelmed with all the gifts that the kids had given him that he began to get very sentimental and he gave me a big hug and a kiss. Since there was mistletoe above the door I kissed him back and said "Merry Christmas, Micky." He then addressed everyone in the room "Thank you all for the great presents and cards." He left everyone in an atmosphere of peace and serenity.

Thursday came rolling along and I became
Continued on page 10

and took time out to sign autographs and talk to us. We thanked him and told him we had to get back to work, so we all waved good-bye to Mike and he waved back and then continued his interview.

Back in the mail room there was a lot of excitement going on. Micky had just received a Christmas present from one of the girls, it was a turquoise blue and green paisley "Hamlet" shirt, Micky was raving about it! As the girl was taking the pins out of the shirt, Micky bent down and gave her a kiss. He said "I'll do that later and who knows, I might even wear it on the show! I think it is outasite!!"

The next afternoon Peter barged in again. I said, kiddingly, "Peter Halsten Thorkelson, don't ever do that again!" Peter's bottom lip started to tremble as if he were going to cry. We all started laughing because Peter looked so forlorn, he joined in on the laughter too, glad to know he had brought a little bit of happiness with him. He asked us how things were and we showed him all the cards we had addressed, five stacks of autographed pictures one and a

---

Micky sure chooses some odd places to take a rest. This pic was taken outside the film studios in Hollywood. That's a sun dial he's parked between his feet.

MONKEES ARCHIVES 1

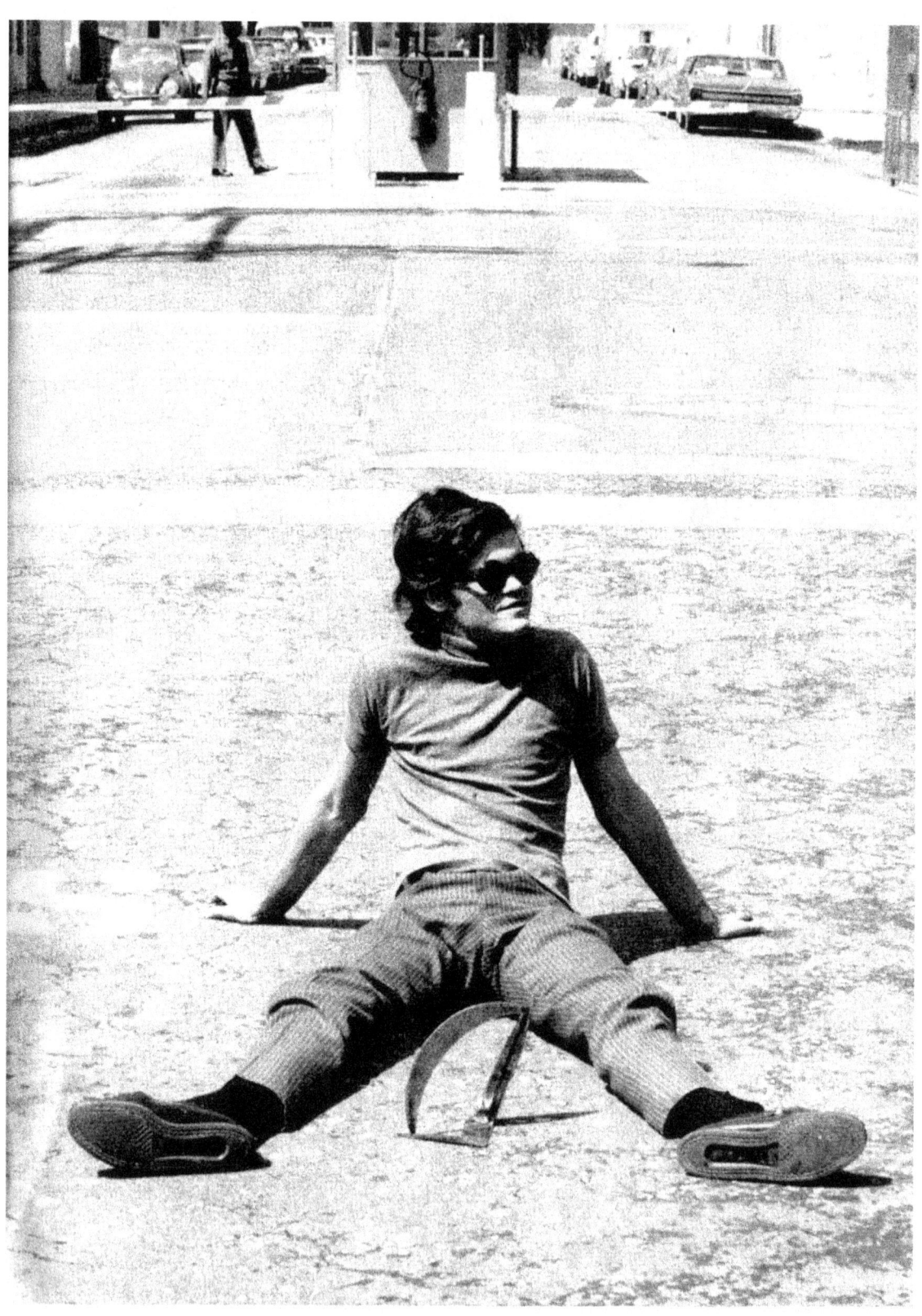

MONKEES ARCHIVES 1

Continued from page 6

acquainted with Randy Creadick, Micky's former girlfriend, she was very nice and not at all big-headed about having a Monkee as a boyfriend. Randy had waist-length, platinum-blonde hair, big blue eyes, a nice figure and stood at 5' 9". Since Friday would be half day Frew asked for volunteers to work until 9 p.m. I'm glad I volunteered because at 7.30 p.m., Micky drove to a screeching halt down in the parking lot. He came bounding up the stairs to pick up MORE mail and presents, one present in particular; two girls presented Micky with a scale model castle, three feet long and one and a half feet high. Micky asked the girls how long it had taken them to make it and what it was made out of; it had taken the girls three weeks to make it and they said "We made it out of anything and everything, plaster of Paris, plastic, cardboard, plywood, marbles, a compass, we put a picture of each of the Monkees in the four windows and put an American flag on one turret and an English flag on the other." The castle was a "beautiful piece of work" as Micky put it; it was painted authentically and had in gold glitter the name "MONKEE MANOR". Micky rushed into the next room to get Bert Schneider and asked him if it would be at all possible to use the castle as a prop in the show, Mr. Schneider replied "I don't see why not!!!"

MICKY FIGHTS

Micky stayed around for a little while longer, signing autographs and pictures, telling jokes, making everybody happy. He showed us how to "stage fight", he picked a girl as his guinea pig and told her to stand very still. He hauled back to punch her and then followed through with a loud "SMACK", Micky had made the sound by hitting the palm of his left hand with his right fist. "A fake right cross" Micky called it; someone asked him to do his impersonation of James Cagney, which he did splendidly and with pleasure. He glanced at his watch and said "Oh, oh, gotta run, Merry Christmas, everybody!!" He bounced down the stairs singing "Jingle Bells" at the top of his lungs.

MONKEE CHRISTMAS

Friday, and hardly any work had to be done, but I managed to find out where each of the Monkees were going for Christmas. Davy was in England, Mike and his lovely family had left on Wednesday for Texas, Peter left on Thursday to join his family in Canada for the holidays. Micky was the only Monkee left, and he was full of Christmas cheer and joy.

Micky had bought a 1967 Lemans Pontiac for his sister, Coco, and an RCA Victor Colour TV set for his Grandmother. Micky, Ric Klein, and David Price (Peter's stand in) tried every possible way to get the television into the back seat of the new car.

Although it was a pretty tricky job, Micky, Ric and David managed to wriggle the set into the car. We were watching them from the office balcony and when they had finished we all yelled "HURRAY FOR MICKY, RIC AND DAVID!!!" They said, very modestly, "It was nothin' ". Micky was running around pounding his chest and making noises like Tarzan, then he went into a fake coughing spasm. Ward Sylvester, the show's assistant producer, gave Micky a crate of wine as a Christmas present, Micky thanked him very much and then blew kisses to everyone; as he climbed into the new car and drove off he waved to every single person in sight.

During the second week things weren't as hectic, because the Monkees were on tour. There were a lot of odds and ends to clean up and when that was finished the volunteers remaining to help had a chance to meet such people as: Bert Schneider and Bob Rafelson—Producers, Jim Frawley—Director, Coco Dolenz, Micky's sister who had dropped by on business; and Tommy Boyce and Bobby Hart—Composers.

I am now six thousand miles away from Screen Gems and the Monkees, but I wish I could go back this Christmas and once again be a part of the happy pandemonium.

NEXT MONTH: Micky talks about his life now! Another great Monkees Monthly Competition

MONKEES ARCHIVES 1

★ SEVENTY MINUTES ★
★ OF SUPER-SPECIAL ★
★★ SHOWMANSHIP ★★

You know what the knockers are saying: "The Monkees can't play and sing well on stage. Just wait until you see 'em—you'll realise they are frauds!" Oh yeah? Well, so happens they won't have long to wait before the Monkees DO all come to Britain and put on one of their super-special stage shows... that's if all the current plans come off. And they'll make those crabby old critics eat their words, one by one —and I hope it gives them indigestion.

UNFAIR

For a start, it's darned unfair to criticise a stage act before you've even been along to see it. And the Monkees are all hopping mad about this because they KNOW, from experience in America, that they've produced a stage act which is really out-of-sight and fantastic. It's taken time, a lot of money, and a lot of courage. And it's great. What's more it runs for SEVENTY minutes, which is about twice as long as you'd get from some of those you-know-who groups who've been hugging the headlines for a long, long time.

PREVIEW

So let's picture the scene at a Monkee concert—kinda give you a preview of what will surely be tearing up the British Isles before the year is out. Imagine a packed auditorium, audience seething with excitement, buzzing audibly as it gets near the boys' stage routine. There are other artistes, good ones, but the stars are the Monkees. You can actually feel, hear, experience the excitement mounting. There's a fifteen-minute interval. Next on . . . THE MONKEES! The announcer's voice rasps through the public address system. "The great stars of television, of records, of everything!—the one and only, the fabulous, the great MONKEES"—and a solid sound wall of screams and roars as the boys come on, single-file, and move to their instruments.

BEST EQUIPMENT

Amplifiers are there in abundance. Not any old amplifiers. For this is the very best equipment produced. Hear Mike Nesmith explain: "What we do on television—that's us. That's our talent, What we do on stage is purely us as well ... but it's another side of us. The two sides don't have to be related. It's a complex show, a complicated bit of stage work. It takes a lot of effort out of us and those responsible back-stage.

"No, we don't want to play out-of-doors. These massive stadiums in the States... you just take the people's money and you run. Most of them can't see you. It just isn't fair. If you're gonna charge people quite a lot of money they're entitled to see all of you, all the time, and you have got to entertain them.

"So it's indoors for us. We

☞ This special piece of Monkee equipment was designed to tell if people have big heads.

use the best equipment we can—and we paid for it. Out of our own pocket. We wanted to make sure it was the best. We carry a screen projection unit so we can show clips from the television series during some of the numbers— you know, comedy bits to tie in with the songs. We have magnificent sound equipment, costing between ten and thirteen thousand dollars, all specially created for us by Vox. We have special guitars . . . the best to suit my style and Pete's style. Micky plays the best drums. And we run through several changes of costume, because we believe that people pay to SEE something different as well as hear something and we keep running on and off changing into different clothes."

An expensive act, then. But worthwhile, seeing as how the boys have always played to packed audiences, some of whom have paid nearly a hundred thousand dollars to see the fantastic foursome. So on stage they come, ready to go, knowing that a long act is ahead of them. Mike says the first twenty minutes are spent putting down rumours that they can't play.

In Trouble

At one concert, as he waited to go on stage, a backroom bloke said to him: "Tell me, is it TRUE you don't play on stage." Said Mike, smiling wryly: "If it IS, I'm gonna be in a heck of a lot of trouble in about ten seconds' time."

The general pattern of the stage act doesn't change— only the audience reaction varies . . . from "stupendous" to "incredible". They do nine songs as a group. They open with "Last Train To Clarksville", which is a guaranteed riot-raiser, even if it didn't get to number one in Britain! Then comes "She's So Far Out She's In", and "You Just May Be The One", and "I Want To Be Free", and "Giant Step", and "Papa Gene's Blues", and "Sweet Young Thing", and "Standing On The Corner" and then "Mary, Mary". Already, you'll note, they've done what would normally add up to a complete act.

Pete's got his own method of taking the creases out of a lawn

Take Turns

They take turns on the lead singing. Micky sticks on drums even when he takes lead. Mike sings HIS solo stuff, standing slightly awkwardly, hand often cupping the microphone. Peter bounces, but mixes his facial expressions in a constant change from momentarily serious to ear-to-ear grin. And Davy, constantly shaking maraccas or a tambourine, is more mobile than the others simply because he isn't burdened with a guitar. Davy reacts beautifully to any fresh sound-barrier breakthrough by the audience. He's a showman; and he loves every single second of being up there in the spotlight.

Then, the nine numbers they bring on a separate over, the boys split up. Usually backing group, to keep the continuity going. Davy may nip back and take over drums, just for a few moments. Micky reaches for the hand-mike and introduces Peter's banjo solo. Pete plays "East Virginia Blues", strumming furiously, peering closely at the neck of the instrument through the more intricate passages. And the audience clap along, on the beat, off the beat—who cares? It's audience participation. And entertainment.

So Peter then introduces Mike, who strides longlegged across the stage, in a change of outfit and does his R and B (plus Country) type number, "You Can't Judge a Book". A brilliant change of mood— and there's more to come. Davy, little Davy, grins on from the wings and launches into his Broadway-show number "Gonna Build A Mountain", reflecting his background in big-success musicals. Then Mike nips on, introduces Micky, who turns the whole atmosphere upside-down again by roaring into a sort of James Brown opus "I've Got A Woman".

Climax

Now this act, showing the boys both as a group and as individuals, comes to its climax.

Above. Woolhat in his favourite sitting position, hands on knees.
Below. Davy, Mike and Micky standing in front of that incredilbe Monkeesmobile on the set of the " Ghost Town " show—remember the one?

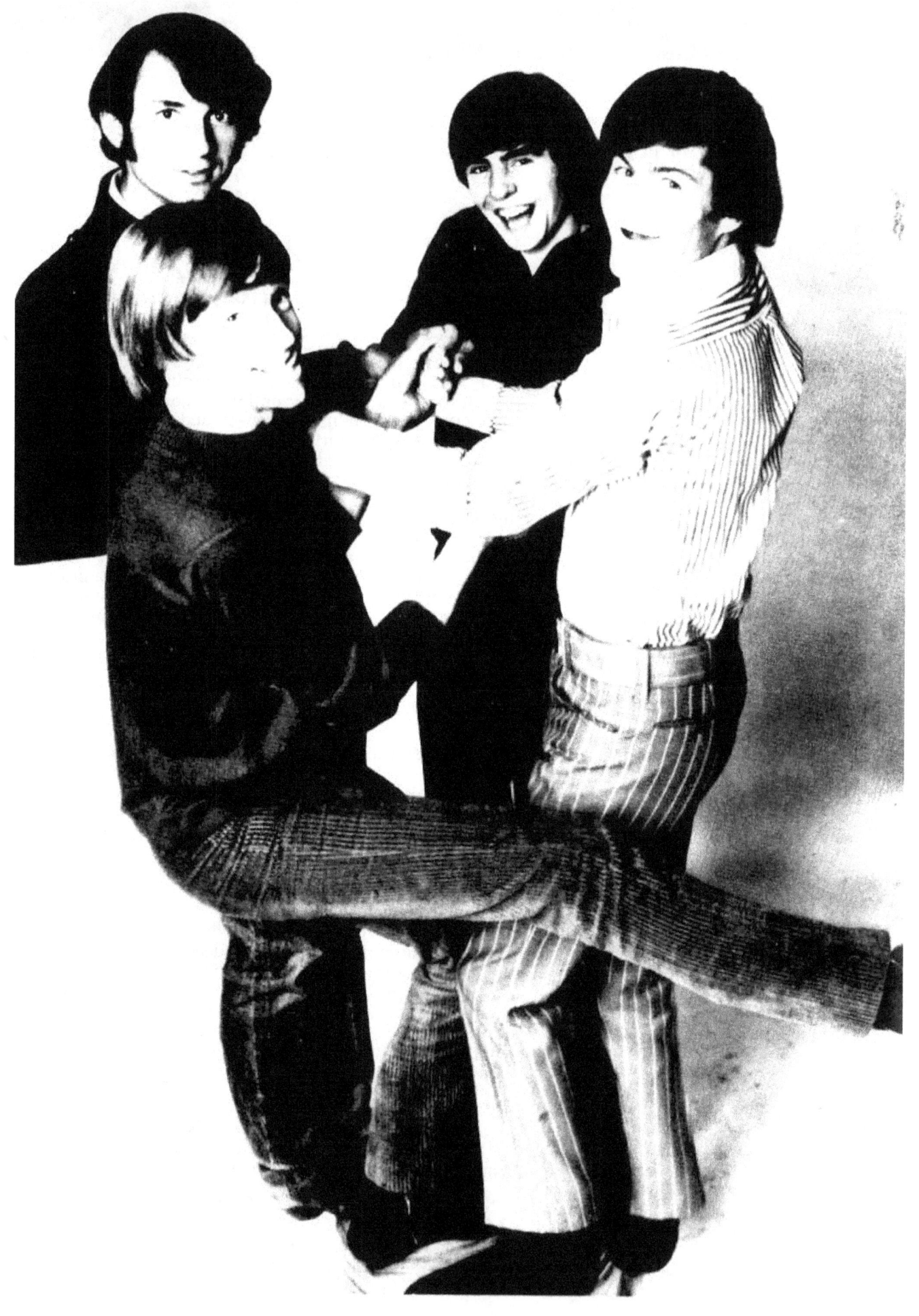

SEVENTY MINUTES OF SUPER-SPECIAL SHOWMANSHIP

Continued from page 11

They all return, take up instruments again . . . and finish off with "I'm A Believer" and "Stepping Stone".

That's it. Audience goes mad, curtains have to be lowered on seventy minutes of action that is, by any standards, first-rate spectacle and entertainment. Produced for the boys largely by a young man, David Winters, who got the Monkees going on movements AND projection. They act themselves, though. This is high-powered personality-selling as well.

17,000 Audience

Hear Micky Dolenz for a moment: "We played to 17,000 in San Francisco. And newspapermen who had knocked us suddenly switched. You've gotta see these Monkees, they wrote. Give them a chance. And it'll take time for this to happen through the world, because it's all happened so quickly for us."

And backstage at a Monkee show? You don't see them drinking or smoking—only Davy lights up "when he gets nervous", says Mike. Says Peter: "Our big worry is when we get into 'Stepping Stone'. That's the moment when the fans either get up on stage OR are held back by the cops." Peter and Mike spend hours playing cards, while Davy chats with everybody in sight. Mike phones home to his wife Phyllis every night. And he's the great worrier, checking every item of the sound equipment in every theatre. He says: "We know that people can't really hear everything if they're screaming. BUT if only a few can understand that everything is O.K. sound wise then all the expense is worth while."

Worrier

There are stacks of presents left for the boys at every theatre. They look at all of them, make notes of the addresses of the senders. But as they usually fly in their own aircraft (along with friends like David Price and Rick Klein and David Pearl and personal managers), they can't take the presents away. They make sure they go to a local hospital.

Micky, on a concert, treats his drums with reverence . . . setting them up absolutely right every time. Mike, previously quiet, revels in being in front of big audiences. Peter is a sort of safety officer, begging the fans to stay in the seats so none of them gets hurt. Micky carries embrocation because he sometimes grazes his back in his slides during his own part of the act.

Changed

Everybody who knows the Monkees well has remarked how they have changed, have built confidence, as a result of the truly tremendous receptions they've had on every show.

And after a concert? It's back to the hotel for a soft-drink session, maybe with some specially-invited fans. Or possibly a visit to a local club—they had a ball one evening in an impromptu cabaret with Brenda Lee. Or maybe even a straight cab-ride to the local airport to get moving for the next day's date.

The Monkees ON STAGE are brilliant. And if there's anyone who still says "I'm not A Believer" . . . well, they'll soon see. And soon!

The End

The Monkee Fire Brigade in Trouble

MONKEES ARCHIVES 1

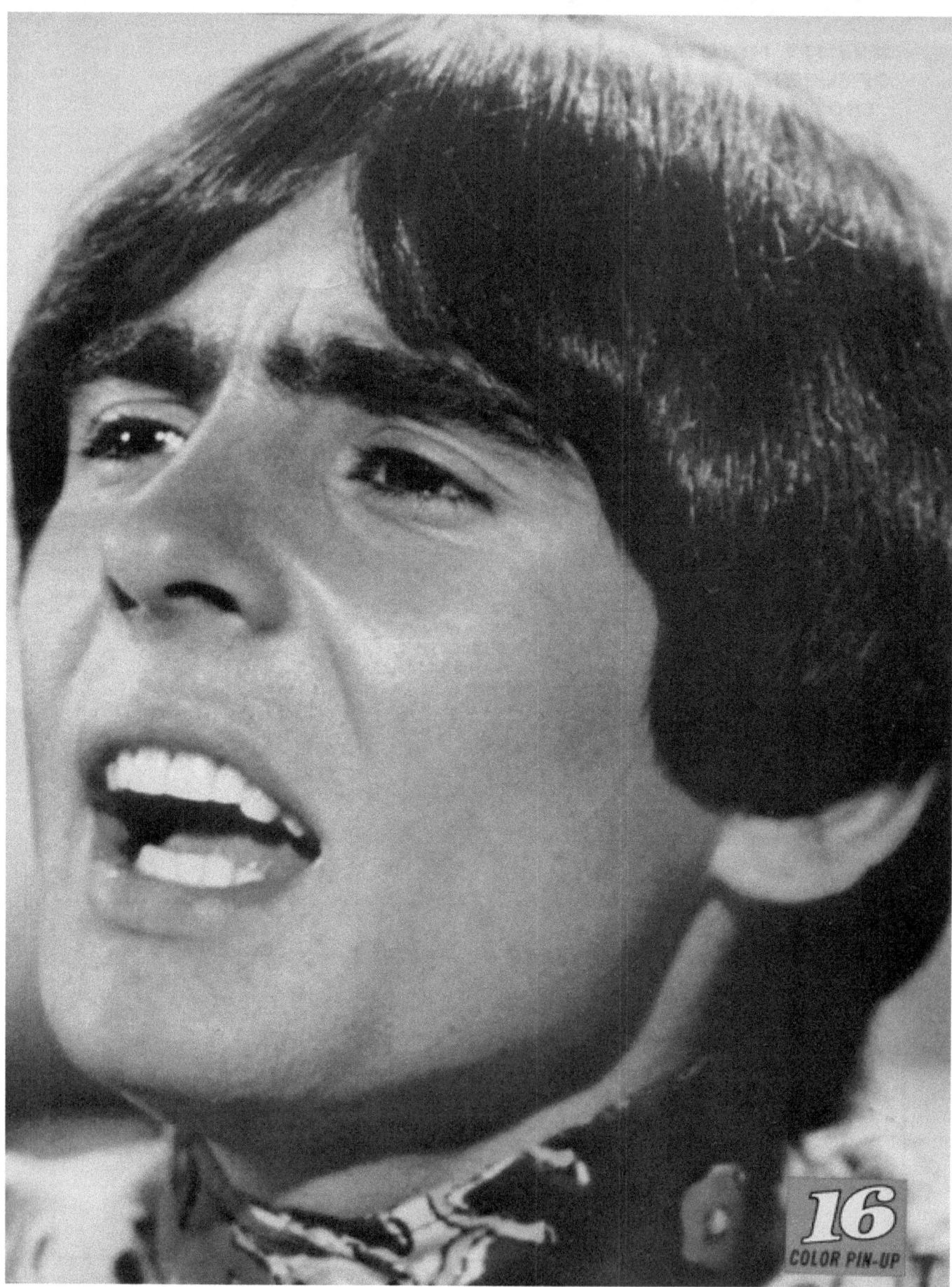

MONKEES ARCHIVES 1

SHOULD THEY HAVE BEEN RELEASED?

asks JACKIE RICHMOND

So the fabulous Monkees are the latest group to walk into a right load of criticism... and it's definitely not their fault! Cause of the panic is that old, and highly-controversial business of record companies releasing near-prehistoric discs by artists made BEFORE those stars have made the grade in their own right.

You know the way it works. Someone makes a record. Either it isn't released at all, or it is pushed out and makes no progress. The tapes are buried away somewhere in the cellars of the recording company. Not even the artist himself remembers the sessions. And then, some years later, he finds himself a star on the strength of brand-new recordings. Everything goes well... until the original disc company remembers those ancient old tapes. And they release them, hoping (quite obviously) to cash in on the star's new popularity.

MICKY SINGLE

Now where do the Monkees come in on this scene? Well, there was the release of an old Micky Dolenz single "Don't Do It", on the London label. Micky made this originally for the Challenge label in Hollywood—and, in fairness, he wrote the song himself. At the time of cutting the disc, it was a reasonable rock'n'roll performance, sung with a good tough edge to the voice. And REAL Micky fans will probably enjoy it immensely as a souvenir of the star's talents, no matter how long ago it was made. BUT... the critics latch on to it and say that it is well below standard and that Micky obviously was below form and that the record isn't worth buying.

WHAT A NERVE!

One letter to a pop magazine went like this: "I think record companies have got a nerve putting out records made by Micky Dolenz and Davy Jones BEFORE they became Monkees. Fans should organise a massed protest and march on the headquarters of the record firms guilty of this stunt."

Micky's problem was purely over a single. The flip didn't even feature him—it was, for the record, "(We Wear) Lavendar Blue" by a group called Finders Keepers, whereas Davy was landed deep in controversy over an LP "Davy Jones" which was made for the American market a couple of years ago—while he was on tour with "Pickwick".

So what's wrong with the LP? For a start it WAS aimed at the Americans. It's full of old-time variety songs, delivered with either a blatant Cockney accent or a fruity North-country one. The Yanks are obsessed with this sort of "folk-British" vaudeville material —especially the mums and dads. But what was right two years ago 'cross the Atlantic is NOT what Davy wants to be heard singing now.

When Davy was in London I asked him about these tracks on Colpix from so long ago. "Crikey," said he, "I've forgotten about THEM. All I hope is that nobody gets hold of them and releases them in Britain."

And Micky was even more adamant. "Sure I made some records early on in my career. But I'm not proud of them. I've learned a lot since then and I just hope someone's burnt the masters." Neither wanted them released. But what the artist wants doesn't matter in this business.

MONKEES ARCHIVES 1

What a clever photographer—he got two Pete's into one pic!

Davy and Micky have become international figures and the record companies make no bones about their desire to cash in on anything remotely connected with the boys. All's fair in love, war and pop music .. that's the theory. So material which can so easily be sub-standard is whipped out —along with outstretched hands to collect the cash.

Don't get me wrong. It's not ONLY the Monkees who get into this sort of trouble. Think of Tom Jones —now voted number one singer in Britain . . gets "It's Not Unusual" to the top of the charts . and out come recordings made for the late Joe Meek which didn't sound even remotely like the current Tom Jones. The Beatles, too. They got to the top and suddenly a Continental company found singles like "My Bonnie Lies Over The Ocean", and shoved them out as Beatle singles—even though the boys had simply been paid a tiny fee to act as backing musicians (unknown) to the "star"—Tony Sheridan.

And the list goes on and on. Simon and Garfunkel— became stars and found an old company had put out an LP of them when they were known as "Tom And Jerry"! "Nothing like us", says Paul Simon—but nobody cares. What about the very early Scott Walker records? Or Roger Miller's oldies pushed out after "King Of The Road"?

So the rather sad Davy Jones and the put-out Micky Dolenz are in good company. But that doesn't make it any more fair. You might remember big arguments on "Juke Box Jury" over this very subject, with David Jacobs coming down heavily on the fact that it didn't do the artists any good at all.

Yet there are two sides to it. Might as well be completely fair about it and explain what the record companies feel. They find an artist and spend money on recording him. So he doesn't make an instant impact. Hard luck? Yes, but

MONKEES ARCHIVES 1

they are entitled to hang on to the tapes for just as long as they like. If that artist pushes off to another label, then clicks .. well, as I was saying all's fair in love, war and pop music.

It's simply a matter of cashing in. Doesn't apparently matter whether the artist is actually HARMED by releasing old gear . and in any case if he's switched labels why should his old company worry about it? Sounds terribly ruthless but that's what money-making is all about.

One record executive explained: "We sink money INTO an artist, and give him a chance. Another way of looking at it is that we are investing in him. We're entitled to get a return on our money. Anyway, quite a lot of fans like the idea of having samples of how their idol USED to sound."

DON'T SELL

Yeah? Well, it's strange that these old-hat recordings don't seem to make much progress in the charts. The Beatles did, to some extent, but they didn't half holler about how annoyed they were that people should cash in on their new-found reputation. Like the Monkees, they take great care with all their new discs and reputations can be wrecked if less-careful selections are flashed around the shops.

If I were Micky or Davy, I'd be hopping mad—as they are. They read reviews of these early discs and must feel sick inside as critics sharpen their knives and knock their efforts. Critics don't always take care about finding out the background of a record—they judge the early "efforts" as being true of the artists' current ability.

No, releasing old records really isn't fair to the artists —or the fans UNLESS it is made clear when the recordings were made. In the case of the Monkees, neither Micky nor Davy sound now anything like the way they sounded a few years back.

Sure, fans who understand the scene will still want the records. But it's surely different when the artists get BLAMED or CRITICISED for performances which they'd forgotten all about in the dim and distant past.

Looks like two bits of two guitars that Mike is playing. Actually it's an Hawaiian guitar.

MONKEES ARCHIVES 1

MONKEES ARCHIVES 1

THEIR VERY FIRST PRESS CONFERENCE

On Thursday, June 29, just over 12 hours after flying into London from Paris, The Monkees attended one of the largest pop Press Conferences ever held in Britain. Gathered in the huge Buckingham Suite Ballroom of Kensington's Royal Garden Hotel were more than 300 reporters, magazine writers, press photographers, radio interviewers and camera crews representing TV and cinema newsreels. This was the first time The Monkees had given a Press Conference of this type, a surprising fact which emerged during the 20 minutes of intensive questioning, which formed the main part of the function. And all the while, as answer followed answer, movie equipment whirled and a hundred cameras kept up a constant clickety-click rhythm. Maybe ten or twenty thousand photographs were taken. Many of these you will see in magazines during the coming months.

Meanwhile, every word spoken by **THE MONKEES** during the entire Conference is to be preserved on these pages. This month there is only room to print about half of what was said. The rest of the questions and answers will appear in the September issue.

Q.: CAN YOU TELL ME HOW MUCH YOU EARN IN A WEEK AFTER YOUR MANAGERS, AGENTS AND ASSOCIATES HAVE EACH TAKEN THEIR SHARES?

DAVY: Er, I clear about three and a tanner, four bob, I dunno. No, we make quite a bit of money but personally most of my money goes in taxes to support all kinds of American officials.

Q.: YOU COME HERE SURROUNDED BY A SORT OF MYTHOLOGY ABOUT BEING A PRE-PACKAGED GROUP AND UNDER CONSIDERABLE ATTACK FROM THE CRITICS. DOES THIS MATTER TO YOU AND DO YOU THINK IT IS TRUE?

PETER: No it doesn't bother us that we come under attack. As far as we're concerned you can't help that. These stories about us being a pre-packaged group, I mean in the sense you mean the words, it is quite true.

MICKY: Jolly good!

MIKE: It's pretty much the same way everybody else forms a group whether it's John Lennon walking down the street asking Paul, Ringo and George to join him or whether someone puts an ad. in a paper. You've got to start somewhere.

MICKY: The original idea was to be a television show and the musical kind of group, the record-making thing kinda happened as an extension. It wasn't intended to be like this, as big as this. And it just so happens that we four get along as well in the recording studios as we do on a stage. It kinda worked pretty groovy.

Q.: WHAT THOUGHTS HAVE YOU ALL GIVEN TO WHAT YOU'RE GOING TO DO WHEN THE SERIES GOES OFF?

DAVY: We know it's sold for another year in America and we have a pretty good chance of making it another year after that. I should think, in about six years from now we'll still be playing together, I suppose.

MICKY: We'll probably go off and do different things—like one of us or two of us, and then

MONKEES ARCHIVES 1

MONKEES ARCHIVES 1

three and then four, and then one of each and two of another... you know, you never can tell just whatever kind of... whichever way the wind blows.

PETER: I hope that's perfectly clear!

DAVY: I didn't understand a thing!

Q.: IS THE FEATURE FILM YOU'RE GOING TO MAKE LATER THIS YEAR OR EARLY NEXT YEAR GOING TO BE AN EXTENSION OF YOUR TV SERIES OR MADE ON AN ENTIRELY NEW CONCEPT?

MICKY: We'd like it to be an entirely new concept. If you've any ideas please let us know. Anybody! Mail 'em in! We're looking for really groovy ideas.

Q.: MICKY, AFTER YOU'VE FINISHED YOUR TV SERIES ARE YOU GOING TO CONTINUE WITH YOUR POP CAREER?

MICKY: It's impossible to get out of the pop world when you're in it. Because you take it along with you. In forty years from now the people I'm playing to now I'll be playing to then. I mean they'll still be my fans if I'm popular and it'll be pop, but it'll be something different. I intend to stay in the field of entertainment. I'd like to get into production and movies and records and shows and films and making candle stick holders on my lathe. And I'm getting into electronic music and I'm trying to discover anti-gravity... and all kinds of things like that!

Q.: WHAT'S THE POSITION WITH YOU AS FAR AS BEING DRAFTED INTO THE AMERICAN ARMY IS CONCERNED?

PETER: They're not doing it to me yet.

MIKE: I've been in and served more or less.

DAVY: I haven't been in yet and I don't think I'm going to go in. I'm still thinking about it. They won't call me up. Too short.

MICKY: Medical.

Q.: "ALTERNATE TITLE" WAS ORIGINALLY "RANDY SCOUSE GIT", I BELIEVE. I DON'T SEE ANY REFERENCE TO THAT LINE IN THE LYRIC. CAN YOU PLEASE TELL ME SOMETHING OF WHAT THE LYRIC IS ABOUT?

"Hey Peter, you're supposed to be up here!"

Will Micky and his friends save the poor old lady?—See page 21

MICKY: The title I heard on a BBC television show called *Mr. Rose* (In fact the programme was "Till Death Do Us Part" but Micky probably watched both programmes—Editor.) I don't understand a lot of what they say here. Somebody was walking around and somebody said to him "Randy Scouse Git". I thought it was the name of one of the characters and I used it as the title. The lyric hasn't anything to do with anything. I was in England and I was sitting in the Grosvenor House Hotel and I was just writing down things that were happening and things that people were doing and saying and, like, birds out on the sidewalk were yelling and waving and screaming. Each one of those things has a legitimate and very valid and very uninteresting meaning.

Q.: WHEN YOU PREPARE FOR A PRESS CONFERENCE LIKE THIS DO YOU ANTICIPATE THE LINE OF QUESTIONING OR DO YOU AGREE ON A CERTAIN LINE THE ANSWERS OUGHT TO TAKE?

MICKY: We've never had a press conference like this. It's the first one ever. It's really neat too.

Q.: DID YOU DO ANY PREPARATION FOR IT?

DAVY: We had breakfast this morning!

MICKY: We've been asked the same questions before, but not in this kind of circumstance.

Q.: I'D LIKE TO ASK DAVY JUST HOW FAR HIS PLANS AS AN INDEPENDENT RECORD PRODUCER HAVE GONE AND, IF HE IS RECORDING GROUPS, WHO ARE THEY?

MICKY: The Beatles!

DAVY: Yeah, I have a group called The Children. They're a Texas group, six boys and one girl. We cut three tracks at a recording studio in Hollywood. Turned out well.

MICKY: I didn't even know that!

● MORE PRESS CONFERENCE QUESTIONS AND ANSWERS NEXT MONTH

MONKEES ARCHIVES 1

MONKEE CONCERTS: DAVY SAYS AUGUST

THE MONKEES will definitely play concert dates in Britain this year, and, according to Davy Jones, they could take place as early as August at provincial venues as well as in London. The Monkees intend to start their round-the-world trip in July—visiting four different continents—and they are currently planning a brand-new stage act completely different from their presentation in Britain last year.

Davy Jones flew into London last Friday for two weeks of TV interviews and business discussions. He told the NME: "The Monkees will be going out on the road in July. We plan to visit Hawaii, South America, Japan, Australia, New Zealand, Holland, Germany and Sweden, as well as Britain.

"We shall play concerts in London, Glasgow, Edinburgh, Birmingham and my hometown of Manchester. They would be some time in August."

However, promoter Vic Lewis regards August as an unlikely period for the Monkees' British concerts. He commented: "I have heard nothing yet from the group's management in Hollywood—and, in any case, I would think it is now too late to book venues for August concerts."

Lewis considers November as the most probable month for the concerts—and this supports the view expressed by Micky Dolenz when he spoke to the NME last week.

Davy revealed that the Monkees are involved in a lawsuit with Screen Gems over the group's name. He said they would like to break away from Screen Gems—the company to which they are contracted—for all activities apart from films and TV.

With Davy having been expected in Britain for nearly a month, he was asked to explain the mysterious delay in his arrival here. "I went away for two weeks on my own, to think things over and get away from it all," he said.

MONKEE BREAKUP?

Is it true that the Monkees are breaking up? If it is, I'm awfully sorry. I have been a fan since they first came on the scene and I would hate to see them split.

Theresa Kendall
Louisville, Ky.

The Monkees aren't exactly breaking up, but it is now official that Peter Tork is leaving the group. Peter is busy with his own company, Breakthrough Influence, and has a lot of other plans which we'll be telling you about in the next issue of TS.

As for the other Monkees, they plan to remain together. And, as things stand now, they don't intend to replace Peter and will be a threesome instead of a foursome.

Among the things to come for the "new" Monkees is what they hope will be a "change of image" where they can truly be themselves. More about that in the next issue, too.

MONKEES ARCHIVES 1

WELCOME MONKEES!

IN front of a crowd of 18,000 screaming, hysterical fans, Monkee Micky Dolenz leapt into the moat at the Hollywood Bowl as the climax of the group's first, sell-out concert in Southern California!

The zany Monkee jumped into the massive moat, which separates the stage from the box seats at the world-famed Bowl, at the end of his "solo" portion of the Monkees' stage show, when he does his James Brown imitation, with Mike trying to lead him offstage with a cape!

The Monkees, unfortunately, were just too far away from the crowd to achieve any kind of rapport. Both the boys themselves and the audience became much more involved watching the slides, film clips and lighting effects projected on a giant screen above and behind the group as they performed.

Dressed in burgundy doublebreasted velvet suits, floral ties and black patent leather boots, the group zipped through all their single releases and most of their "Headquarter" album.

Earlier, Mike sang in a white suit with white patent boots and lace-cuffed shirt, without wool hat, "You Can't Judge A Book"; Peter in white sweater and pants sang "Cripple Creek," accompanying himself on banjo; a tuxedo-clad Davy sang "Gonna Build A Mountain"; and Micky, wearing brown slacks and a bright red jacket with a shiny print shirt, sang "I Got A Woman Way Over Town."

The main difference in this act from the one in January at San Francisco's

HOLLYWOOD
Tracy Thomas

Cow Palace was the addition of several new instruments and the switching around of instrumental roles.

Twice Davy handled the drumming chores; first when Micky came out front to play a kettle drum and sing "Randy S" and then toward the end of "Mary, Mary" when Micky came down again. Davy also tackled the electric organ while Peter stepped up to sing "Auntie Grizelda."

Peter switched constantly from bass to organ to piano, while Mike stayed on guitar, except during "Shades Of Grey", when he played electric steel guitar.

The throng of fans went wild at every mention of the Monkees' name and greeted every song opening and close with frantic applause and screams, although my inner applause meter told me that the noise never reached Beatle proportions—you could always hear the music and what the group was singing.

Among the warm-up acts were Ike and Tina Turner with the Ikettes, who were strangely added to the bill. I say "strangely" as the 10-14-year-old fans were not at all familiar with the Turners, who were polished but felt out of place.

MONKEES ARCHIVES 1

One Michael Nesmith album for the price of three!

For those of you who really didn't listen, Michael Nesmith and the First National Band's three albums (Magnetic South, Loose Salute, and Nevada Fighter) are, when stripped down, a trilogy. Yes! A trilogy. Play Side 2 of each record consecutively and you'll hear one continuing saga of the old West. And it's going to surprise you.

When we questioned Mr. Nesmith on his concept (so that we could sound smart when we were telling you about it), the verbose Mr. N. drawled, "It's about what it's about."

Finally, after much prodding, we pinned him down to stating that the six tip-off songs in the trilogy were "Beyond the Blue Horizon," "Hollywood," "Listen to the Band," "Hello Lady," "Texas Morning" and "Tumbling Tumbleweeds." He also was quick to say that none of these were his top 40 successes; they're confined to Side 1.

The six tunes (as well as a lot of other choice stuff) are ingeniously spread out, for maximum sales potential, (clever cowboy, that Michael), in the aforementioned three albums.

But, listeners, take heart. You don't have to plunk down bread for all three at once — though it would be nice if you did — because you can enjoy the glorious melodies of Michael Nesmith and the First National Band individually. The albums, taken one at a time, are very good music. Good enough to rate reviews like these:

"The music (in Magnetic South) feels so good that you can just tell the musicians were smiling when they recorded it." —San Diego Underground.

"The album is good... Loose Salute by Michael Nesmith and the First National Band is one of the hippest country rock albums in some time, certainly the most listenable." —Rolling Stone

"His albums, always beautifully produced, just get better and better" said Record World of the trilogy's final album, Nevada Fighter.

And to help you merchandise these albums, a batch of goodies have been whipped up by the busy beavers in our sales promotion department. They include a counter display which folds up and fits into a record box, a full color poster of Michael and a rack strip (also full color!).

So, together or apart, you've got it. Music that reflects the old West and the old westerner. By Michael Nesmith. A cowboy for today's America.

```
Loose Salute      LSP-4415
                  P8S-1633
                  PK-1633

Magnetic South    LSP-4371
                  P8S-1636
                  PQ8-1636
                  PK-1636

Nevada Fighter    LSP-4497
                  P8S-1705
                  PK-1705
```

RCA Records and Tapes

MONKEES ARCHIVES 1

DAVID and MICKY

HIGHLIGHTS OF THE MONKEES' TOUR

Here's the inside story of what really happened to Davy, Micky, Mike and Peter on their outasite summer splash!

By David Price

IN PARIS, Peter had a great time clowning in this old-fashioned swimming suit. He lost a lot of weight on the tour. None of the Monkees have a weight problem. If you've seen the show, you already know why.

MIKE NESMITH, above right, missed Phyllis right from the beginning of the tour. When we got to England he called her and flew her over. The other Monkees spent most of their time in Paris sightseeing. It was outasite.

MONKEES ARCHIVES 1

About the author: David Price is Davy's stand-in on the Monkee TV show and also in charge of the Monkee's equipment on their tours. He always travels with them wherever they go and keeps Monkee Spectacular and TiGER BEAT readers right up to date on what's happening.

Everybody keeps asking me . . . "What's it like to really live with the Monkees?" Well, it's quite an experience in more ways than one. So, in this article I'm going to tell you some things that happened on our tour and then you can judge for yourselves . . . what it's like to live with the Monkees.

Paris

When we did the shooting of the Monkee show in Paris last July, I had a chance to get to know the boys better than ever. You see, in France, they're unknown and this made it easy for them to walk around the streets without any fans bothering them.

Mike was more cool than ever and got a great charge out of just roaming the streets and not signing any autographs. Mike's really interested in a lot of things and this three day spree gave him a chance to stroll around, look at different art objects, and study people. I remember he said how good it was to be able to look at everyone else for a change instead of having everyone staring at you.

Peter the Frenchman

Peter's the only Monkee who can speak French so he probably had a better time than the other three. He talked to everyone, and he got around a lot better because he could ask for directions in the right language. Peter makes friends very easily. Some people have told me that they think Peter is very hard to get to know. This is only true if Peter doesn't dig the person. Actually, Peter is very friendly and open to people he likes being with.

Micky and Samantha

Sam flew over to Paris to see Micky while we were there. She had been to Paris many times before and she showed Micky all the craziest clubs in town. If you remember, Sam was also Micky's guide around London last year when he went there on his vacation. For those of you who want to know about her, I think Sam could be described as a quiet, considerate kind of girl. She's very calm in disposition; quite different from Micky. She has this feminine quality about her. She rarely thinks about herself first; always the other person.

MICKY AND SAMANTHA IN PARIS

MONKEES ARCHIVES 1

Anyway, one day in Paris, Micky showed up for the day's shooting wearing a French policeman's hat. Nobody knew where he got it and Micky wouldn't tell. We knew he didn't buy it, though. To this day, it's still a secret, but it is one of his favorite hats.

Davy and Clothes

We filmed a whole day in the Flea Market in Paris. This is sort of an open place where they sell almost everything you can think of. Davy bought a fabulous black stovepipe top hat for himself. When the director saw him in it, he asked Davy to wear it in the show. So when you see this segment next season on TV, you'll know that Davy's wearing his own hat.

He also bought a blue military jacket and he wore this in the show, too. Davy can't resist buying clothes ... for himself and any of his friends who might be along.

Girls in Paris

There were no actual dates for the Monkees in Paris. The boys did hang around with some of the French girls who worked on the TV segment we were filming. They tried to teach Micky, Davy and Mike French, but there just wasn't enough time to learn anything.

Opinions on France

The Monkees really flipped over the beauty of Paris. But, none of them really dug the French food. Everyone kept wanting a good, old fashioned steak dinner and in Paris the French put sauce on everything. One night Mike found a really groovy Hungarian restaurant and he thought the goulash was outasite.

MONKEES ARCHIVES 1

FILMING IN PARIS, the Monkees had a great time. They are not famous there so they could film right on the streets without any disturbance from fans. The girls pictured on these pages are all French. They were hired for this particular segment of the Monkee show which you'll be seeing this season over NBC-TV on Monday nights.

MONKEES ARCHIVES 1

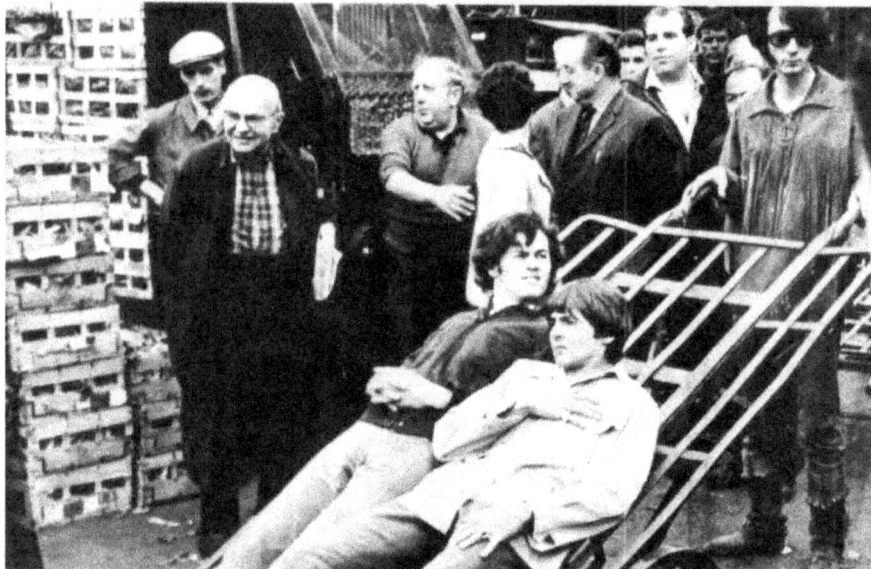

London Lowdown

The big news about England was the fact that there were more people at the Monkees' press conference than had attended Winston Churchill's conference in World War II. Most of us don't remember back that far, but it really had been the most important press conference in the history of England and now the Monkees' had topped it.

It was really a groove being backstage with the Monkees before they went out before the 400 English newspapermen who were there to question them. In case you don't know, the English newsmen aren't known to be the world's friendliest. In fact, they love knocking American performers and it would have pleased them if the Monkees had been really stupid in their answers. Fortunately, I can tell you that all four Monkees responded well to the questions and were quite witty in their replies.

I won't bother repeating the questions they asked because you probably know all the right answers already. But I will tell you that the reporters tried to get the Monkees to say something controversial like John Lennon's statement about Christ or Paul McCartney's statement about drugs. The Monkees were all too smart for them. They just joked back at the questions and the reporters loved it.

Mike was asked more questions than any of the other Monkees because he seems to be the quietest and they were trying to get him to talk. Davy wound up doing most of the talking and you know Davy, he's a very groovy conversationalist. I think Davy was more at ease than the others because England is his home.

Concert Getaways

The concerts were all groovy in England. They gave five and almost all of them were sell-outs. A funny things happened at the Friday concert. One of our security men spotted a boy in the audience who resembled Davy. He had long hair and everything so the officer asked him to come back stage.

After the concert our security guards used this boy as a decoy. All the fans thought he was Davy so they mobbed him and let the other Monkees get away. This trick worked so well, we may use it at other concerts.

Big Beatle Party

There was a big party held for the Monkees and the Beatles came, but we won't talk about that here because in another section of the magazine there's a whole story about the Beatles and the Monkees.

MONKEES ARCHIVES 1

Vic Lewis presents the
MONKEES
AT WEMBLEY

Friday June 30
Saturday July 1
Sunday July 2

LONDON PRESS CONFERENCE was a great success. The Monkees are very good about answering questions, even for reporters who are trying to get them to say something stupid. They listen carefully to the question, then reply with lots of wit and charm. Their conference in London was the biggest one ever held. More reporters turned out to see them than had ever turned out for a Beatles' press conference. The boys were very happy about the whole event.

Shopping in London

East Indian clothes are very big in London right now. You know, the long Mandarin coats and things like that. Davy flipped over these and bought quite a few. Carnaby Street is really out now in England so Davy shopped at Dandy's Fashions and places like this.

Phyllis flew in to see Mike in London and the two of them ran off to Biba's to buy some new clothes for Phyllis. Mike also bought a new Mini (auto, this is) in London. Mike and Phyllis really dig buying things, but then, I guess we all do.

Speaking of buying things, Micky did the most outasite thing you've ever heard of in London. He arranged to buy one of these big two decker London buses. You know the ones I mean . those where the people can sit on the top floor outside and then there's an enclosed bottom side. Well, his plan is this. He's going to have the bus shipped over to New York and then drive it from New York to California after the inside is decorated in a real groovy style. Who knows, Micky may be driving through your own town soon.

Dates in London

Micky didn't date anyone but Samantha in London. But Davy dated several different girls for various parties. Peter had little time for girls because Brian Jones of the Stones, who Peter met in Monterey, was busy showing Peter all the spots of interest around the city.

Davy did get a chance to have a quiet two day reunion with his father. Mr. Jones was feeling well when Davy visited him and this made Davy very happy because Davy has been worried about his father the past few months. When Davy got back from the visit, he was all smiles. The relationship between Davy and Mr. Jones is one of the finest I've ever seen between a father and son.

Back to the U.S.A.

The pace in the States was just as hectic as overseas, but I'll tell you all about that in this month's TiGER BEAT (October issue) on sale at your local newsstand on September 7th.

MONKEES ARCHIVES 1

AN AFTERNOON WITH DAVY

Davy has friends all over the world and sometimes they get a chance to visit him in Hollywood.

Just recently some of Davy's old mates from England paid him an unexpected visit. They are playing with a professional soccer team, so while they stopped off in Hollywood, Davy got several opportunities to see them. He also got a brief chance to play some soccer with them. This is something Davy has missed very much. He loves all sports, but especially soccer.

MONKEES ARCHIVES 1

WHEN DAVY'S SOCCER buddies came over from England to play in the pro games here, they invited Davy along to a practice session.

HE COULD HARDLY WAIT to change from his Monkee boots to the regulation soccer shoes. Davy hadn't seen many of the boys since they went to school together back in Manchester.

(Continued on next page)

MONKEES ARCHIVES 1

NOTICE THE ANGLE at which Davy "dribbles" the ball. In soccer, the rules say only the goalie can touch the ball with his hands. Davy had a great time!

THE BOYS HAD a grand time romping through their usual practice session. They all agreed Davy hadn't lost his skill at the game. Below, that's Davy diving head first at the ball!

MONKEES ARCHIVES 1

AFTER A ROUGH work-out, Davy took his friends to one of his favorite men's stores and treated them to anything they wanted. At left, the salesgirl couldn't resist asking Davy for his autograph. Davy never minds this.

A MINI-SKIRT FOR DAVY? We prefer him in slacks and skirts, but Davy always loves to joke with people. The boys left the shop with many goodies and many memories of a groovy day with their friend, Davy.

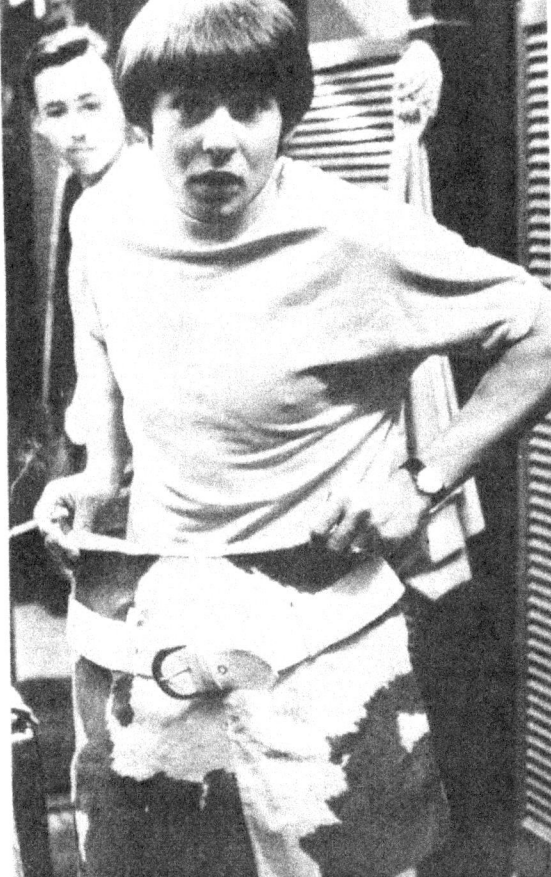

MONKEES ARCHIVES 1

MONKEES ARCHIVES 1

THE MONKEES IN PARIS

Paris, for sure, will never be the same. Not since those galloping Monkees turned up there to do some film shots for a programme which we'll probably see sometime in the New Year. In fact, there are some Parisians who swear that the old Eiffel Tower visibly rocked to its foundations when the boys were let loose to clown around as they wanted for the benefit of the film cameramen.

BEGINNING

But let's start at the beginning, as all good stories should. The Monkees were due in Paris a few days before arriving in London for their sell-out shows at the Wembley Pool. So as not to alarm the gendarmes, their spot of French leave was kept highly secret. As it happens, the secrecy wasn't necessary . . . because, believe it or not, the Monkees are not very well known in France!

Can you imagine it? Micky and Davy walking along a street in, say, Birmingham or London without being instantly recognised? Or Peter sitting, nose buried in a book, in some Manchester coffee-bar and nobody taking any notice? Or Mike strolling through flower-gardens in Liverpool, firing away with his camera, and nobody giving him even a first glance, let alone a second?

But the Monkee telly-shows were on in France at this time. And the French fans were, as they often are, very slow in latching on to a newish group's records.

Add in the planned secrecy, then, and you have this picture of the Monkees and all their mates arriving in Paris straight from America and checking in, under their own names, at the luxurious George V Hotel, which is just off the Champs Élysées . . . one of the most expensive "pads" in the whole of Europe. . . .

Managers Bob Rafelson and Bert Schneider were there, plus a lot of friends—and Samantha Juste who turned up mid-way through the visit to see Micky. The boys roared into the hotel, with Micky shouting to one of our reporters there on the spot: "This is our French shooting season. Anybody seen my guns?" And they flew up to their suite of rooms, beautifully furnished and with a massive selection of soft drinks already there on ice.

Though they were tired after a long flight, the boys made plans not to waste the first evening on French soil. True, Micky decided to stay in the hotel, but Davy and his entourage went out to some recommended night-clubs, like the Castille and the Cupole, where they could hear the music the French fans were digging then. Mike just wandered round the nearby streets, window-shopping by lamplight and soaking up the atmosphere of a city he'd wanted to visit since he was a kid at school.

☞ The Monkees getting off the plane at Paris Airport.

Peter played it real cool. He armed himself with a book (a VERY serious tome with a long title but which added up to being about the psychology of religion) and he went from cafe to cafe sampling the local wine and coffee. Every so often he looked up to watch the "passing world" as he put it, but mostly his head was lowered to his book, a frown of concentration on his face.

Quite a bit later, they exchanged notes at the hotel. Said Davy: "Honest, it was great to be able to go out without being recognised. Maybe if we'd all been together it would have been different, but this way we had just one night away from being on show as a Monkee. Fantastic . . . a knock-out evening."

JUST A JOKE

Micky said: "Oh sure, but you'd hate it if nobody recognised you anywhere" but he was joking. And the boys agreed that it was like being in a different world and that they really enjoyed being in the middle of their fans.

And then it was bye-byes for a few hours. With the promise of something quite unusual in the Monkees' schedule . . . a complete Sunday off. None of 'em could remember when they last had twenty-four hours to themselves without any commitments at all, like an interview or a phone call or a picture session or something. . . .

Well, the best-laid plans and all that. In fact, the boys all slept rather later than they wanted. It was lunch-time when they split up and went out on tours of exploration. Paris on a Sunday is a wondrous city. The boys went, in two separate groups, round Versailles, which was the court of King Louis XIV in the eighteenth century. And they took pictures of the local characters and they sampled French delicacies of drinks and food. Walking and sightseeing is a tough business and soon they all felt rather tired. So it was agreed (in fact, it was ordered by their management) that they'd all have a very early bed-time that night.

MONKEES ARCHIVES 1

Shooting on the Monday was due to start very early indeed. Would you believe 6.30 a.m.? The boys hardly could for this was earlier than they had to report back home in Hollywood for their series. Anyway, the alarm calls did the trick and the boys gathered in the foyer of the hotel bang on time. Peter Tork took on the role of interpreter because he speaks French quite well.

FLEA MARKET

So off they went to the Flea Market. No, it's not a place that sells, or even encourages, fleas. It's a place famous for cheap and second-hand bargains. Micky immediately broke off to buy a beautiful slave bracelet for Samantha... "I'll have it hammered on her," he said. Another joke. But he later took her back to the market to show where he'd got it. Micky really flipped over the things on display ... said he'd like to buy the whole market and have it shipped to America.

Davy bought a military coat, double-breasted and from the French Army style of the First World War. He also collected a ring, antique of course, which he said he'd give as a Christmas present. And Davy, by now right in the spirit of things, bought an old Bedouin throwing dagger which he said would have pride of place in his home.

They were filmed rushing among the strange old characters in the Flea Market. They sat together at a pavement cafe, just watching. And they agreed that they thought Paris one of the most beautiful places they'd seen, though they weren't, all of them, too keen on some of the aggressive salesmen they'd met that morning.

And it was another fairly early-to-bed evening. Micky stayed in his hotel room, with Samantha. The others tried new night-spots.

Tuesday was another busy, hectic day. First there was a filmed sequence at a swimming pool, the boys wearing old-style costumes and hamming it up in the way of the old Keystone Kops. Point was that this was sort of free-style filming—the cameras kept on running and the boys did pretty well what they wanted. Which meant a very crazy scene indeed. They clowned around in an old cemetery, they roared through a fair-ground. And they started work on apparently trying to demolish the Eiffel Tower.

Even though they weren't known to the locals, they attracted huge crowds, watching "the mad Americans". They steamed up and down the Champs d'Elysees in an old jeep, getting the spirit of driving fast in Paris as everybody does. And there was the inevitable traffic jam. For three hours they choked the traffic because of the sightseers.

BONNET

Mike had one sequence where he lifted the bonnet of the jeep—and showed astonishment when it simply came away in his hand. Fine ... but the cameraman "shooting" this incident found he'd run out of film. They tried it again but by this time two gendarmes were leaping up and down in anger, so they scrubbed round it. Micky decided his ambition was to climb the Tower from the outside and made a pretty good stab at making it to the first platform!

In fact he had a real mountaineering instinct on this trip. Next day they took a canal trip, also filmed. They went by the Flea Market again and Micky improvised a horrific climb up the side of a building there ... reaching the second floor, then blowing kisses to the girls watching. Two of the boys leapt from a moving car. Davy jumped 15 ft. from a building and turned over dangerously when he hit the ground.

For another sequence each Monkee had a girl-friend, enrolled by Bob Rafelson ... but other locals got too enthusiastic and they ended up with about seven each! "Bad planning," said Bob. "Good planning" chorused the Monkees. And they were filmed on the banks of the Seine. One of the most chaotic incidents in the history of Paris was now coming to an end ...

There was a last meal at Maxim's, one of the plushest of all restaurants. A quick return by Micky to the Flea Market to buy a silk square for Sammy.

Then, on the Wednesday, on to a plane arriving in London at 23.30 at London Airport ... to a huge welcome from fans.

'COME ON MICKY, QUIT THE COMEDY!'

TOP: Davy, Micky, Mike and girls driving down a Paris street in their jeep.
BOTTOM: The boys' road managers dressed as French gendarmes.

MONKEES ARCHIVES 1

BRIAN VISITS THE MONKEES
AND FINDS PETER TORK IS LEAVING...

PETER Tork, the flop haired "slapstick innocence" element in the Monkees, has left the group. Lovable, but far from simple, Peter was known for his folk background and excellent banjo playing as well as his zany antics in the Monkees' television series. Just back from a brief visit to America, Julie Driscoll, Brian Auger and the Trinity met all four Monkees in Los Angeles and later, Brian revealed the story to RM.

"We were filming a Monkee special with Madman Jack Good producing and it was there we were told that Peter was leaving the others to involve himself in recording and producing other people. Mike, Mickey and Davy gave him an exquisite gold watch with the inscription "From All the Guys Down at Work", which I thought was a rather amusing anecdote. When the filming began, the Monkees wandered in one by one, picked up their instruments and began playing this simple melody, "Listen to the Band". Then the Buddy Miles Express, another U.S. group and ourselves descended on them and started a disconnected jam session all round them. We kept this up while they, undaunted, continued with this simple tune. Eventually, we twindle our music down and into their song until everyone is raving away at "Listen to the Band". At that point it becomes a complete explosive jam session built around that tune.

MIKE'S HOME

Mike Nesmith invited us to his Bel Air home afterwards. This being our first trip to America we were already stupefied by the scene there and we had no idea what to expect from the home of a Monkee. Julie wandered off somewhere in the depths of Los Angeles, so I pulled Lobs (bassist Dave Ambrose) from hiding in his room and we all boarded the Rolls Mike ordered to fetch us. After a rather scenic drive through the millionaire section we pulled up to a huge iron gate, which at the driver's touch of a control panel in the car, swung open with mysterious ease. The door to this huge house was of course equipped with a monitor into which we announced our arrival. The inside was indescribable. Mike had his own recording studio with two Hammond organs and all the necessary sound fixtures. We immediately lurched into another jam session. I went mad on the organ while Dave looned furiously on his bass.

Later Micky Dolenz and Davy Jones arrived. Micky went into the drums and Davy sat goggle-eyed throughout. When we finished and the fuses were nearly all blown, we all felt like we'd just ploughed the North forty. It was then turkey time. From Mike's actual radar oven, came a golden brown bird (fowl type) with all the trimmings. We ate as much as thirty people would and sank back into a little digestive hibernation.

A few days later, we had a press reception and played for the journalists and guests. Jeff Beck, Arthur Brown, Buddy Miles and a load of others showed up, plus all four Monkees.

JULIE DRISCOLL, BRIAN AUGER and the TRINITY

PETER TORK—Leaving the Monkees

Davy was still goggle-eyed and told us he'd never seen anything like it. Of all the Monkees though, Mike is the one who really has it all together. We had gone over expecting to find four rumbustious teeny boppers and found instead four —and particularly Mike — switched on musicians with valid things to say about music and the present scene. We look forward to our return for a tour some time early this new year.

MONKEES ARCHIVES 1

Mickey, Davy, and Mike wish Peter the best of luck and success!

TO PETER - NOW ON HIS OWN!

We can see it all now.

For the next few months, the magazine stands will be blazing with ridiculous cover lines such as "The Hot Intimate Sizzling Spicy Real Low-Down Dirty Reason Why The Monkees Had To Fire Peter Tork" and other such ridiculous krap.

Well, we hate to spoil everyone's fun, but there just isn't any hot, intimate, sizzling, spicy, real low-down dirty reason why Peter is no longer with the group. And he wasn't fired. He left of his own free will.

You'll also be hearing all kinds of fabricated nonsense about how the group could no longer get along and how they didn't part friends and assorted garbage of this ilk.

Don't believe a word of this bilge, either. The Monkees got along just fine. The group started out as four total strangers, but they came to mean a lot to each other personally and that's really pretty groovy when you think about it.

As for not parting friends, that's really dumb. They're ten times better friends than they were two years ago. I first heard of Peter's impending split with the group from Davy Jones' best friend several months ago. However, it wasn't official then and I was asked not to mention in print what I had been told in confidence. So I didn't, and as far as I know, this is the first time the news has been announced.

The reasons why Peter left the group are really rather difficult to completely explain. It's as simple as him wanting to do his own thing, but it gets rather complicated when we get into exactly what his own thing is. He has so many interests, like record producing and other areas of music and right this moment he and Bobby Hammer (a close friend who lives in Peter's guest house) are working on a film which they hope will be the first of many.

I'll know a lot more about Peter's plans this time next week because in a few days I'm going to have dinner at his house and should have all kinds of groovy information for you soon.

It may be awhile before even Peter himself is fully aware of the direction he wants to take. Remember, he's been busy day and night for a very long time, being a Monkee, and it wasn't an easy job. This is really the first time he's had a chance to think things out, and the more he thinks, the groovier his ideas will get, I'm sure.

You will no doubt be hearing all sorts of wild speculation about who is going to take Peter's place in the group, and you'll hear everyone from Sajid Khan to Henry Gibson suggested as possible substitutes. Well, again, don't listen. At this writing, the Monkees have decided not to replace Peter. Instead, they'll be a threesome.

They may change thier minds sooner or later, of course, but as of now, it is their decision not to add another member.

I'll have more news on the subject of the Monkees' and Peter's future in the next issue of TS, at which time I'll be coming back to work as the editor again. (Whee!)

In closing, I would like to say that I feel the Monkees are going to surprise all of us, and so is Peter. This group has been put down by critics and fans alike because of their "teenybopper" image and some of their music, and I'm not saying that the put downs weren't or were deserved. I am only saying I think they're going to surprise a lot of people with what they can come up with now that they're free to make decisions on their own and do, at long last, their own thing.

END

MONKEES ARCHIVES 1

RHINO AUGUST

AUGUST 1987 RELEASES RHINO RECORDS 1201 OLYMPIC BLVD., SANTA MONICA, CA 90404

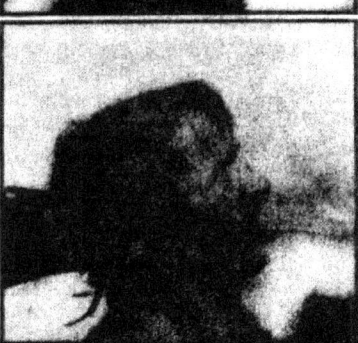

BACK WITH A SPLASH!

First all-new recording in a generation

THE MONKEES:
"Pool It!"

(Compact Disc RNCD 70706) (Album RNIN 70706, Cassette RNIC 70706, $9.98 List)
[UPC #'s — Compact Disc 8122-70706-2, Album 8122-70706-1, Cassette 8122-70706-4]

NEW ARTIST!

Rhino is proud to present the first new MONKEES album in two decades! Similar in approach to the classic Monkees albums of the Sixties, Rhino has searched for the best songwriters available and hired pop producer extraordinare, Roger Bechirian (Elvis Costello, Squeeze, and The Undertones), to make certain this album embraced the production values and sound of the Eighties, yet retained all the energy and creativity of the original Monkees. Rhino will be charging ahead with this album, as we mount a full-scale promotional campaign that includes a video by Bill Fishman and Preacher Ewing. Considering that their TV show is syndicated in all the major markets, with the Nickelodeon Channel viewers just voting The Monkees as their #1 favorite group (by a 2-to-1 margin over the #2 group!), and with the group touring to sold-out stadiums all summer, it's obvious that all the elements are in place to insure The Monkees' new album will be the best-selling album of the summer.

★ This is the first new Monkees album in 18 years!

★ Produced by the renowned Roger Bechirian, it has the sound of the '80s, yet retains the style and spirit of the great Monkees classics of the '60s.

★ Nickelodeon viewers just voted The Monkees as their #1 favorite group.

★ Once again, their TV show is syndicated in all major markets throughout the country.

★ The group will be touring all summer to sold-out arenas across the country.

★ The Monkees sold over 2 million albums last summer.

Marketing Tools

★ Four-color poster

★ Flats

★ Individual Monkees Poster cut-outs

Will be a Smash CHR Single!

TENTATIVE TRACKS INCLUDE:
DON'T BRING ME DOWN MIDNIGHT (I'D GO THE) WHOLE WIDE WORLD HEART AND SOUL COUNTING ON YOU
SINCE YOU WENT AWAY LOVE YOU FOREVER MOVIN' IN WITH RICO SECRET HEART LONG WAY HOME
GETTIN' IN EVERY STEP OF THE WAY

Other Monkees titles available on Rhino (All $8.98 List):
"The Monkees" (Album RNLP 70140, Cassette RNC 70140)
"More Of The Monkees" (Album RNLP 70142, Cassette RNC 70142)
"Headquarters" (Album RNLP 70143, Cassette RNC 70143)
"Pisces, Aquarius, Capricorn & Jones Ltd." (Album RNLP 70141, Cassette RNC 70141)
"The Birds, The Bees & The Monkees" (Album RNLP 144, Cassette RNC 144)
"Head / Original Soundtrack" (Album RNLP 145, Cassette RNC 145)
"Instant Replay" (Album RNLP 146, Cassette RNC 146)
"Present" (Album RNLP 147, Cassette RNC 147)
"Changes" (Album RNLP 70148, Cassette RNC 70148)
"Monkee Flips" (Album RNLP 113, Cassette RNC 113)
"Live - 1967" (Album RNLP 70139, Cassette RNC 70139)
"Missing Links" (Album RNLP 70150, Cassette RNC 70150)

MONKEES ARCHIVES 1

At The ...And Convention Now!

Their First Order Of Business?! After All These Years It's Still *You!*

Davy Jones, Micky Dolenz and Peter Tork were the Monkees combination that decided to go out on tour in '86. By now Michael was well established as a video and filmmaker and he had little time to get away for a tour. To touch base with their fans of these last twenty years, the three Monkees attended the Philadelphia convention organized in their honor by Ed Riley and Maggie McManus, longtime fans and Monkees newsletter editors.

It was in August that Davy brought his wife Anita and daughters Sara (left) and Jessica to the three-day bash. While there was lots of Monkees memorabilia on sale, Davy brought some rare items to share during the question and answer period. He told stories from the past in a joyful and animated way and even played some rough demos of his new solo singles "Incredible" and "After Your Heart."

Peter Tork shook hands with emcee Fred Velez as he stood next to a huge blow-up of the Monkees 45, "Last Train To Clarksville." Peter was a very congenial host and answered even the most personal questions about his alcoholism gracefully. The audience of old and new Monkees fans filled out lots of question cards during their visit to the Society Hill Hotel, ever curious about what makes these boys tick!

Peter was a very congenial host and answered even the most personal questions about his alcoholism gracefully.

Now it was Micky's turn and he was tickled to talk to fans. He stayed past his allotted time and really didn't want to leave, but as always, there was lots more to do on a tour that would pass through over a hundred cities in a very short time.

How did that incredible reunion with Michael turn out? Turn the page and be there!

MONKEES ARCHIVES 1

DAVE CLARK'S DAY WITH THE MONKEES
told by Dave Clark

ANN MOSES INTRODUCED DAVE TO DAVY ON THE SET

MONKEES ARCHIVES 1

Here's an inside look at everyone's favorite group — told by Dave Clark

Dave Clark was reluctant to tell us his story. He had been invited down to the Monkees' set and didn't want them to think he had come for any publicity reasons. We explained that by telling us the story he could share his experiences with all the Monkee fans, so he agreed. Here is his story...

During his two week vacation, Dave Clark was invited to visit the Monkees set by their producers. When he arrived on the set, the Monkees were busy filming a scene in their set "house."

Dave's immediate reaction to the whole set up was one of surprise. He couldn't believe the casual atmosphere that prevails at all times —the director calling out instructions and the Monkees ad libbing terribly funny lines.

Davy Meets Dave

When the scene was finished, Davy Jones glanced up and noticed Dave watching from the back. Annie Moses introduced Dave to Davy and Davy seemed very excited. It was unusual, since the Monkees are so often meeting big stars, that Davy was so enthusiastic. He called to Peter who was pouring coffee nearby, "Come here, Pete, I want you to meet Dave Clark!" Peter, too, was eager to meet one of the long-time pop leaders.

Conversations during the filming breaks centered around the Monkees successes and Dave's, as well. Dave and Davy often chatted about England and then Davy laughed, "I have to tell you about a really funny incident. You know, I remember seeing your show at Carnegie Hall in New York when you first came over here three years ago! I really dug 'Glad All Over' and 'Bits and Pieces' and I was really excited about seeing your group in concert. At the time I was playing in 'Oliver' and my hair was a little darker than now, about the color of my eyebrows.

"So I was sitting in my seat and the group had come on stage and of course, everyone was screaming. All of a sudden a little girl in the row in front of me turned around and pointed at me and shouted 'That's Dave Clark's brother!' Before I knew it, there were girls all around me and grabbing at my clothes, so I had to leave! I was really disappointed I didn't get to see your whole show."

Clarksville No Hit

Dave asked the Monkees if they weren't excited about playing for London for the first time and Peter told Dave, "Our first record, 'Clarksville' wasn't a hit over there. When we finally did make the charts, even number one, there were lots of knockers, so we really want to show them what we can do!"

Later I talked with Dave about his opinions on the Monkees and this is what he had to say:

Opinions

"There has been so much comment on the Monkees, good and bad, and I always like to form my own opinions, so I was really happy I had the chance to meet them and get to know them. I think the groups that are knocking them and
(Continued on next page)

MONKEES ARCHIVES 1

ANN MOSES with DAVY

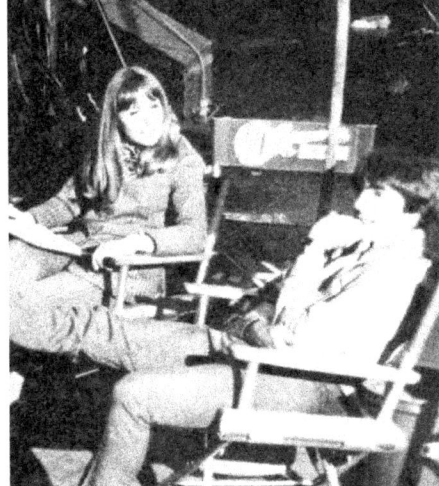

(Continued)
saying they don't play their instruments and they're not good performers are wrong. You can't knock success! I wonder if those who are knocking the Monkees could do as well? Ninety-nine per cent couldn't do a quarter of what they've done!

"I usually don't go down to film sets, but I was invited and I went out of curiosity. I planned to stay a half an hour and I was so impressed that I stayed all afternoon. I think they're very talented people, they have a great sense of humor and the way they ad lib is very natural.

"I was surprised to hear that they filmed each episode in three days. That just seemed unbelievable to me. Then I found out that they work like a machine together. If they weren't as professional as they are, they couldn't do it. I also found them very much down to earth. They're not big heads at all!

"There have been remarks that the Monkees aren't good musicians. And we talked about this on the set. I told them that when I first started someone asked me 'Are you a good drummer?' and I said, 'No, I don't consider myself a good drummer,' which I don't. There are thousands better than me, but there are thousands worse.

Manufactured Group

"They've been criticized for being a 'manufactured group', but it doesn't matter if someone spends millions of dollars on a publicity campaign if the kids don't like your records they won't buy them. If they don't like you, they won't turn on the TV. You've got to have that little bit of magic, that little bit of magnetism. Obviously, that's what the Monkees have!

"I think the Monkees are the biggest thing since the Beatles. I went to Peter's home for dinner and we spent the evening talking about music. I found him to be a very talented guitarist. People say they're not musicians, but I think Peter's a brilliant guitar player.

"A lot of people don't realize they've been around for years — working and roughing it. Davy Jones worked in the states for six years, so you can't say that's getting to the top the easy way! I think it's great — Davy being English, going out of the country unknown and coming back and being treated like a king. It's a great achievement.

"I found Davy and all the Monkees to be very down to earth. I'm for all of them. They're great!"

MONKEES ARCHIVES 1

MONKEES ARCHIVES 1

open for..... MONKEE BUSINESS

Is it a bird, is it a plane, or is it a Monkee, zooming around like sixty, getting into all kinds of good things?

Chances are, it's a Monkee. Besides making records and telly specials and going on tour with their fabulous show (which includes a sword swallower, would you believe) and rehearsing weekday afternoons at a Hollywood niteclub, the Monkees are doing some pretty neat things individually as well!

First of, Davy Jones has really been going great guns making appearances on his own. This more or less got started with his guest star thingy on "Laugh In" (see pix here if you missed that one, and if you didn't!). Then he bopped on over to England for a solo stint on Tom Jones' super variety show, and he was such a hit on that, he went back for an encore a few weeks later.

DAVY ACTIVE IN TV - HERE, A SCENE FROM "LAUGH-IN"

MICKY, AND WIFE SAM, NOW OWN "ONE-OF-A-KIND" BOTIQUE SHOP

Davy has been spending his free time, which there is so little of again for him these days, working on his singing and--are you ready for this--dancing. Davy, as you know, really got his start in musical comedy, and we wouldn't be a bit surprised to find him back on the stage one of these days in something even groovier than the "Oliver!" he got his start in.

Davy isn't exactly taking dancing lessons, but he is spending a lot of time working out, when he has time. When a person stops dancing for any period of time, you really have to work at getting your breath control back. Or, when you first start dancing again, getting your breath, period. Davy's past that point, of course, and you well know it if you saw him larking about in that dance number on Tom Jones, but he still has a way to go before he feels totally up on dancing again.

When he's really back into it, just think. We may all be going to the theater and on opening night the curtain rises and there he is. Wow. It boggles the mind, baby.

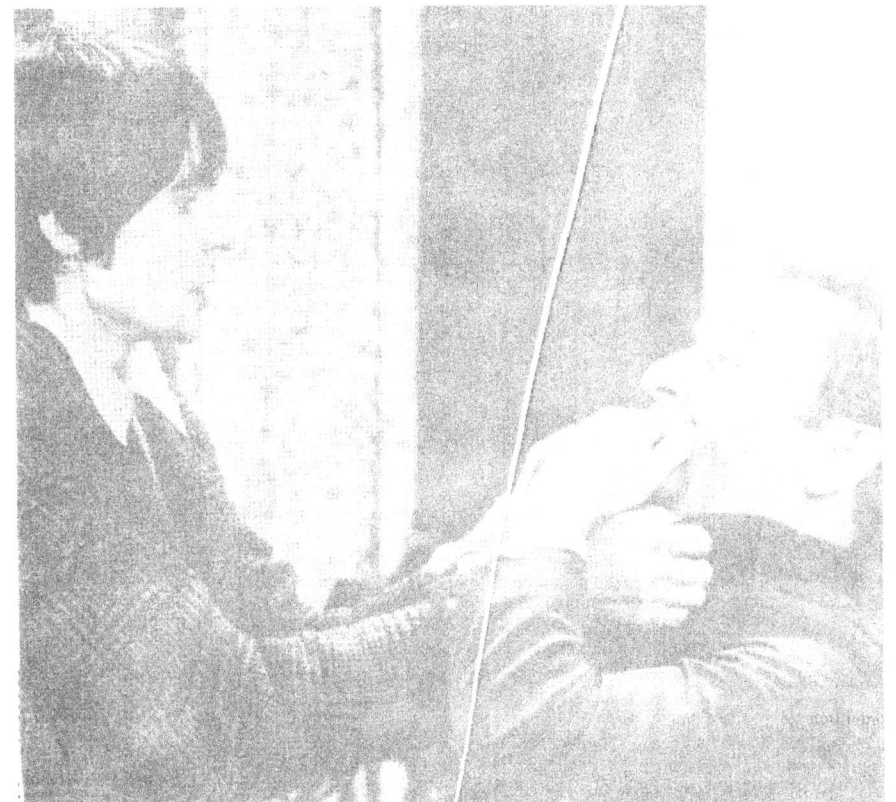

MONKEES ARCHIVES 1

Micky has something altogether new going, as well. Actually, his wife Sammy is a lot more involved than he, but together they have taken a large first-floor dentist's office on Santa Monica Blvd. in Hollywood, recarpeted the place, painted the inside (Micky did the walls and doors and Sammy and friends painted the woodwork) and stuck butterflies and flowers all over the outside (Sammy was in charge of that, too) and called it "One Of A Kind."

It is now open for business and is one of the neatest boutiques you ever did see. They have small quantities of jewelry, paintings, scarves, and middle-sized quantities of gorgeous clothes that Sammy made herself. She actually crochets whole dresses and that kind of thing! What talent. All that and gorgeous, too.

What you do is go into the store and either buy something Sammy has already made, or you find a fabric you like (some of which she brought back from Japan when she went over on tour with Micky) and Sammy will make it up into the dress of your choice.

MIKE, TALENT-SCOUTING

The place is very groovy and very tasteful at the same time, which is a pretty difficult point to make. Sammy is at the shop herself in the afternoons, and she often brings baby Ami Bluebell along in a basket.

Ami was there the day we went over to look around "One Of A Kind" and she has to be the most adorable baby in the world. She doesn't look like Micky or Sammy. She looks like Micky and Sammy, with her daddy's nose and mommy's mouth and that sort of thing. Honestly, she is the most incredible combination of two beautiful people we've ever seen.

Incidentally, everything in the shop is, as the name implies, one of a kind.

Sammy has been working on items for the shop since way before Ami was born, and is really excited about the prospects of being a "businesswoman." She has always wanted to open her own shop, and now with Micky away a good deal of the time again, or very busy, this gives her something to do, and something very groovy.

By the way, when the guys are out of town, the girls get together occasionally in the evening and one recent weekend they celebrated the opening of the shop with a groovy champagne supper at Mike and Phyllis Nesmith's house, way up in them thar hills. The view from Mike's house is spectacular, especially at night, and particularly through a glass of burbly.

Speaking of Mike Nesmith's house, about a year ago he threw one of the neatest press parties that ever happened. He invited every reporter in existence up to that beautiful pad in the sky to preview his first album on his own (production-wise), "Mike Nesmith Presents The Wichita Train Whisler." Only all he did was play the album in a room where you could go in and dig it if you wanted to listen, and give you a free copy on your way out. Other than that, the party was minus the usual hype and everyone had a ball not to mention the best appetizers that ever lived (huh?).

Anyway, that record has really paid off for Mike. It sold well and it caused a lot of talk because it was an excellent blend of country, rock, jazz and classical sounds.

As a result of this album, Mike has been associated with Paramount Pictures Music for the past year, and Dot Records (which is part of Paramount) has just announced the finalization of an exclusive production agreement with Mike, calling for lots of goodies to be produced by Mike's American Wichita Company.

PETER NOT DECIDED

Mike is now talent-scouting for performers who will have appeal all the way up and down the rock music spectrum.

His first artist is an old friend of his named Bill Chadwick. They worked together and knew each other well before Mike became a Monkee, and they're back together again!

Bill's first record for Mike's company will be "Talking To The Wall" b/w "If You Had The Time," both written by Bill.

Also, Mike has discovered a quartet called The Corvetts, and is now recording them. It's a bluegrass-country-pop oriented group, featuring the highly diversified talents of John Ware, Jeff Hanna, Chris Darrow and John London.

Besides doing all of this and being a Monkee too, Mike has gone back to college! He's attending classes at U.C.L.A. and wants to get his B.A. in history just as soon as possible!

How's that for three groovy guys really getting into a little bit of everything? Some Monkee business!

MONKEES ARCHIVES 1

EVOLUTION OF THE MONKEES
from fame to fortune!

MONKEES ARCHIVES 1

MONKEES ARCHIVES 1

Meet Peter Tork's New Group

ALWAYS LAUGHING AND SINGING, "Release" sends out good vibrations to everyone. Their music reflects their way of life, too, in that most of the songs are happy tunes.

"Release" is the name of Peter Tork's new group and what an exciting group they are! "Three is a quorum for our group. We sometimes have four. We're thinking of having a rotating fourth," says Peter.

The current fourth member is Judy Mayhan, who Pete is also promoting as a solo writer and vocalist. The rest of the group consists of Peter on lead guitar and vocals. Ripley Wildflower on bass and vocals and Peter's girlfriend Reine Stewart on drums.

Their current repertoire consists of two of Peter's songs, one of Ripley's songs, a Slim Harpo number called "Mailbox Blues," two of Nick Thorkelson's songs and even an old Monkee Tune called "Take A Giant Step," done in a very different style.

They hope to have their sounds on records soon, so watch for this groovy group to come your way!

PETER PLANS to let his hair grow and grow. "Release" practices every day at Peter's house in North Hollywood.

MEET "RELEASE"—They are from left Ripley Wildflower, who's part Indian, Judy Mahan, who Peter is also producing as a solo vocalist and writer, Peter and his girlfriend Reine, who has been playing drums for two years.

MONKEES ARCHIVES 1

MONKEES ARCHIVES 1

A MONKEE CONCERT

Their Hollywood Bowl Smash!

By Bruce Barbour

(Bruce, at left, puts another Monkee adventure on paper in every issue of TS. And he knows what he's talking about because he's Mike's brother-in-law!)

Bowl Photos by Tad Diltz

Back again . . . . this time backstage at the Hollywood Bowl and just minutes after the Monkees first personal appearance in their home city. The show can only be described as another fabulous success for the Monkees.

First to appear on stage were the Sundowners, the group replacing the Candy Store Prophets as the Monkees back-up band and the same group that played behind the Rolling Stones on their personal appearances. The Sundowners started the show with a medley of some of their own original material and some of the better known Rolling Stones hits, and then made way for Lynn Randell, the seventeen-year-old singer who's the number one vocalist in Australia. Lynn and the Sundowners did about a forty-five minute set and then a short intermission was called to give everyone a chance to prepare for the second half of the show which belonged to the Monkees.

Let me stop for a minute and bring you all up to date on the conditions here at the Bowl. Every seat was sold out weeks ago and the place was packed, even though it has been overcast and rainy looking all day. Although the fire regulations would not allow standing room tickets to be sold, a total of 18,600 fans were here tonight to see the Monkees play.

The security people have turned the backstage area into a kind of fortress to protect the Monkees against the many hundreds of overly enthusiastic fans who try to break through at every concert. When the Monkees' limousine rolled inside the barricade

Continued on next page

MONKEES ARCHIVES 1

Above: Mike working out with maracas at the Bowl. Right: Big boy Pete plunking away!

a few minutes before they were to go on stage, the entire backstage area was sealed off completely and no one was allowed to enter or leave until the show was over.

The Monkees made their appearance directly following the intermission, entering through two huge phony amplifiers which I think I described to you in my last article. The roar from the crowd as they made their appearance was deafening, which answered any questions anyone might have about the Monkees popularity in the city of Los Angeles.

The show consisted mostly of songs taken from the new album which was first released just a few weeks ago. Davy, Micky, Peter and Mike each did solos backed by the Sundowners and I think that once again, as in Toronto, it was Micky who topped off the evening by bringing about mass outbreaks of fainting and hysteria in the audience.

Micky came on stage combing his hair, threw his comb out into the audience and started into his James Brown version of "I Got A Woman!" Getting really involved with his singing and kneeling on the stage sobbing into the microphone, he was led off the stage twice by Mike, but broke away and ran back to the microphone each time. (I described this particular number of Micky's in detail in the July issue of Teen Screen.) This time however, after breaking away from Mike and doing a flip back to the microphone, Micky finished his song AND THEN THREW HIMSELF INTO THE POND WHICH CIRCLES THE STAGE! This took everyone completely by surprise, including everyone connected with the show. One of the Sundowners ran over and helped Micky out of the pool and the most incredibly loud applause I have ever heard followed him as he ran soaking wet off stage. Micky was back minutes later in a dry set of clothes for the Monkees last song of the Hollywood Bowl concert, "Stepping Stone."

I've got to tell you how they escaped from the Bowl without being mobbed. An armored car had been parked directly behind the stage door throughout the entire concert and all of the kids naturally assumed that this was the way that the Monkees would leave. Little did they know that the man who built the famous Monkee car, Dean Jeffries, was parked on the other side of the stage in a battered '56 panel truck complete with cracked windows and chipped paint waiting to sneak the four Monkees through the crowd, which is exactly what he did. The truck was so old and terrible looking that it didn't even draw a second glance, and that's how they made their getaway.

I only have one more thing to add, and that is that the Monkees' managers and producers chipped in and rented PJ's (a huge night club here in Hollywood) for an entire night and threw the mother of all parties in honor of the Monkees' success at the concert. Each one of the Monkees was allowed to ask anyone he wanted to come to the party, and the final guest list was so star-studded that it staggered the mind. Mike even went so far as to invite the entire staff of the Free Press, Hollywood's underground newspaper. Music was provided by the Penny Arcade and the Gordian Knot and I think that all in all, it was the most fabulous party I've ever been to.

That's about all this month, except that the Monkees are just getting ready to go on a two-month tour to London, Paris and thirty cities in the United States. Rest assured that you will get all the facts about the tour firsthand when everyone gets back in September.

Bruce

MONKEES ARCHIVES 1

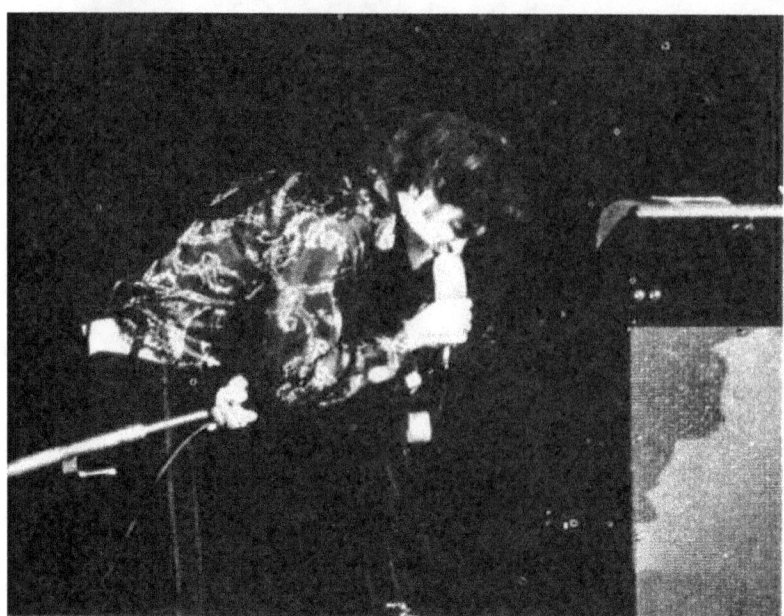

Above: Micky kneeling on stage, blowing everyones mind. Right: Mike helping Micky of the Bowl stage.

Left: Returning to the stage, Micky leaped into the pool and the place went wild! Above: a sundowner helps him out of the water as applause roars!

WCFL TeenSet

JUNE, 1967

35¢

A WCFL/TeenSet Exclusive: Concert Countdown Scrapbook!

The Monkees Recording Sessions

Way Back When with Peter and Davy

Fabulous Monkee Pinups! Monkees Contest!

Ridiculously Beautiful Raider Pinups

Beatles! Turtles! Spencer Davis Group! Association!

See Barney Pip turn into peanut butter on page 11!

MONKEES ARCHIVES 1

WHAT PETER HAS LEARNED FROM MICKY

How many times have you met someone you just didn't like? Someone who seemed to be *everything* you didn't like? Someone whom you didn't have the slightest interest in getting to know any better? Yet you did get to know them better and you found that they were actually wonderful friends and great people?

That's what happened between Peter and Micky. Peter just didn't like Micky when he first met him, yet there was nothing he could do. Both of them were now Monkees and that was that. So they *had* to get to know each other better and Peter found that instead of being nowhere, Micky was actually right where everything was at.

MICKY IS NOWHERE

"When I first met Micky I thought he was nowhere. I thought he was right out of 'Reader's Digest'. He seemed to be everything I stood against: second hand humor, second hand situations, everything. I thought, well, they hired him because they needed someone with professional experience. Period.

"You see, when Micky was in Circus Boy he didn't have anyone at all around that was his age. His whole life was spent in pleasing adults—it was the heaviest experience of his life. So that affected him a lot.

FULL-FLEDGED GENIUS

"Then I got to know him and he grew and evolved and got bigger and bigger and bigger. He just didn't stop growing and now I think he's a full-fledged genius. He's really one of the brilliant people of our time."

When the Monkees first started, there was practically no time when they *weren't* together. There was just too much to be done in a very short space of time. So Peter and Micky were thrown together nearly twenty-four hours a day and Peter began to really know him. They would talk and argue and discuss things for hours on end because during the long waits in filming and recording there was nothing else to do. At first their discussions were endless circles: Peter had his ideas and Micky had his and the two just didn't have anything in common. And Peter, who is always searching for Truth, would always put Micky's ideas down as not being logical or valid. But over a period of time, Peter began to change his ideas. Maybe Micky had something after all.

PETER SAW THE LIGHT

"I used to say things like, 'Micky, don't you know that that's not right? It has to be this way,' and he'd tell me, 'No, man, that doesn't matter.' Well, after a while I discovered that he had been *right!* Whatever it was, he had been right and I'd been wrong. That's the sort of thing that really got me thinking. His attitude would have seemed to be so wrong to me, yet I'd find out that it was so right. I'd get overwrought over nothing.

"Then there would be something that I wouldn't think was worth much and he'd be fascinated. I'd tell him, 'What's the matter with you? Man, you're hung up on the wrong kind of thing,' and he'd tell me, 'No, man, this is where it's at.' Well, *again* he'd turn out to be right."

IDEAS THEY SHARE

Peter would do a lot of thinking after these things happened. Maybe Micky was actually a couple of steps ahead of Peter and it had been Peter who was out of step! Peter began to re-think all his opinions and arguments in the light of what Micky thought. Eventually he came to the realization that Micky was doing a lot more teaching to Peter than Peter was doing to Micky!

"Now we share our religious and philosophical viewpoints, which are very similar. For instance, we both believe that God is not a man sitting on a throne somewhere. We both think that this viewpoint is simple, childish and inaccurate. Anyone who worships this sort of God is worshipping an idol, not God. We both believe that peace on Earth can only begin with me, which is pretty much the basis of everything.

WHERE THEY DISAGREE

"Where we differ is in political opinions. For instance, do demonstrations accomplish anything? Are they worthwhile? I think demonstrations are vital and necessary. I think Micky feels that demonstrations can be done without. I don't think he feels they accomplish anything worthwhile. Now this may not be an entirely accurate representation of his views, but I think that this is basically what he feels. I know he doesn't feel them to be as worthwhile as I do.

"We both feel that the Monkees show could be broadened greatly. Right now we think the series is too square and restricted. There are lots of things that we could be doing that would be good things, but we aren't."

TRUE FRIENDS NOW

Another area where Micky has taught Peter is hobbies. Peter's spare-time activities are mostly things like reading, playing different instruments, composing songs. Micky's spare-time activities are, for the most part, things like building his gyrocopter, making things like wire lampshades, recording his album of children's music.

"I enjoy a lot of the things Micky does, but not to the point of participating. It's enough to just watch him do the things he does and I learn a lot that way."

Micky and Peter have become very close since they started working together. As both of their viewpoints have changed, they have found themselves in closer and closer accord. They have taught each other much about life and their work. The two who at first didn't like each other are now true friends.

MONKEES ARCHIVES 1

PETER GROOVES ON JAPAN

MONKEES ARCHIVES 1

Peter's pretty well-traveled. He's up on a lot of languages, especially French, and he knows about many places. The United States is familiar to him, from New York to Los Angeles, and he's been to England and France on tour. Also, he's been studying like crazy many Eastern ways of life. But he still wants to keep on moving and seeing the world, learning about all kinds of people.

"I'd love to go to England and France again. Of course, when I go back to France, it won't be as easy because the Monkees show has just been sold over there and I won't be able to walk around unrecognized like I could the first time.

MULTI-LINGUAL

"As far as languages go, besides French, I used to speak German. I learned a little Spanish when I was in Venezuela. My father was working in Caracas for a year and I was there with my family for six weeks right in the middle of my beatnik period.

"One place I'd really like to go is Persia. Now, the *Indian* style of thing is for a 'guru', or teacher, to gather his students around him. He sits cross-legged and teaches and they sit cross-legged and listen.

"But in Persia I've been told that you have what's called a 'Sufi' which means a brother. These cats are also very hip and very aware. If you go to them and say 'Listen, we want to gather around and have you just teach us your ideas,' he'll say 'Beat it. If you want to watch me, you go stand a good distance off and watch me but don't get in my way. I have my own life to lead'."

All these places are very fascinating to Peter, but there's one place that he wants to visit more than any other and that's Japan.

JAPAN TODAY

"I think there's something incredible happening in Japan today. It's about the Japanese spirit and it doesn't pertain to recent history. The last hundred years don't count. But before that, the spirit was very evident. And again, just now, I think the spirit is coming to the fore.

"The Japanese are very simple, you know. Some people are now looking to India in their search for enlightenment because they think they can pick up a lot of help there. But I think the Indian way of life is a little too cluttered for my way of thinking.

"Of course I do enjoy Ravi Shankar's Indian music but that's because he's a genius. He's spent his lifetime just to involve me in his music and I'm very happy to let him do that. I dig involving myself in his music because it's truly enlightening to hear.

"But the Japanese spirit and religious concept is much simpler than the Indian. They believe that awakening will come to you in a single second. It'll just come to you in this great big flash, where it's all at. It's called the Doctrine of Sudden Enlightenment.

LEARNS LANGUAGES

"I'm now learning to speak Japanese from the Berlitz Japanese teacher. In the Berlitz school you're only supposed to speak the language you're learning, but sometimes we talk in English too. Some of the words I've learned are 'empitzu' which means 'pencil,' 'Ohaio' which means 'Hello' or 'Hi' and 'Nihongo' which means the Japanese language itself.

"When I go to Japan I'd like to go to Kyoto most of all. Kyoto is the former capital of Japan and it's the center of the Zen Buddhists. Zen Buddhist temples are all over the place and I'd like to go there just to pick up on the vibrations."

Without a doubt, Peter will make it to Japan before too long, because when he sets his mind to do something, it gets done. And after he gets there, the country will never be the same. Wherever Peter goes, he learns from the people he meets and the things he sees. But everyone who meets Peter always learns from *him* too! You can't help it because he's a super-fascinating person chock full of super-fascinating ideas!

MONKEES ARCHIVES 1

Mike's Troubadour Days
...as club owner Doug Weston remembers them

(It's impossible to miss Doug Weston in a crowd. For a start, he's over seven feet tall and wears a Beatle haircut! But more important, Doug owns the Troubadour, a famous folk club in Los Angeles which has launched people like the Smothers Brothers and Roger Miller, as well as rock groups like the Sunshine Company and Nitty Gritty Dirt Band. And a very special person is also an alumnus of Doug Weston's Troubadour—none other than Monkee Mike Nesmith!)

I first met Mike about three years ago when he came to my club, the Troubadour, and auditioned for me. He was trying to get into a blues bag at the time—doing sort of a slick R & B act for the "better" nightclubs. But this didn't work out too well for him and he went out on tour with some rock and roll show.

The second time I met Mike was right after he had decided he wasn't happy with what he was doing and had joined one of Randy Sparks' groups. Finally he decided he wasn't happy with that either.

But I really got to know Mike when I hired him as my hootmaster for the Monday night hootenannies at the club, a job he held for almost two years.

MIKE'S TALENTS

And from the first time I ever saw Mike on a stage, I respected his talents. I could see right away that he was a bright young man and he has a wit, a nice country wit.

Mike did a very good job as hootmaster. He had spontaneous humor and a light way of introducing the performers. It's an involved job, too,

MONKEES ARCHIVES 1

and Mike had to take care of scheduling the acts, handling the performers, and plan a show as well. And he did the job nicely.

Finally Screen Gems came to see Mike and they were equally impressed with his talents. They had called me for prospective talent for The Monkees and Mike was one of the many people I referred to them. By this time, both Mike and Peter were being seriously discussed for the parts.

Don't think I mean to say that I got them the gig. Nothing could be farther from the truth—they got the parts on their own talent. I just suggested Mike, and if I'm not mistaken, I think Mike is the one who sent Peter down to audition.

FOLK BAG

A lot of people now involved with The Monkees, like Mike, Peter and their producer, Chip Douglas, basically hung out at the Troubadour. It's a folk club but we also have hootenannies but we also have all kinds of music. And remember that both Mike and Peter came out of the folk bag.

Mike helped develop a lot of people while he worked as hootmaster at the Troubadour. You see, he had control over scheduling—who would go on when—and he could arrange certain people to be on at the best times.

Occasionally Mike himself could get on stage and play. He had already put several discs out under the name Mike Blessing, though I don't know where the Blessing came from because he was using Mike Nesmith at the time and he was always talked of as Mike Nesmith.

Peter likewise played the Troubadour (all this was happening for the guys just when their careers were ready to break). He was working at the time as a dishwasher at the Golden Bear in Huntington Beach and he came up one night to audition. He seemed quite charming and I could tell that he really had something going for him but that he was still trying to get himself together. He played the Troubadour for several weeks and then he was asked to audition for The Monkees.

BIG AUDITION

After the audition, Peter went off to New York to wait until Screen Gems announced the results. Mike found out he'd been chosen for The Monkees and then I think Mike realized Peter would be called back from New York for the part. Peter returned and the filming started. Peter continued to play the Troubadour for three or four months but then his filming schedule just got too heavy and he had to quit. But he and Mike still come back and perform once in awhile.

It's interesting to see the difference in audience reaction before and after The Monkees. Before, Mike and Peter would get moderate to good response. Now when they play the audience just goes wild! And Mike particularly has retained some of the special stage humor which set him off before the series began.

Now as I look back on Mike's Troubadour days, I can remember some really funny incidents that happened and the great way he had of handling them.

For instance, we were always bugged by promotion people who would try influence to get their client on first instead of using our first come, first served method. Mike had a good way of taking care of these people without alienating them, even though they were the kind who were basically just trying to con their way into the hoot rather than wait their turn.

CLEVER MIKE

When something like this happened, he'd come strolling over to me with the troublesome person in tow and I could tell by the glint in his eyes what he was up to. He'd say, "Gee, we really have a difficult problem here," in mock seriousness. You see, he was playing a game with the other person and he'd already communicated to me just by the look in his eyes that here was a person trying to use favoritism.

Then he'd go through a long story, telling me how difficult it was to help this person out and he'd go on and on and I'd nod in agreement. But actually, I knew Mike was going to work it out his own way and the performer would play in the same spot Mike had originally assigned him, despite what his promotion man tried to do. But don't misunderstand, Mike always handled people very fairly—he's an extremely fair-minded person.

STOCKING CAP

Mike was quite a spectacle in those days, too. He wore his stocking cap all the time and, of course, levis and colorful shirts. He'd do a set every once in awhile and I think he did an occasional gig at other clubs, too. Meanwhile, he worked on recording sessions and I know he did a lot of songwriting.

Looking back now, I think there is something people who want to get into show business could learn from Mike (and Peter's) Troubadour days.

Mike realized that success is hardly ever instantaneous. It takes serious work. Mike wasn't just a performer waiting around to be discovered on the streets. He took an active role in his career. He performed every occasion he could. He was seriously trying to break through.

Mike didn't just come out of the woods. He didn't fall into a Cinderella thing. He knew that success is a matter of being in the right place at the right time, and **being there frequently!**

MONKEES ARCHIVES 1

DAVID TALKS

MONKEES ARCHIVES 1

ABOUT FRIENDSHIP

Friendship has always been very important to me but I never realized quite how valuable it was until I became a Monkee. You see, after you become successful there are always a lot of people who want to be your "friend" for reasons that have nothing much to do with real friendship. When this happens, it's great to have true friends that you can depend on, no matter what.

I've been very lucky in having lots of true friends all my life. Now that I'm a Monkee, these true friends are the people that mean the most to me in the whole world. I know that whatever scrapes I get into, or whatever moods I might feel—my friends will be there.

But just because you call some people your "friends" doesn't necessarily mean that they have anything in common. My friends don't. All my friends have different qualities. I just know that someone is a real friend and I couldn't really tell you how I know.

CHARLIE ROCKETT

For instance, Charlie Rockett was originally a friend of Mike Nesmith's. He came from San Antonio to Hollywood with Mike and he and I met out here. We hit it off well from the beginning and then he needed a place to stay so he moved in with me. We wrote some songs together and our friendship just sort of grew. Now he's got his own place but we're still good friends, of course.

Charlie had a friend, Steve Pitts. You see, in Texas Charlie and Steve and Mike and David Pearl—they were all buddies. Well, when Mike became a Monkee all his friends just got to know everybody and I got some good friends.

MONKEES ARCHIVES 1

ARE THE MONKEES GOING HIPPIE?

Dear Monkees,

Please don't become HIPPIES! I love you just the way you are. Don't ever change because I couldn't stand it all over again.

The very first time I heard your record, "Last Train to Clarksville," it made me happy because there were such happy things coming out of the record. Then, when I saw you on TV, I just couldn't believe how cute you were.

You've always made me smile and laugh, that is, up until now. Now I'm worried about what's happening.

P.D.
Chicago, Ill.

BACK TO OLD STYLE

I think the Monkees look like hippies! Before, I thought they were the greatest, but now I'm not so sure. Since Micky has his hair curled and wears that thing that looks like a rug, he's not my favorite anymore. Mike and Peter aren't too bad but their sideburns are too long. Now Davy's my favorite. His haircut is nice and short and I hope he'll keep it that way. If the other three would go back to their old style I'd love them just as much as Davy. (Still I'm a true Monkee fan.)

G.D.
Providence, R.I.

WE CAN DIG IT!

My friends at school have been talking lately about how the Monkees have turned into hippies. Well, I think that's outasite! The beautiful beads, which I love wearing myself, are so colorful. I think Davy and Peter look the cutest ever in their Indian rajah coats. Micky looks great in his American Indian headdress. Don't change, you all look super groovy!

C.N.
Anaheim, Calif.

What do YOU think about the Monkees? Let us know how you feel by writing to Monkee Spectacular, 1800 N. Highland Ave., Hollywood, California 90028.

MONKEES ARCHIVES 1

DAVID TALKS ABOUT FRIENDSHIP

DAVY AND HIS BUDDIES always have a great time wherever they go. Last summer on the tour, when the Monkees weren't working it meant play time for everyone. Here's Davy with some of the Sundowners and Ric Klein.

MONKEES ARCHIVES 1

HENRY DILTZ

NEKO

DAVID PEARL

CRAZY STEVE

Well, back to Steve Pitts. He's really funny. He went down to the Troubadour one night and we all went to hear him and he was telling these funny stories and everybody in the place just cracked-up. The stories were as funny to the people who didn't know him as they were to us. He and I wrote some songs together, too. He went back to Texas a few weeks ago to get married and everyone went down for the wedding.

BEST BUDDY

David Pearl is my best friend. David Pearl is the best friend I've ever had. He's been the most helpful to me as a person and to my career. He handles all the business parts that I often don't get the opportunity to take care of. David Pearl is my best friend because he's never, ever held out his hand to me for anything. We do all the same things, go to all the same places, everything.

He's becoming a personality in his own right. He's got his own national fan club in England and he gets mobbed wherever he goes. He's really getting to be big and I'm all for it.

HOUSE MATE

The only person who lives with me now is Lindy. Lindy is the brother of a kid who was in "Oliver!" with me, now he's in "Mame". Lindy is nineteen and he's in college—he goes to school every day. I'm friends with his family, all of them.

Neko is another friend of mine. I've known him for quite a while, now, and he's often up at my house. He's an artist and he draws groovy pictures of us and the Beatles. He does a lot of different things for us and sometimes he even gets into the Monkee act. On tour once he brought some cotton candy on stage for all of us and we ate it during our act. It really looked groovy.

PHOTOGRAPHER HENRY

Then there's Henry Diltz. Henry is the photographer we work with most. He's so great to have around because he's never up-tight. He just takes picture after picture and we often don't realize he's there. That's important because after you get photographed as much as we've been you get really tired of photographers who make a huge production out of taking a picture.

As you can see, there's really nothing that my friends have in common except that they're my friends. Each one of them is my friend for a different reason and yet I like every one of them.

I know, too, that whatever happens in the future with the Monkees that my friends will continue to be my friends. Those are the kind of friends to have.

MONKEES ARCHIVES 1

Micky In the Monkee Movie!

The Monkees New Movie is Movin' and Groovin' and Mighty Micky is right in the thick of all the outasite action!

Treasure these precious pix of your cuddly curly-headed fave as he dances across the desert in the most outasite, zany action-packed adventure that ever blew the roof off your neighborhood movie house on a super-dooper Saturday afternoon!

MONKEES ARCHIVES 1

BEATLES & MON

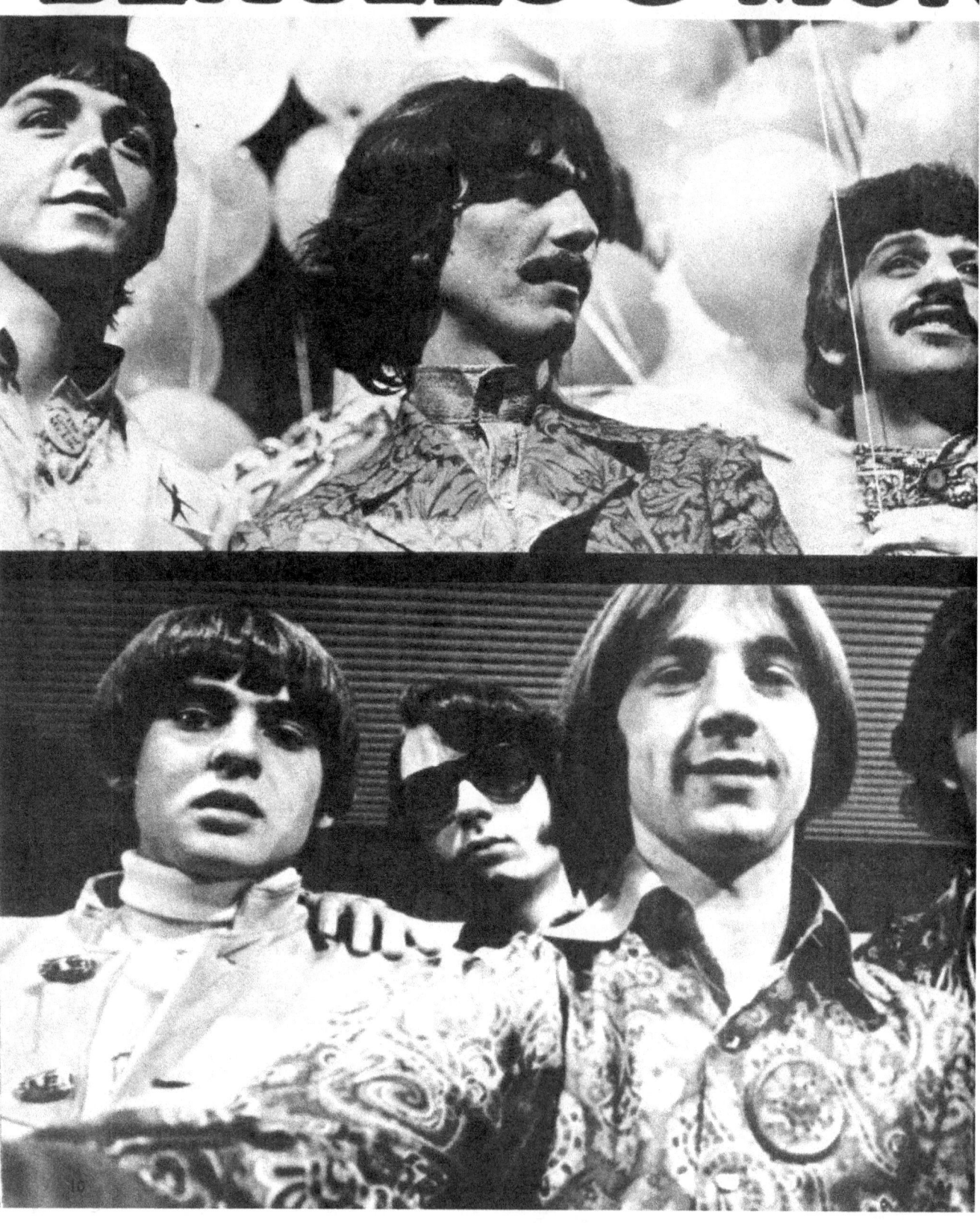

MONKEES ARCHIVES 1

KEES HOW ALIKE ARE THEY?

This summer the Monkees and the Beatles got together in England and had an outasite party that both groups are *still* talking about! It was the first opportunity the two groups had had to get together, all of them, and talk as much as they wanted and both groups took full advantage of every precious moment.

It was a time of renewing old friendships and forming new ones. There was laughter and singing and dancing, but beneath it all was the solid bond of true friendship. It was a friendship quickly formed, for both groups saw in each other the things they each valued most.

Mike, of course, had met John Lennon and the others on his vacation to England this year and Micky had met Paul McCartney at the same time. So, except for Davy who went to see his father, all the rest of the Monkees got to meet all the rest of the Beatles and a fantastic time was had by all.

THE PARTY

The party started early in the evening and lasted until the sun was peeping over the rooftops. Micky sang and danced both Monkee and Beatle songs while Peter and George Harrison huddled in a corner, talking. Each of them is interested in the same serious subjects: Eastern philosophy and religion, classical music and the more serious problems of the world. Ringo stayed home with Maureen, who was expecting their second child, so Peter wandered over to his house during the evening to see him. They climbed into Ringo's treehouse and talked until six in the morning.

During the long evening some very interesting facts were revealed. The Monkees and the Beatles have more in common with each other than either of them had expected. And it became obvious that both the top British group and the top American group were both changing in the same direction. Their music, dress and actions were becoming more and more of a kind, and this could mean that the whole direction of modern music is moving in the same direction.

THEIR SIMILARITIES

First of all, both groups are intensely aware of their music. They want to perform the best music they are capable of performing, and they are coming to find that the best ways of each of their groups are very much alike.

Both groups have members that are especially interested in the deeper subjects of philosophy and religion and the effects of these things on human life.

Both groups are very much aware of the influence they have on their fans and on the whole field of popular music. And both groups have been very much identified with their own countries.

THEIR CLOSENESS

Because of these similarities, both groups are finding that their thoughts on such external things as how they should dress sometimes are similar. The clothes each of them wears are very up to the minute with lots of bright colors.

All of these things mean that in the near future you'll probably be able to find more and more similarities between the Monkees and the Beatles because these are the two most outasite groups ever!

MONKEES ARCHIVES 1

MICKY

Micky was out of show business for quite a while, then he joined the Missing Links—did you have any doubts about that venture?

I had a lot of doubts about the success of the group. I don't know if Micky knows that, either. First of all, the group wanted him to sing in a style that wasn't his own. He's singing with his own voice now instead of trying to force a style. He wasn't with the Missing Links exactly, they **lived** in the house with us!! It was a Micky-the-Musician Mission-type thing. The boys were all very nice, they really were.

Was it hard for you to watch the group struggle?

No, because Micky knew what he was getting into. If he had really been starving (I know Micky has a lot of pride, but he also knows that we're with him all the way), he would have certainly written home, which he did not do. So I know he wasn't sleeping on a cold, damp park bench at night. It didn't hurt me, though I thought it was a little unnecessary. But the experience of going out by themselves, Micky going out by himself, seeing at first hand what it's like, it was good.

What did you think when Micky first told you about the Monkees?

I never knew a great deal about it. I knew he was going to audition for a part, but not much more than that because I was in Northern California and he was in Hollywood. That meant talking long distance or writing (and Micky's letters are sometimes not too easy to read. He writes faster than he can think). The importance of it didn't strike me, because there are series and there are series. That it would ever hit as fast or as big as it has—I really didn't think along those lines. As far as I was concerned, I knew if it was the best thing for him, he would get it, that's all.

What were your first impressions of what the Monkees would be like?

Micky called me and told me (I remember that)—The Monkees, the name didn't strike me at all because I'd listened to the Byrds and the Animals and the Beatles, so the name didn't affect me at all. I said, "Well, what is the plot?" He said he couldn't tell me. I said, "Real handy, what do you mean you can't tell me?" He said, "I just can't explain it!" I said, "Micky, does it have a story?" And he said, "Would you believe—no?" He explained that it was on the idea of a Marx Brothers thing, the camera angles, and knowing a little bit about it, this made sense to me.

My first impression was that it would either be a completely kooky nothing (real great for two or three-year-olds maybe), but I didn't really understand it or know what it was about until I saw the pilot. Then I realized they had something very different. I'm not a big TV watcher, but I liked it.

MONKEES ARCHIVES 1

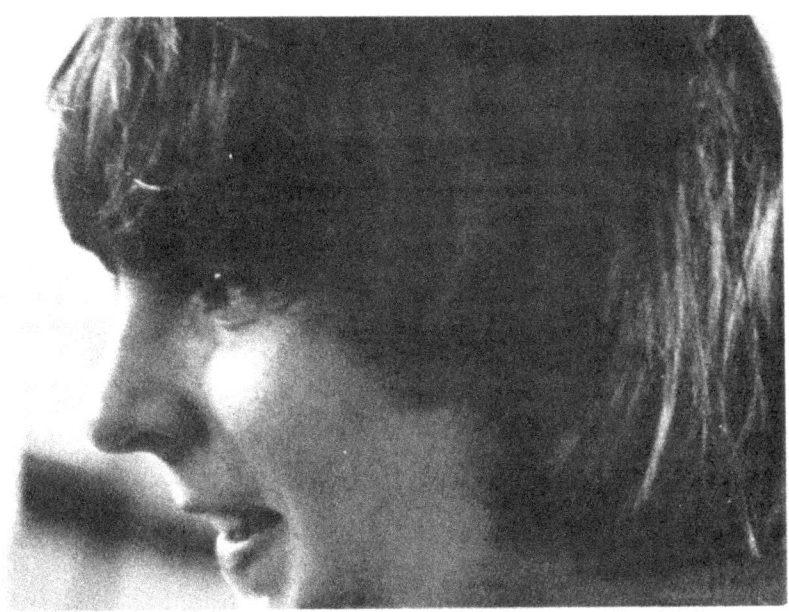

A PHOTO-GRAPHER'S VIEW of the MONKEES

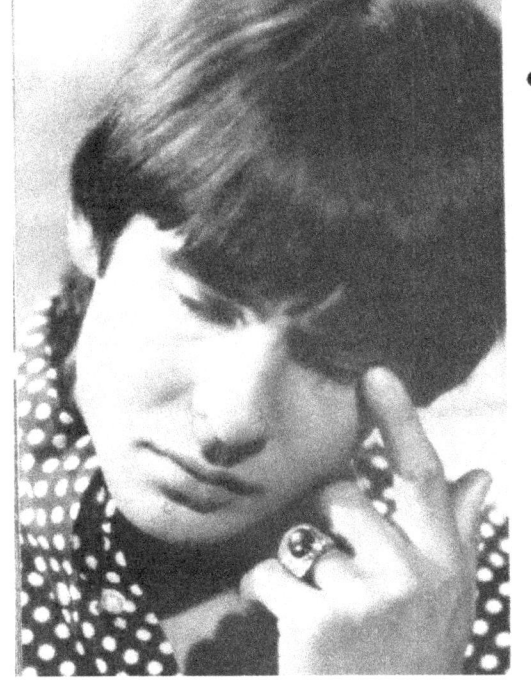

Bob Custer, Tiger Beat and Monkee Spectacular's Official Photographer, tells his personal impressions of Davy, Peter, Micky and Mike.

MONKEES ARCHIVES 1

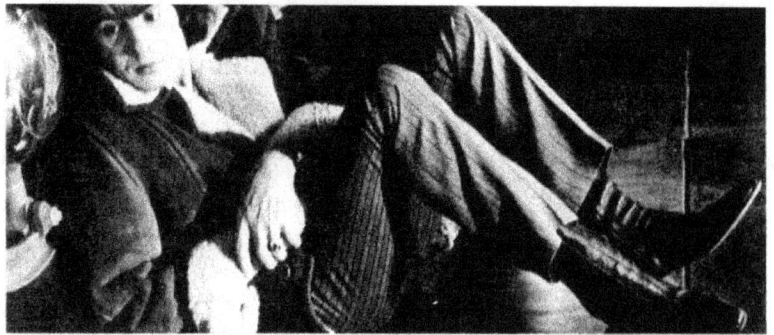

Q. When did you first meet the Monkees?
A. Back in September of 1966. There was a big press party to introduce the Monkees; they showed the pilot and a couple of segments of the show and everyone met all of the guys. I could see right away that Davy was extremely talented and that Micky was the wild one in the group. I didn't get any vibrations at all from Peter or Mike that day.

Q. When did you first photograph them, other than the party?
A. At the "Last Train to Clarksville" promotion, then at the Columbia Ranch where they were filming. I didn't know any of the Monkees personally at this time.

Q. When did you first get to know them personally?
A. Well, it was in December. I had a studio sitting with Davy and when we started I was just another photographer to him and he was just someone else to photograph as far as I was concerned. He was very tired and sleepy that day—he had been working awfully hard—and so he wasn't expecting much from the session. I shot seven rolls of film that day and they turned out fantastic—really great. You couldn't tell that he was tired or anything. He saw what I could do and so he wanted me to shoot him some more. We got to be better and better friends, session after session.

Q. How is your relationship with Davy today?
A. We have a sort of built-in trust. He comes over to my house a lot, even when we aren't shooting, just to talk or listen to music. It gives him a chance to unwind. When I'm shooting on the set we have a sort of game going. He'll do something really crazy unexpectedly and dare me to get it on film. I always do, and it's a good thing because he always checks later on to see if it's on the contact sheets.

Q. What are your impressions of the other Monkees?
A. I've only done studio sittings with Davy and Micky, although I've caught them all on the set. Micky is hard to pin down to get the shots you want. He's always in non-stop motion. I'll just get the lighting fixed correctly and my camera set and then he'll be off before I get the chance to take the picture! He's always clowning around. When I want a serious picture it's hard because I'll finally get a serious look out of him and then before I snap the shutter he's back to clowning. Mike doesn't want to smile for the camera, though he does smile on the set. Whenever he sees me start to take a picture, off goes the smile immediately. Even if he's laughing with other people, if he sees me with the camera he'll stop laughing right away, before I can get a picture. Peter is a challenge. If he gave me the opportunity I could really photograph him like he's never been photographed before. There are great depths to Peter that I want to get on film very much.

MONKEES ARCHIVES 1

Q. What sort of makeup do you use to photograph them?
A. Sometimes we use a light liquid base when they're very tired. I like to photograph them without makeup, and the guys prefer it too, but when they're working so hard and they're so tired and all you just have to use makeup. We never use anything on the eyes or lips; I have them wet their lips before I shoot. Micky uses hair spray sometimes, but he has to because of the way his hair is. It's difficult to keep in place and he moves around so much you have to do something.

Q. What makes them impatient when you're shooting?
A. The hot lights. It's easily over a hundred degrees under those lights and the glare is terrible. Sometimes when they're very tired I have to add another 500 watt bulb and that's murder. I try to shoot fast but when I add that 500 watter you can't believe how hard it is on the guys.

Q. Do you know of any special things that the guys do to protect their looks or preserve their energy?
A. Well, Davy works out with barbells and tries to eat health foods as much as possible. Peter eats a lot of health foods too. That's the main thing—good foods that don't have sugars or starches in them.

MONKEES ARCHIVES 1

Q. What do you respect most about the Monkees?
A. The desire they have to really be good performers. They'll all go out of their way to give a really good performance or do most anything else they feel is necessary, no matter how little they might personally want to do it at the time. Micky has come in to be photographed after working twelve hours straight at the studio. He's had Sally wash his hair and then he's come over, ready for a session and dead tired. Davy comes in when he's about to drop from exhaustion, because he cares about his responsibilities and his career.

Q. Who is the easiest to photograph?
A. Davy, by far. He's a true professional. Most of the time I don't even have to direct him, he just gives me different poses — good ones — one right after another. He's great to work with.

Q. Where do you feel the Monkees will go after the series stops?
A. I feel that Micky and Davy will be super-stars, they've just both got it in huge quantities. Mike and Peter, I believe, will develop other talents, like songwriting and producing, because they already have these things deep within themselves.

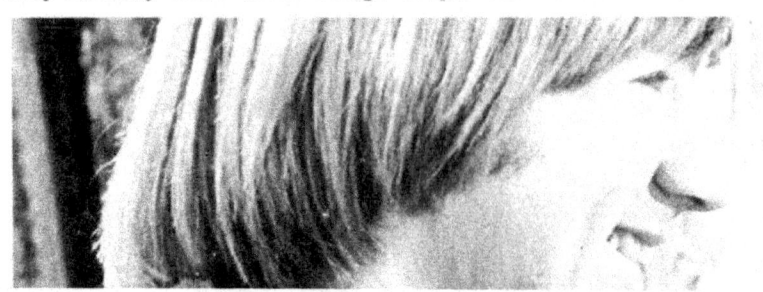

www.ingramcontent.com/pod-product-compliance
Lightning Source LLC
Chambersburg PA
CBHW080450170426
43196CB00016B/2745